HEART

Shift

HEART
Shift

THE **2** DEGREE DIFFERENCE THAT WILL
CHANGE YOUR HEART, YOUR HOME, AND YOUR HEALTH

JOHN TRENT

BROADMAN
&HOLMAN
PUBLISHERS

NASHVILLE, TENNESSEE

0-8054-3063-6

Published by Broadman & Holman Publishers
Nashville, Tennessee

Dewey Decimal Classification: 248.84
Subject Heading: CHRISTIAN LIFE \ DISCIPLESHIP

Leading From Your Strengths™ is a registered trademark of
Insights International, Inc. in Scottsdale, Arizona.

Unless otherwise noted, Scripture quotations are from the NASB,
New American Standard Bible, © the Lockman Foundation, 1960,
1962, 1963, 1968, 1971, 1972, 1973, 1975, 1977; used by permis-
sion. Also used is *The Message,* the New Testament in Contemporary
English, © 1993 by Eugene H. Peterson, published by NavPress,
Colorado Springs, Colo., and KJV, King James Version.

1 2 3 4 5 6 7 8 09 08 07 06 05 04

To two men who continually help me shift my heart toward the Lord and toward new growth in ministry, Bob Leenhouts and Doug Childress. And most especially, to my beloved wife, Cindy, who for twenty-five years has used "two degree changes" to help me become a better man, husband, and father.

Contents

Part 1: *How Did I Get Here?*

Chapter One: Waking Up Miles Away from Where You
Want to Be   3

Chapter Two: How a 2 Degree Change Can Ruin or
Renew Your Life   13

Chapter Three: Taking That First Step into a Kingdom
of Change   33

Chapter Four: Nine Reasons You'll Never Change—and the
One Reason You Must, Part I   49

Chapter Five: Nine Reasons You'll Never Change—and the
One Reason You Must, Part II   61

Part 2: *The Five Things You'll Need Now*
That You're Ready for Real Change

Introduction to Part 2: The HeartShift Life-Change Process   77

Chapter Six: Three Key Factors in Making Your
HeartShift Real   81

Chapter Seven: Setting Up a Memorial Marker to Celebrate
the Day You Made a HeartShift   91

Chapter Eight: Getting a Clear Starting Point for Change Today   105

Chapter Nine: Why You Won't Succeed without a 33 Group   127

Chapter Ten: Your Opportunity to Join a Unique Online
Community of Friends   139

Part 3: *Putting 2 Degree Changes into Practice*

Introduction to Part 3   147

Applying the 2 Degree Difference to Strengthen Your Faith

Chapter Eleven: It's Always Been the Small Things, Saints   151

Chapter Twelve: Daniel and Samson through a 2 Degree Lens   161

Chapter Thirteen: The 2 Degree Difference Quiet Time   169

Chapter Fourteen: The 2 Degree Difference Church
and Small Group   183

*Applying the 2 Degree Difference to
Strengthen Your Marriage and Family*

Chapter Fifteen: The 2 Degree Difference and a
Stronger Marriage   187

Chapter Sixteen: The 2 Degree Difference for Parents and
Grandparents   203

*Applying the 2 Degree Difference
as a Key to Better Health*

Chapter Seventeen: The 2 Degree Difference and Better Health   215

Conclusion

Chapter Eighteen: Final Thoughts on Making a HeartShift
and Long-Term Change   225

Appendix

Appendix A: Seven Keys to an Effective HeartShift Small Group   227

Appendix B: Three Sermon Outlines for a HeartShift Series   231

Notes   245

Acknowledgments

Very special thanks need to go to the entire Broadman & Holman publishing team, who saw the vision for a book on "small things" making a big difference in people's lives.

In particular, I'd like to thank my good friend and editor, Len Goss, who has provided encouragement and support, as has Kim Overcash, whose last minute production heroics is worthy of a medal—and my deepest thanks.

And to the Insights International team, most especially my fellow laborers and greatly valued friends, Rodney Cox and Eric Tooker. Their gift of a passcode for each book will make all the difference in many people making a HeartShift in their lives.

Part 1

How Did I Get Here?

CHAPTER ONE

Waking Up Miles Away from Where You Want to Be

*H*ow did I get here?" the character asks.

It's a formula that's been used for generations in classic children's tales, adventure novels, and feature films. Someone wakes up, opens his or her eyes, and discovers that everything has changed.

In literature, it's Rip Van Winkle waking up to discover himself covered with the dust of decades after lying down under a tree for a short noontime nap. It's a New England blacksmith in Mark Twain's *A Connecticut Yankee in King Arthur's Court* who opens his eyes to find an armor-clad knight's lance-point leveled inches from his heart. For Gulliver, it meant awakening to find he'd been tied up by hundreds of tiny evil creatures bent on his immediate demise.

You see the same situation pictured time and time again if you go to the movies or spend time at your local video store. It's Bill Murray waking up to find another day stuck on rewind in *Groundhog Day*; or a mother and daughter waking up to discover they've traded bodies in *Freaky Friday*; or Joe waking up to find that he doesn't have a body at all in the black-and-white classic *Mr. Jordan* (which was remade as *Heaven Can Wait* in the 1980s and remade again in 2003 as *Down to Earth*).[1]

Why do so many novelists and producers rely on this tried-and-true plot device? Because, as impossible as it may seem, it still rings true with us at many levels. In a way, people every day, *perhaps even you*, wake up to find that in a critically important area of life everything has changed. In the blink of an eye, you're miles from where you ever thought you'd be.

> *People do indeed wake up one morning to find that everything has changed people like William, Sarah, and Ray.*

WILLIAM'S STORY

Back in the days before club sports and coaches who demanded that junior-high athletes focus on one sport, William did it all. In high school he was a three-sport letterman: football in the fall, wrestling in the winter, baseball in the spring. The track coach even let him run in meets that didn't conflict with his baseball schedule. Only five-feet-nine-inches and 140 pounds, he had the strength to climb the dreaded exercise rope all the way to the top of the gym using only his arms, blast out sixty sit-ups in two minutes to win the president's blue physical fitness ribbon, and run the mile in 8:30 without even breathing hard.

Then William opened his eyes one morning and found that everything had changed in regards to his health.

In what seemed like the blink of an eye, William was now thirty years from high school and age fifty-one. Instead of picking up physical fitness ribbons, William had picked up (or rather packed on) 85 pounds to his 140-pound fighting weight. Once able to do crunches and sit-ups nonstop, now just bending over long enough to cut his toenails was a struggle that left him breathing like a horse. He'd long since lost his six-pack abs, and his standard joke to his friends was that he now carried around the whole case! Forget running the mile in under nine minutes. He laughed that the only thing he jogged now was his memory. But what wasn't funny was the day he had to be helped off the treadmill by the nurse after *walking* all of seven minutes.

For all the jokes he made about his health and physical condition, the humor was actually motivated by fear, particularly from his doctor's reports. William was a medical meltdown waiting to happen.

How did I get here? he thought to himself.

He closed his eyes, and William was back in high school, in a huddle, barking out a pass play and then leading his football team up to the line of scrimmage to take the snap from center. But when he opened his eyes, the person looking back at him in the mirror looked like he'd swallowed the football! High blood pressure. Pants uncomfortably tight even after he'd broken down and bought his first size 42. "Border-line diabetes," the doctor had said. "Possible restricted arteries." "Further tests are needed immediately." An entire laundry list of fearful predictions.

William isn't the only one who wakes up one day and can't believe his health has somehow evaporated. There are thousands of Williams and Wilmas across our country who share the same fearful wake-up call. For nearly everyone there is a shared sense of amnesia. If asked, a common response is how, despite the passage of time, there was no real conscious sense of moving from A to B much less from A to F on their heath report card. Time indeed sneaks up, without an inner alarm ever going off to warn them that they are inching closer and closer to a medical crisis.

Ever been there?

Ever realize how quickly you'll be there if things don't change?

Ever given up and thought you've wandered so far from good health and a healthy weight that you can never get back to where you want to be?

As you'll discover in this book, there is a way to wake up instead of giving up on good health. There is a way to drop pants or dress sizes and keep from dedicating more and more shelf space to doctor-ordered prescriptions.

For some readers, discovering that they can indeed make important health changes will be the most important shift they make in their life story. But for many others it won't be the fear of clogged arteries or shortness of breath that opens their eyes to the fact that important things have changed. It will be waking up to find a treasured relationship in ruins. Every day, far too many people wake up miles from where they ever thought they'd be in their marriage or family relationships.

SARAH'S STORY

When it came to Sarah's courtship and marriage, pick or mix any positive metaphors that come to mind, and they would most likely have applied: **Camelot. Two-foot putt. Off to a great start. Rock-solid foundation.** Sarah met Tom on a blind date that turned into a dream date. They were both committed Christians. In fact, they were the only outspoken believers in their respective fraternity and sorority. When it came time for the All Night Match Date and Dance, they were unwilling to shack up and instead stayed up all night talking and sharing and even praying together. That started a friendship and courtship that was a blueprint for success. He went to her father after two years of dating to ask for her hand. She went on a cross-country car trip with his mother for two weeks to cement their relationship. The two of them plugged into a great church with a top-notch couples' class. Then came the twins, and then another blessing, this time a boy. Mentally flipping through these snapshots of a near perfect past was what made where they were now so shocking and unreal.

Is he going to show up? Sarah asked herself as she sat in the small waiting room outside the counselor's office. Of all people, Sarah never thought she'd be in such a place. Not that there was anything *wrong* with counseling, *but her? Tom?*

She could close her eyes and think of the missions trip to Guatemala before they had kids, the romantic Alaskan cruise on their tenth anniversary, the long vacation drive to Disney World with the kids just last summer, the way they'd been in leadership positions at the church for years.

But when she opened her eyes, Tom still hadn't arrived, and somehow Sarah wasn't surprised. He'd been so tied up with work for so long. She'd been so busy leading her Charity League chapter and plowing time into the twins and especially making sure their youngest child didn't feel left out. (Twins have a way of making other siblings disappear.) Sure there'd been "heated discussions" and distance at times. And yes, if she was honest, the passion had cooled off considerably over the years. *But what woman with three children under ten had time to be passionate?* she asked herself.

As she tried in vain to focus on an article in a months-old waiting-room magazine, she thought, *I should be home. The twins have practice, and I've got so many calls to make.* But instead, she sat in a counselor's office, miles from her home, and miles away from where she ever thought she'd end up in her marriage.

Sarah isn't alone. There are far too many Sarahs and increasingly more and more Toms all across the country who wake up one day to discover they're in a marriage that's in ruins. To top it off, what's so confusing is that there was never a clear-cut, wrecking-ball reason for the collapse. In the marriage there was no adultery. No drug or alcohol addiction issues. No job loss that caused incredible financial pressures. No piling on by intrusive in-laws that finally became so heavy it shattered the relationship. Despite all this, the relationship was in ruins and seemingly over such small things.

RAY'S STORY

What troubled Ray most was something invisible to others. Ray didn't struggle in his marriage, which was as healthy as it had ever been. And it certainly wasn't his health. To the irritation of his coworkers and even occasionally his wife, Ray's measurements hadn't changed since high school. On the outside he was still six foot even, 32 waist, 34 inseam, 15½ collar.

But deep inside Ray knew something had shrunk to almost nothing.

If his wife or best friends noticed, no one had said anything. But for Ray there was a nagging, heavy feeling present nearly every conscious hour—*even though he knew it had to be just that, a feeling.* It was like something had died inside him. For Ray, that something used to be his everything—his faith in Christ and his love for a God who had, at one time, been so incredibly real to him.

Ray had come to Christ in college through the lifestyle evangelism of two Christian roommates. His roommates didn't condemn Ray when he came in drunk from a party. They didn't get defensive or preach at him when Ray questioned and even mocked their stand on evolution and the "ridiculous" belief that there really was a Noah and the ark. But they were also the only ones in his dorm who really seemed to listen and provide any comfort when Ray's mother unexpectedly died his junior year in college. That stunning loss led Ray to start asking serious questions about God, faith, and Christ. In their dorm room, on a muddy March day, with his two new brothers in Christ by his side, Ray asked Jesus to become his personal Lord and Savior.

It was a real-deal conversion, and he started off strong. Bible studies. Quiet times. Favorite Christian authors. Dating only committed Christians. Now twenty years, one wife, four precious kids, one difficult internship, and one incredibly successful job later, he should have been the most content person on the block. Instead, he knew something was terribly wrong. He didn't just feel spiritually empty but spiritually dead. How could that be?

In the three cities they'd lived in, they'd plowed themselves and their kids into outstanding churches. He'd gone to all the right conferences, even the big ones with thousands of men. He'd even helped lead retreats at his church, served on the elder board, and met several top national ministry leaders over the years. But now, as he stood in "their spot" in their church sanctuary—at the far back, right-hand corner of the church—he wondered if anyone else felt it was all a sham. He knew it was wrong even to think such a thing, but was what he believed really true? And what really ate at him was, *did it really even matter anymore?*

Why didn't the praise songs seem to move him as they once did? Why did he forget the sermon before he even got to the car in the parking lot? When was the last time he opened his Bible without a pastor telling him to turn to a passage? As he stood next to his wife, all he could think about was how loud and irritating the lead guitarist was in the worship band—never once how great God is.

How did I get here? he asked himself as he turned and looked at his wife, her hands open and eyes shut in worship. His own eyes stayed open as he battled with that terrible, nagging emptiness.

How did I get here?

Granted, William, Sarah, and Ray represent people in crisis. But have you ever felt like one of them? In your health, at home, or even in your heart for God, have you ever felt that the place you're at isn't *close* to where you ever thought you'd be? If so, then you're not alone, and you've picked up the right book. On the other hand, if you've never once been where these three have, then you've *absolutely* picked up the right book. To draw from the apostle Paul's words, "Let him who thinks he stands take heed that he does not fall" (1 Cor. 10:12).

In my own life, and after spending twenty-five years counseling with hundreds of Williams and Sarahs and Rays across our county, I have found that it is incredibly easy for all but a few of us to drift away in one or more important areas of our lives. In fact, it's not just individuals who wake up one day far from where they want to be. In the Scriptures, *an entire home church* got a wake-up call that despite all their good works, things were terribly wrong.

A CHURCH THAT FELL PREY TO LUCIFER'S FALL

A few times in modern church history, a paraphrase of the Bible has come out that sweeps a generation. I'm not speaking about a *translation* that strives for a literal rendering of each word of Scripture (like the King James, New King James, New International Version, or New American Standard). Rather, a paraphrase comes out that seeks to put the Bible in modern English and contemporary terms. In the 1960s, the Phillips Bible (called the "cookbook Bible" because of its distinctive cover) was one of the first that surfaced. It was devoured by new believers trying to understand God's Word. Then came The Living Bible, which has helped believers new and old for decades with its everyday wording. But I'd like to quote from one of the latest paraphrases, *The Message*. Here's how its picturesque language captures how an entire church woke up one day and found they where nowhere near where they wanted to be.

"Write this to Ephesus, to the Angel of the church. The One with Seven Stars in his right-fist grip, striding through the golden seven-lights' circle, speaks" (Rev. 2:1–2). And that Person who looks down and speaks to this church we know in any translation or paraphrase is the resurrected Lord Jesus himself.

Stop for just a moment and try to put yourself in the picture these words are painting. You're in your own church, in your own pew or favorite seat, and suddenly a special guest speaker shows up on Sunday. It's Jesus himself! And from his own mouth, you hear an unexpected message on how you as a church are doing in your walk of faith, and the news couldn't sound any better as he begins:

"I see what you've done, your hard, hard work, your refusal to quit. I know you can't stomach evil, that you weed out apostolic pretenders. I know your persistence, your courage in my cause, that you never wear out" (Rev. 2:3 *The Message*).

Wow! What a laundry list of right actions. Not that anyone was counting in the congregation, but that's seven positive things the Lord highlights they were doing right. (The number seven in Scripture always speaks of completion, perfection.) Even for the godly, I imagine that those sitting in the congregation, listening to those words, were ready for a congratulatory handshake or even a plaque or gold medal for faithfulness.

What an incredible church leadership team to get praised seven times! What devoted members and disciples who had to be making an impact in their community! What honoring words from the Lord Jesus himself! Words like, hard working! Weeding out imposters. Having courage and persistence!

In all humility, of course, if the average church today heard such praise from their Commander in Chief, they would be ready to chant, "We're number one! We're number one!"

But then came the chilling words that said they were not only *not* number one; they weren't even in the right ballpark.

"But you walked away from your first love—why?" (Rev. 2:4 *The Message*).

"What's going on with you anyway? Do you have any idea how far you've fallen? A Lucifer fall!" (vv. 4–5 *The Message*).

While I've mentioned that this is an interpretive paraphrase rather then a literal translation, I feel Eugene Peterson has captured the context of the original languages perfectly in his wording.

Somehow, in the process of doing so many good things over such a long period of time, this church had ended up at Satan's, not heaven's, doorstep! Doesn't that seem almost incredible based on all the "good" they had done? The question the Lord put to them—"Do you have any idea how far you've fallen?"—points out that they didn't know! There was a collective wake-up call that day as the message was delivered, and people must have looked around and thought, *But we've worked so hard! Done so much! Done so many things right!*

How did we get here?

As you'll see in the chapters that follow, even for a church it's not enough to put good "actions" on autopilot and just assume we'll end up where we want to go. As the church in Ephesus discovered, in the midst of doing all those good things, they had drifted from what's best. They had ended up closer to pride and emptiness than God's heart and the warmth of a first love.

Before we move on, remember that most early churches, including this one, were home churches. Not megachurches with six services on Sunday. These were small groups of believers similar to what we'd call home groups, cell groups, or small groups today. And so the question is: Have you ever been part of a small group that just seemed to fall away or fall apart over time? And again, if you have, you're certainly not alone. Far too many small groups, and even large congregations for that matter, began with a cutting-edge commitment that turned dull and ineffective over time.

"Turn back!" the Lord says. "Recover your dear early love. No time to waste, for I'm well on my way to removing your light from the golden circle" (v. 5 *The Message*).

Can you hear that sense of urgency from the Lord, who calls those in the church to make a "shift" before it's too late? There's no time to waste! Now is the time to wake up and see that our collective light as a small group or congregation has grown ineffective and dim, like a candle moved farther and farther from a table it once brightly lit.

It's time we made a HeartShift.

Like it or not, realize it or not, far too many of us are like William, Sarah, or Ray in our personal and spiritual lives, and, if we're honest, like the church of Ephesus when it comes to our corporate worship and church relationships. We've drifted toward a place we never wanted to be—even in the midst of making sincere efforts. It is time we turned back to our families, or toward better health, or to a vital personal faith, or to a loving connection with our brothers and sisters in Christ.

Like an echo from the writer of Hebrews, "Today if you hear His voice, do not harden your hearts" (3:7–8).

Today is the day we need to wake up and begin the journey back toward God's best and what's best for our family, our friendships, and even our fellowship with other believers.

It's time we made a HeartShift.

DISCUSSION QUESTIONS FOR YOUR CHURCH, SMALL GROUP, FAMILY, OR CLOSE FRIENDS

1. Can you think of a book you've read or a movie you've seen that opens with the main character finding that everything's changed? Do you agree that there is an element of truth to such stories where someone wakes up to such dramatic change? If so, why?

2. Do you know someone like William, whose health made a dramatic change over the years? What are two factors you feel numb people to deteriorating health?

3. Can you think of a couple whose marriage mirrors to some degree the story of Sarah and her husband—a couple who were the last ones you'd think would face a marital crisis but whose marriage somehow came apart over time? In an honoring way, share one reason or factor that they (or you, if Sarah's story is your own) felt led to such a thing happening.

4. Has there ever been a time in your spiritual life when you felt, at least to some degree, like Ray? Can you describe what it's like to feel alone in a crowd of worshippers or to harbor secret thoughts of God's reality, even his very existence? What do you think happens to most people who feel that way for an extended a period of time?

5. Dr. Trent uses the church of Ephesus to point out how an entire congregation walked away in their heart, even in the midst of doing lots of good things. How can that be? Do you have a firsthand example of a small group or even a large congregation who ended up far from a "first love" for Christ.

6. With only the information you have right now, respond to Dr. Trent's challenge that it's time to make a HeartShift. In the honesty of your heart, and with a trusted friend or small group, which one of the three areas described would you put at the top of your list—your health, your home, or your heart for God? Is there a fourth area not mentioned here that is really the most important area where you need to make a HeartShift?

CHAPTER TWO

How a 2 Degree Change Can Ruin or Renew Your Life

When asked to share our life story, most of us overwhelmingly describe special occasions and singular events. If we're still in school, the things that mark pages in our life story tend to be a graduation, the prom, opening an acceptance letter from that hoped-for school, or winning (or losing) a basketball championship. If we're believers, it's often the night we came to Christ or the day we were baptized or confirmed. As we get older, it may be the birth of a child, a wedding, a funeral, a divorce, a promotion, or even the day we were fired from a job.

The same thing is true with our view of history. Dramatic events are most often picked as having the greatest ability to turn the pages of history. And in truth, that's often the case. For example, the picture of a mushroom cloud rising over Hiroshima, the sounds of rifle shots ringing out and striking down President Kennedy, or the terrible replayed image of planes being flown into each of the twin World Trade Center towers can indeed shift the plates that lie under entire nations. Viewed another way, these dramatic, often unparalleled historical events can act as huge levers that shift world actions and attitudes.

Dr. Patrick Dixon, a fellow at the London Business School and a committed believer, has been called Europe's leading business futurist. Dixon labels these dramatic historical events as "wild cards,"[1] and their occurrence has sped up over the past quarter century. For the average person, these are huge unpredictable events that force us to alter our daily routines.

Yet for all their power and dramatic effect, if you'll look more closely, it's not just wild cards that become the hinges in history. In fact, far more often it proves to be the smallest acts that produce extraordinary changes.

For example, did you know that modern historians credit a difference of just two feet with the death of more than a million people?

A Difference of Just Two Feet

The date was July 20, 1944.[2] Adolph Hitler had called a supersecret meeting of his most trusted general staff at a small airfield just outside Berlin. The tide of war had turned decidedly against Nazi Germany. The Americans were steadily advancing toward the Rhine, and bombers were now reaching Berlin almost daily. The Russian front was in full collapse. An emergency war council was called, and crucial battle plans were being drawn up by the fuehrer himself.

With the meeting already in progress, Colonel Klaus von Stauffenberg walked inside a small, inconspicuous building. A nobleman by birth, he was actually Count von Stauffenberg, now chief of staff to General Fromm, the commander in chief of the German home army.

Stauffenberg entered the briefing room wearing an iron cross he had won fighting with the Tenth Panzer Division against the Americans at the Kasserine Pass in Tunisia. He also walked into the room minus his right hand and wearing a distinctive black patch over the eye he had lost in close combat. With the three fingers remaining on his left hand, he carried a large, black soft-sided briefcase. Needless to say, with all those badges of courage and sacrifice, no one questioned this officer's patriotism or his presence in the room that day.

Nor did they question why he was carrying a briefcase.

Several of the officers present, including Stauffenberg, had been called upon to bring an updated report to the fuehrer on some aspect of the war. Yet hidden inside Stauffenberg's black satchel, along with his briefing papers, was a time bomb wrapped in an old shirt. Several pounds of plastic explosives had been linked to, of all things, an English-made detonator.[3]

It was a daring plan by a secret cell of Hitler's most senior officers to save Germany, end the war, and sue for peace with the Allies—starting by ridding the Third Reich and the world of the madman Hitler.

Hitler's back was to Stauffenberg when he entered the room. No one noticed as he slowly inched closer and closer to Hitler and then casually slid the black satchel under the table. With incredible nerve he placed the bomb on the inside of one of the large heavy oak table supports, within a few feet of where Hitler sat. Colonel Stauffenberg quietly excused himself from the room. If anyone had asked, he would have told them he needed to be excused to take a prearranged phone call to get an update from a commander in the field. No one asked, however, and Stauffenberg walked out of the room at 12:36 p.m.

At 12:42 p.m., exactly six minutes later, the countdown ended.

When the massive explosion took place, Colonel Stauffenberg was standing back at a distance, looking directly at the small, thirty-by-fifteen-foot building. Bodies literally flew out the windows as everything went up in smoke and flames. There was absolutely no doubt in Stauffenberg's mind that everyone inside the room was dead.

Unfortunately, what Stauffenberg didn't know was that after he left the room, Colonel Brandt kept hitting the large black satchel with his foot. Several survivors remember Brandt being irritated, reaching under the table and sliding the briefcase two feet to his right—away from the fuehrer and on the outside of the thick, oak table support. Five minutes later the bomb went off. Seven instantly dead. Twenty-four fatally or seriously wounded. But Adolph Hitler escaped with only a sprained wrist and a shattered eardrum, and Stauffenberg was captured and executed that same night.

As a direct result of that assassination attempt, Hitler ordered his "final solution" sped up. Thousands upon thousands of Jews and German prisoners were murdered in the months immediately following the blast. Instead of the war ending that day or soon after, the carnage continued for another full year. An estimated one million lives on all sides were lost because of a two-foot difference.

It's not just in a war between nations where we see that the smallest of actions can make huge shifts. In the world of modern-day presidential politics, we've all witnessed how the smallest of margins can dramatically swing an election. In the 2000 election between George W. Bush and Al Gore, if fewer than two votes per polling place in Florida had swung the other way, it would have moved the state from the blue column to the red, and Al Gore would be in the White House today. Nationally, a 2 percent change in four of the most closely contested swing states could have changed the outcome of the election as well.

If small things matter in the conflict of arms or in the fate of a national election, they are incredibly powerful when it comes to our personal lives. For while there are certainly global wild cards that force us to change, for many of us the smallest actions will bring the greatest change. In fact, they can ruin or renew our lives.

HOW A 2 DEGREE CHANGE CAN RUIN YOUR LIFE

I'm a "too frequent" flyer during certain times of the year. That means I get to experience all the joys of increased security, long lines, lost luggage, weather delays, and even the "let's just sit on the plane for two hours before we take off for no apparent reason" delays. At least that's what it seemed like to me one summer day when my plane pulled away from the gate in Austin, Texas.

I'm sure the airline marked down somewhere in large, official-looking letters, "We left on time!"

Indeed, the deplaning passengers had been hurried off, and my fellow passengers and I hurried on our flight in record time. The perky flight attendants had closed the door and cross-checked the cabin as the ground crew pushed us back from the jetway for an on-time departure. The only problem was, we didn't depart. The pilots started the engines, taxied all of five hundred yards towards the runway, and that's where we came to a stop.

"Folks, we just found out we have a paperwork issue we have to iron out," the pilot said. "We'll be stopping here for a few minutes."

For those who travel frequently, being told you'll be waiting a "few minutes" could mean "anytime between now and when your youngest child graduates college." For those of us inside that packed Boeing 727 during the summer, it meant sitting and sweltering on the hot tarmac. (Thankfully, and to their credit, Southwest finally sent out an air-conditioning truck before we all melted!) In that stuffy, claustrophobic environment, we endured minutes that turned into two hours without moving an inch.

Normally, with no phone or e-mail interruptions, I look forward to redeeming the time on a plane by writing, reading, or doing correspondence. But after the battery on my computer ran out, and sitting next to someone for what seemed like forever, I finally stuck up a conversation with my next-door neighbor. He was an engineer from the Houston area.

"Petroleum engineer?" I asked.

"No, I work for NASA," he admitted.

And of course, for the next hour I'm sure that's something he wished he hadn't confessed. Like most people my age who grew up watching the build-up of manned space flight to Neil Armstrong leaving his footprints on the moon, I was an astronaut "wannabe" as a kid.

Here at last was my chance to talk to a genuine missile scientist and ask all my questions about space flight! He was patient and shared some incredible behind-the-scenes stories, including his role in the last *Apollo* space flight. But at one point I hit a nerve when I brought up what I thought was a simple "margin of error" question.

"What are the tolerances you build into the trajectory when you blast off and head to the moon?" I asked him. "For example, after you blast off, could you be just a little off, say like a couple of degrees off on your flight path, without it being such a huge problem?"

"Two degrees?" he said. "Just be two degrees off?"

Out came his briefcase and his hybrid handheld calculator that would make a Texas Instruments T3000 calculator blush and feel like a slide rule. In went the "very approximate" distance of 217,614 miles from the earth to the moon (depending on the time of year and apogee of the moon's orbit around the earth, of course). Fingers flew furiously for a few moments as some Einsteinian calculation continued.

"Be just two degrees off from when you blast off, and roughly taking into account the time and distance traveled," he said as he turned his calculator toward me, "and you'll miss not only your point of orbital entry, but you'll miss the moon by a measly 11,121 miles."

I wrote down that number on a torn off page of a *USA Today* that served as an impromptu notepad. "11,121." I finally left my new NASA friend in peace, but I've never forgotten his conclusion or what it can tell us about the most important relationships and areas of our lives.

Add in enough time and distance, and be just two degrees off and you'll miss your target by miles. I think that thought impacted me so much because it seemed to answer the *why* and even the *how* question of the church of Ephesus I'd been studying so closely—the same group of "committed" folks I described in the previous chapter. Just be two degrees off from a right heart attitude, add in enough time and distance, and an *entire church* can end up miles from God's heart.

In my counseling practice, that same explanation fit like a frame around many troubled marriages I'd seen. Be just a few degrees off as a couple and don't bother to make any genuine course corrections over the months and years, and then watch how you wake up one day and discover you're emotionally miles apart.

For example, I recall the successful red-haired banker and his wife I'd met with in my office. Like Sarah's story in the first chapter, their marriage had gotten off to a great start. But seventeen years had passed, and now they stood at emotional ends of the equator. To make matters worse, a female coworker at the banker's office now factored into the husband's equation. Tragically, from this banker's perspective, it all seemed to add up.

After all, what's easier to do? Make a 180 degree change (or even a 90 degree change) back toward his wife? Or just turn 2 degrees toward a stranger?

What's easier to do?
Make a 180 degree change back toward a loved one,
or just turn 2 degrees toward a stranger?

That conversation on a plane years ago first began to form a tangible picture in my mind and provide an answer to much of the emotional, spiritual, and even physical wreckage I'd seen for decades. What's more, it opened my eyes to passage after passage in Scripture that talks about the importance of small things in a life of faith, peace, and rest. As I began to share these ideas, first with those in counseling and then with many at my conferences over the years, you could see the heads nod and the eyes open.

People instantly got it.

They understood almost intuitively the idea that a small 2 Degree Change could change their life for the worse, given the gradual workings of time. But then they began to understand that the *reverse* was true as well. Amazingly, even small shifts in a positive direction could move a person from ruin to renewal.

How a 2 Degree Change Can Renew Your Life or Relationships

In your mind, picture any one of the couples I've mentioned who woke up one day with their marriage in ruins. (Or feel free to substitute your own marriage, if you've been there, or any couple of your own choosing.) If you've spent any time viewing a conflicted couple, it's like they're standing on opposite banks of a deep, fast-flowing river. The mere thought or encouragement from others to move toward each other seems to bring with it a strong, involuntary emotion akin to having to plunge into that icy cold river and exert tremendous effort to get across. No wonder so many couples settle for tossing loud, angry words across the chasm, trying to get the other person to take the plunge. And no wonder so many people then feel justified with walking away because, "Well, I tried to get him (or her) to move, but it just never happened."

But what if there were a way to bridge that gap between a couple in conflict?

A way that wasn't as dramatic or flashy as flinging oneself into a river (which, as we'll see in chapter 4, is one of the nine reasons so many of us never do get around to making positive changes).

What if there were a way to bridge a gap between a couple in conflict?

But what if there already were a bridge, a footbridge really, between these two people—so narrow it had gone unnoticed and unused? What if there really was a way to move closer so that any need for shouting could stop because they were now inches instead of a football field apart?

And the answer to all those "what ifs" is that such a footbridge does exist, though it is too often ignored, unseen, or less traveled.

There is a narrow way that our eyes tend to miss in all the noise and emotion of our lives. A bridge that can provide a way back to closeness and caring for couples, or to a renewed faith, or to good health for an individual.

That bridge is what I call a HeartShift, and the way we cross it is through 2 Degree Changes. Certainly I'm not the first one to see or describe such a bridge that can take a person from enmity to closeness in a broken relationship. For example, C. S. Lewis uses the word *charity* to describe just such a secret path.

WHAT DOES *CHARITY* HAVE TO DO WITH CHANGE?

C. S. Lewis was a Cambridge scholar and the author of many wonderful books, including the series The Chronicles of Narnia. In my opinion the Lord also gave him a still unparalleled ability to clarify complex issues. In his apologetic classic *Mere Christianity*, Lewis speaks at length about "good and evil." At the heart of doing good, Lewis highlights a Christian virtue called "charity." For Lewis, this word has a two-part definition. One part has to do with "forgiveness," which is something we'll address in the next chapter. But his primary definition of what it means to "do good" as a Christian is by extending charity to others, a word very different from what we normally refer to as charity.

From our seats in this third millennium, charity involves putting outgrown or unwanted clothing on the curb for Goodwill, or dropping an envelope in the collection plate that's being passed for the poor. Yet for Lewis, charity wasn't a token gift given to help those less fortunate. It was a heartfelt decision to choose action over emotion or natural preference as well as a daily virtue that should mark a Christian as set apart from nonbelievers. Here's how Lewis illustrates charity in action: "The difference between a Christian and a worldly man is not that the worldly man has only affections or 'likings' and the Christian has only 'Charity.' The worldly man treats certain people kindly because he 'likes' them, the Christian, trying to treat every one kindly, finds himself liking more and more people as he goes on—including people he could not even have imagined himself liking at the beginning."[4]

Now go back to that picture of a conflicted couple.

The idea of not being able even to imagine liking their spouse again is exactly the mind-set most couples hold on to with white-knuckle grips when they first walk into my counseling office. They can't even imagine rekindling warm feelings of attachment, much less regaining a genuine love for that person they're so angry with.

But again, what if there really were a bridge that still existed between these two, even with all the arguments they've had? What if, over time, they could pick a path that could lead them up to a level of closeness they couldn't dream of reaching in that first counseling session? What if there were a way of relating to each other that could even result in their gaining back a first-love attachment for each other?

"Good and evil both increase at compound interest.
That is why the little decisions you and I make every day
are of such infinite importance."

Sound impossible?[5] Such a bridge back to each other does, in fact, exist, as C. S. Lewis points out: "The rule for all of us is perfectly simple. Do not waste time bothering whether you 'love' your neighbor, act as if you do. And soon as we do this we find one of the great secrets. When you are behaving as if you love someone, you will presently come to love him. If you injure someone you dislike, you will find yourself disliking him more. If you do him a good turn, you will find yourself disliking him less."[6]

Doesn't that sound simple? It sounds almost childish, foolish, or shallow. And yet Lewis's conclusion is absolutely true, is understood only by the mature, is undeniably biblical, and is fathoms deep. There is indeed an amazing secret at work when we take even the smallest steps toward what's right and good. For example, even the most conflicted spouses—lovers who have become intimate enemies over time—can renew a grudging respect, then a like, and then, incredibly, even a love for their spouse. Such a shift will not come by doing that person ill. It can come, however, even if the doing of small, loving acts toward the other person feels at first like acting or pretending. For when it comes to our *actions* toward another (and as we'll see later, even in how we view ourselves), there's something unseen and incredibly powerful behind each act of good or evil. Lewis continues with this transforming thought: "Good and evil both increase at compound interest. That is why the little decisions you and I make every day are of such infinite importance."[7]

Read Lewis's words one more time. Think about them, ponder them for a moment. Do they seem to ring true and reflect what you know of Scripture? Do you think his use of the words "infinite importance" is hyperbole and exaggeration, or are they really true?

And now read how Lewis fleshes out that staggering thought: "Good and evil both increase at compound interest. That is why the little decisions you and I make every day are of such infinite importance. The smallest good act today is the capture of a strategic point from which, a few months later, you may be able to go on to victories you never dreamed of. An apparently trivial indulgence in lust or anger today is the loss of a ridge or railway line or bridgehead from which the enemy may launch an attack otherwise impossible."

Lewis was writing immediately after the deep shadows cast by World War II and was drawing his analogies from that tragic time when hating former enemies seemed so easily justified. However, Lewis expounds the thought that the little decisions we make every day will move us gradually toward more good or toward evil.

It's the Small Marks on Our Soul That Will Shape Our Lives

Remember my NASA friend on the plane and how far off we can miss our target by being just two degrees off course? C. S. Lewis and this space engineer have much in common. One looks at what being on or off target means over a great physical distance, while the other reminds us that in a journey through eternity, even the small acts count. Lewis writes, "Remember, we Christians think man lives for ever. Therefore, what really matters is those little marks or twists on the central, inside part of the soul, which are going to turn it, in the long run, into a heavenly or hellish creature."[8]

For Lewis, and throughout Scripture, it's the small things that count in a big way toward eternity. But that's so hard to see! From our daily life perspective, it's easy to think that just a few cigarettes a day can't matter much because we can't see decades ahead to our dying too early of lung cancer.

It is absolutely true that the small steps we take today are either moving us along a road toward increasing light and love, or we're taking steps toward complete darkness. There are no other roads, no middle-ground choices. To use another analogy, if we're up to our chin in the surf, facing an unrelenting incoming ocean tide, the water will only become shallow and our situation less dire if we turn and walk toward the beach. Life will only get better if we begin to make the small choices that over time have the power to rescue and redirect us.

Standing still simply isn't an option for those who choose life. Doing nothing isn't neutral but often fatal.

"Therefore, what really matters is those little marks or twists on the central, inside part of the soul, which are going to turn it, in the long run, into a heavenly or hellish creature."

To go back to yet another analogy, can you now begin to see the outlines of that bridge I mentioned that can connect a distant spouse, or be used to renew a flagging faith, or that can even help restore a body that's too far out of shape? Even the smallest of acts, what I call "2 Degree Changes," count greatly. In fact, for most of us our most important personal changes won't happen by waiting for a huge wild-card event to change our life situation. Relying on that one big break that will somehow transport us from A to Z is a great way to become or stay broken.

In our health, putting all our hopes on that magic pill that will take off those sixty-five pounds with no effort, overnight, all without negatively effecting our health, can almost guarantee our waistline will expand.

With our finances, convincing ourselves that we're going to win the lottery this week or hoping a rich relative will pass away and leave us thousands isn't a winning strategy to erase our debt. It's the small changes in our spending or saving that can, over time, lift that burden.

In a conflicted marriage, it's not *knowing* that our spouse will never change, and therefore feeling justified to do them ill, that will change a hurting marriage. Evil doesn't beget good. It's doing small things, 2 Degree Actions—regardless of our feelings, that will assuredly change *our* attitude toward them, and perhaps even theirs towards us.

For example, I've seen the "tipping point" come for a severely conflicted couple when a husband started pulling out his wife's chair when she sat down at a restaurant. A hundred times he had told her, "I'm a different person. I've changed." And each time his words carried all the weight of steam. But that small act of moving to her side and pulling out her chair was something she couldn't explain away, and it began eating away at her hate.

Similarly, regarding our spiritual life, I've seen men and women whose love for Christ had grown cold make a small turn toward the Lord by just starting with simple sentence prayers at night. Amazingly, they soon discovered that Jesus hadn't moved or deserted them after all.

And finally, I've seen a discouraged woman begin a successful path toward better health by starting with the first small step of cutting down from two desserts to one. While some might find that humorous or even silly, that small step began to strengthen the resolve that changed that woman's life and finally brought her success in moving toward better health.

Still not convinced? Still uncertain that great relationships and successful life changes should start with a HeartShift that puts us on the right path and then becomes habit and undeniable reality by small acts, small 2 Degree Changes? Then instead of looking at the calculations of a NASA engineer or at the arguments of C. S. Lewis, let's look at a time when the Lord Jesus himself clarified to the disciples how the path to the heights of greatness begins with the smallest of steps.

LISTENING IN ON A PRIVATE CONVERSATION

Have you ever had the incredible embarrassment of having your boss or a coworker unexpectedly walk into the room right in the middle of your conversation about him or her? There's no hole to crawl into near the water cooler, nor was there any place to hide in the village where Jesus asked his disciples a pointed question: "What were you discussing on the way?" (Mark 9:33).

Busted. That must have been the disciples' feeling when Jesus' words caused their jaws to drop but no words to come out. That's because during their long journey on foot, we're told, they'd been discussing which one of them was the greatest.

In the disciples' defense, most believers have had those conversations at times. Most of us are good at pointing out to others our potential and promise. We're quick to explain why we deserved that raise, why anyone else *but us* should be downsized at work or RIFT'ed if we're in military service. And even if we are humble enough not to voice such prideful words aloud, that sense of liking to get ahead of someone else lies deep within us. That's particularly true if we dislike or hold a grudge against that person. For example, who among us hasn't been cut off by an extremely rude driver on the freeway, and then inwardly exalted when we later see his car pulled over by the police or stopped dead in its tracks as our lane of traffic speeds past?

Doesn't that bring an inner voice that shouts, *Yes! I won!*

We keep score in our culture, and who wins counts.

What's sad is, that very human characteristic of arguing "I get a bigger half than you do!" came out right after Jesus had finished talking about sacrificial love and about how their world was about to change dramatically, tragically. To see that, let's back up a few verses to the context of the disciples discussing who was the greatest. For as we look closer at this passage, we'll receive not only a lesson in real greatness but in small 2 Degree actions as well.

In Mark 9:31 we read, "For He was teaching His disciples and telling them, 'The Son of Man is to be delivered into the hands of men, and they will kill Him; and when He has been killed, He will rise three days later.' But they did not understand this statement, and they were afraid to ask Him."

Fear lies at the heart of procrastination.

It was no fun talking about losing Jesus or imagining him slain, so they put off talking about subjects that were so disruptive. It was confusing to think that Someone who could calm the waves and call forth the dead was now talking about laying down his life. To think about such massive changes was disquieting so, faced with a long journey on foot, why not spend the time talking about something that made them feel better or at least bigger?

In fact, if things were changing so dramatically, then why not talk about who had done the best or was owed the most or deserved the greatest share? If things were changing, then why not add up their winnings? Why not talk about what's in it personally after investing three years of sweat equity walking with Jesus?

These were guys, after all, who were a resurrection and Pentecost away from being saints. They were calloused fishermen and once-crooked tax collectors. Real people like us. If the game was close to over, at least some of them wanted to know, "Who won? Who's the greatest?"

Can you see that, just like the church in Ephesus, it's possible to be around Jesus—in this case *literally*—and still end up miles from where he wants us to be? Thankfully for those of us seeking to follow Jesus, we have his Word and the biblical record of what happened next.

Watch how Jesus first challenged his disciples to make what I'd call a HeartShift, to realize they were off course and to make a decision to move in a different direction. And then look at how he laid out for them a path that would allow them to arrive exactly where he wanted them to be. For Jesus such a path or bridge to real greatness isn't crossed by taking big steps or doing big things but by the smallest of actions—2 Degree steps. That comes out as the lesson begins: "Sitting down, He called the twelve and said to them, 'If anyone wants to be first, he shall be the last of all and servant of all'" (Mark 9:35).

Whether you call it a HeartShift or a mind shift or a paradigm shift or any other kind of shift, Jesus began by challenging them to make a huge shift in both their mental and emotional perspectives. That day along the road, they may have been on the right road to their destination, but they veered way off course from the subject of their discussion—greatness. To reinforce that fact, Jesus went even further to give them a picture of just what he (and his heavenly Father) meant by greatness.

"Taking a child, He set him before them, and taking him in His arms, He said to them, 'Whoever receives one child like this in My name receives Me; and whoever receives Me does not receive Me, but Him who sent Me'" (Mark 9:36–37).

What an incredible privilege to get to peer into the classroom the Lord Jesus set up for his closest followers. For example, did you notice how Jesus didn't start off by telling them how wrong they'd been? There's not a negative word about their prideful talk, or any verbal attacks about how dull or dense or full of themselves they'd become. Why?

Jesus didn't have to beat them up, because conviction already hung heavy in the room. His one-sentence question: "What were you discussing on the way?" (v. 33), had instantly stopped their lengthy conversation.

Remember, Jesus was as fully man as they were. He already knew what their conclusions would be on the subject of greatness, and he knew they were wrong and off course. So Jesus didn't waste time discussing the wrong answer with them. There's no use having a struggling golfer hit another hundred balls with the wrong grip.

Instead of shaming them, it was time to gently but firmly change their stance and grip, and Jesus did just that by first "sitting down." Perhaps in a movie or in college you've heard about the "chair of education" or the "chair of the history department." That's a reference to the fact that in ancient times, rabbis or even kings "sat down" when they issued a solemn message or official decrees. (Picture the gravity behind the words of our own president when he sits down in the Oval Office to address the American people.) Here, Jesus "sits down" and begins training the Twelve on this subject of greatness.

Though they had remained silent about what they had talked about, Jesus spoke up and gave them the answer to their question, Who's the greatest? Those who want to be first must learn to be the servant of all.

It's not the celebrity but the servant who pictures greatness. Greatness will not be found by looking at the beautiful people strutting down the red carpet and holding aloft their shinning awards. To see an example of greatness, you would have had to show up hours earlier to see those who worked to lay down that red carpet that allowed others to look so good.

Servants do the small things, the little things that help others succeed. Servants focus on the small, often uninspired tasks that make something better or cleaner or closer. And to illustrate his point powerfully, Jesus gave his disciples a living object lesson.

Before he spoke a word, Jesus put a child in his arms.

Did you know that every time we see Jesus with a child, there is appropriate, meaningful touch?[9] The Person in the room who knew the most about greatness used the smallest one in the room to make his point.

The disciples, faced with the prospect of their world turning upside down, had opted instead to discuss who would end up on top. Who was owed the most? Who would gain the most? Who should receive the most after all they'd done? Now the Lord answered their question: "Whoever receives one child like this in My name receives Me" (Mark 9:37).

So that's it? Help children if you want to be great?

If that *were* the right answer to what they'd discussed, and if it *were* what Jesus had said, then the disciples would have been right on target in their discussion about greatness. For whether it's the disciples in Jesus' day or interns trying to impress Donald Trump in our own, people think that greatness is reserved for the one who moves from "the bottom of the pile to the top," from obscurity to celebrity status. Greatness is all about having the most, being the best at what we do, knowing the most, or gaining the most attention. Or in this case, helping the most children.

If that were true, if Jesus had defined greatness as helping *children*, then whoever helps the most children wins. It's all about size and scope and "reach" and programs and numbers and BHAG (Big Hairy Audacious Goals).

It's all about doing it for *the children.*

But that's not what Jesus said.

The disciples' focus was wrong. If Jesus hadn't sat down himself and then sat them down, they would have gone on being off course when it came to greatness. Without his challenging them to make a HeartShift and live it out with 2 Degree steps in the right direction, they would have spent years striving toward what they thought was greatness and the whole time have been on the wrong road!

If they had kept thinking that greatness was all about doing the most for the most, they'd never have gotten close to what Jesus thought was great. Now I'm sure that they would have accomplished laudable things. Certainly they would have been helpful to many children. They might have even gotten praised seven times, like the church at Ephesus, for all the good they'd done. But they'd have been off course and getting more so each day when it came to hitting the target of real greatness! Instead, let's let Jesus answer the question of what "greatness" is and where it really lies.

Jesus didn't say, "Whoever receives *children.*" From his chair he said to them, "Whoever received *one* child like this one in My name receives Me."

Think about Jesus having that one child in his arms as he spoke. If greatness was about helping the children, he could have surrounded himself with every child in the neighborhood for dramatic effect. But just as dramatic, if too often overlooked, Jesus held just *one* child. It was a picture they couldn't miss.

The disciples were thinking "large ball" equals greatness.

Jesus told them it's "small ball" that counts.

They were thinking it's all about helping "the children" or "humankind."

Jesus said it's about receiving one child, this one child.

The disciples couldn't have missed his point that day.

But we do on so many days.

We still give the biggest awards to those with the biggest social service agency. We still applaud the celebrities who add their names to causes that help so many. Jesus says you're great, even if you "receive just one."

It's so like us to think it's the big things that matter the most.

It's so much like Jesus to sit us down, tell us we need to make a HeartShift, and point out that it's the little things that are really important. For Jesus, it was faith the size of a mustard seed that could move a mountain. It's the tiny bit of leaven in the loaf that could raise the whole lump of dough. It's reminding Martha that it wasn't all about doing extra credit things for Jesus; it's that one thing that her sister Mary did right.

C. S. Lewis wasn't exaggerating; instead, he was echoing the words of Scripture when he wrote about how the smallest acts and smallest decisions could set us on the right course and keep us on the right path. It's the small acts of goodness that can move us increasingly toward doing more and more good until we reach our heavenly home.

Good and evil both increase at compound interest. That is why the little decisions you and I make every day are of such infinite importance.

It's the small things that take advantage of the incredibly powerful secret of compound interest.

It's things like reaching out and putting our arms around *one* child.

Or opening one car door for our spouse (instead of giving her that look that says, "What's the matter, your arm broken?").

Or skipping one dessert.

Or reading one verse a day in our Bible or uttering a one-sentence prayer at night.

WHERE THE RUBBER MEETS THE ROAD

In the next chapter, to flesh out this thought that can seem so foreign to who we are and what our culture says, we'll look at several more biblical examples of what it means to make a HeartShift and a 2 Degree Change. But I don't want to close this chapter without giving you a homework assignment that can give you a literal feel for what I mean by a 2 Degree Change.

To do this, I'm going to ask you to do something that I know will play to every American's strengths. It might surprise you to know that in our 50/50 nation, where we're split down the middle on everything from politics to ethics, there is one thing every American agrees on: that they're a "better than average" driver.

Every survey of Americans shows that self-perception, so let's go driving as a homework assignment that can give you a feel for both a 2 Degree Change and a HeartShift.

Go out and sit behind the wheel of your car. If there weren't so many hungry trial lawyers on the streets, I'd ask you to actually start your car. However, since we live in the real world, just sit behind the wheel of your car in your garage or carport, put your hands on the steering wheel, close your eyes, and imagine you're driving on a wide, flat street.

After you *imagine* pulling out from your driveway, begin to accelerate as you start down the street. On your imaginary drive, pretend there are no other cars behind or in front of you. It's a beautiful day, and there are no potholes or stop signs or cars parked anywhere along the long, absolutely flat street in front of you.

Also, since you're using your imagination, let's make it a *new car* you're driving. Showroom fresh with tape marks still on the window where the dealer sticker was attached just hours before. In other words, everything works, everything's new, and every system is factory tight and aligned to exact dealer specifications.

With all that going for you as you start out on your drive, now make sure you're right in the middle of your lane. After making sure you're going as straight as possible, gently, carefully let go of the steering wheel. (Perhaps you can see now why we're *imagining* that you're driving!)

You're on a flat, open road in a new car that's perfectly aligned, so why bother to steer? Just step on the gas, put your hands behind your head (you can even close your eyes), and enjoy the ride.

If you actually do that, how long do you think it would take for your car to begin to drift? And how much longer before your new car ended up wrecked or in the ditch, or at least rammed into the side of the road?

Do you get the picture behind this homework assignment?

Because you are a better-than-average driver, you know that to stay on the road and stay out of serious trouble, you constantly have to make small, minor course corrections.

2 Degree Changes.

Dozens of small shifts of the steering wheel on a trip to the store.

Hundreds of them on a trip to the next town.

Even if the road is wide and flat and your car is in great shape, the car won't steer itself. That's because there is no autopilot on a car. *And now you know that there's no autopilot in your spiritual life, or your health, or in your marriage, or as a parent, or friend, or grandparent, or at work,* or *in ministry,* or *as a student.* And now I hope you have a feel for something else as well.

If your hands *have* been "off the wheel" for any length of time, then you're drifting toward problems whether you realize it or not, and you will only move in a positive direction by making a decision to get back to driving. That decision, that *HeartShift,* gets your hands off your lap or untangles your fingers from behind your head and gets them back on the wheel and doing the small things it takes to get back to being that better-than-average driver . . . or person.

If you're serious about keeping your relationships out of the ditch— or getting them yourself out of the ditch and back on the right road— then life is all about making that HeartShift and those small, minor, consistent, 2 Degree adjustments.

There is no autopilot on a car, and there is no autopilot in your spiritual life, or your health, or in your marriage, or as a parent, or friend, or grandparent.

Throughout the rest of this book you'll discover more verses and encouragement to make a HeartShift in the most important areas of your life and to live that decision out with small 2 Degree Changes. You'll also be challenged to start your own "33 Group" to support these changes, to join a unique online community of those committed to change, to enlist your home church as a HeartShift church if you'd like, and you'll even get the opportunity to pinpoint your strengths and find a starting point for change by taking an incredibly powerful online assessment.

But before we get into the process of change, we need to make two stops. First, we'll look at several powerful, biblical examples that can help us understand more clearly and dig more deeply into just what I mean by a HeartShift and 2 Degree Changes.

And then, just before we jump into a change process presented in this book, I'll urge you to stop and face the barriers to change that stand in front of you. In fact, I'll share nine reasons you'll never change and then share that one reason you must.

QUESTIONS FOR DISCUSSION WITH A SMALL GROUP, SPOUSE, OR CLOSE FRIEND

1. Do you agree with Dr. Trent's assertion that history, and our life history, is most often measured by events? If so, what are some page-turning events in your life story?

2. Dr. Dixon's study of "wild cards" is certainly sobering. Share how a "wild card" event in the past has impacted your life. As a group or with a friend or couple, tell what you think might be a probable wild card we'll have to face in our future? Is there any way to prepare for such an event?

3. What's easier for you to picture—how a small change can ruin a life or renew it? Explain your answer.

4. Dr. Trent says, "Add in enough time and distance, and be just 2 degrees off, and you'll miss your target by miles." Can you think of, and share, an example where these words fit like a frame around a friend or family member's actions?

5. Dr. Trent obviously puts great weight on C. S. Lewis's comments: "Good and evil both increase at compound interest. That is why the little decisions you and I make every day are of such infinite importance." As a group or with your spouse or friend, dig into that statement for a few minutes. What do you think Lewis is saying? Can you think of a biblical verse, person, or situation that backs it up?

6. Jesus shows that the starting point for real greatness starts with holding one child. Does that encourage you as you see Jesus focus on small things? Why or why not? Can you think of another time when Jesus had people focus on one thing? (As a hint, think of two sisters in Scripture whom Jesus knew well.)

7. Did the driving analogy that ends this chapter and highlights the need for constant 2 Degree Changes make sense to you? Did you realize how many small changes you make just to keep your car going straight? Can you think of how this analogy might encourage you as you seek to make changes in your life story?

John
IVERS
FOR
COUNTY
COUNCIL

Mark 9:33

Page 7. Ray's Story
Page 12
Page 24 - 29 Read

Than Read 📖 Where the
Rubber meets the
Road.

Than Talk about their
life - are your hands
on or off the steering
wheel?

(812) 882-8872

CHAPTER THREE

Taking That First Step into a
Kingdom of Change

It's time to take a closer look at two terms that have surfaced throughout the first two chapters: HeartShift and the idea of making a
2 Degree Change. Because it's always best to show and tell, I'd like to
let two dramatic biblical examples help show off and define both terms
and demonstrate practically what they can mean to your life and mine.

Both stories are found in the Old Testament. In the first we'll see a
man who indeed woke up one day to find his world radically and tragically changed.

WHEN SMALL THINGS LEAD TO GREAT THINGS

In God's Word, there was a soldier who had earned a place of great
power, prestige, and influence. Here's how the Scriptures picture him:

Now Naaman, captain of the army of the king of Aram,
was a great man with his master, and highly respected, because
by him the LORD had given victory to Aram. The man was
also a valiant warrior. (2 Kings 5:1)

Have you noticed how some people just seem to have it all? The
confidence of their superiors. The respect and admiration of their peers.
The courage of their convictions and even the physical strength to com-
pete with the best. Seemingly, the hand of God on their every endeavor.
Such a man was Naaman, a man of undisputed personal courage and
great positional power.

Yet in a cruel twist of fate, he would now lose it all.

That's because Scripture tells us that he was a leper.

On whatever day Naaman first noticed the unmistakable sign on his skin that he carried the ancient world's most deadly disease, a terrible countdown clock began ticking. With each passing hour his wealth, power, and privilege was being eaten away. *Literally.* That's because leprosy wasn't just a minor inconvenience but a death sentence. It was a slow, creeping, terrible way to die that would relentlessly strip him of all his dignity, physical prowess, lofty positions, and closest relationships. Mighty warriors had failed to kill Naaman on the battlefield. Now a tiny microbe would bring down Aram's best. But as sad as his situation was, this is actually a story of hope.

In the previous chapter, we saw how Jesus used a child to instruct the disciples on greatness. In this story we're introduced to another child who had the courage to speak up and tell a shattered man and his wife that things can change. "Now the Arameans had gone out in bands and had taken captive a little girl from the land of Israel; and she waited on Naaman's wife. She said to her mistress, 'I wish that my master were with the prophet who is in Samaria! Then he would cure him of his leprosy'" (2 Kings 5:2–3).

No one except the king held a position of greater power than Naaman. As such, you can be sure that whatever remedies were at hand when his leprosy had appeared had already been hurriedly and fervently tried. None worked.

Not only was there no remedy with leprosy, but remission wasn't an option. Leprosy, like a pitiless cancer, wouldn't stop until it had disfigured and finally killed its victim. Yet it was not only the leper who was sentenced to suffer. For that person's family there came a terrible burden as well. Never again could they touch or hold their loved one. Take just a moment and imagine never being able to touch your spouse or child again. For Naaman's wife, it meant she could hold him only at arm's and word's length now, and do her best to endure with him the long, slow wait until his death.

Yet even with such a dire diagnosis, there remains a stubborn hope when we deeply love someone. It's the kind of hope that makes us hyper-alert to some unknown or unpublished remedy. And so it was that Naaman's wife grabs hold of the alternative medicine offered in the words spoken by a young slave girl.

The slave child seemed so certain, so convinced that in the land of her birth lived a prophet of God who could help her master—and not just help him bear up under his symptoms but provide him with a full pardon from the death sentence he faced.

If this young girl's words really were true, then there was hope. And yet Naaman, the great warrior and statesman, must both accept the advice of a child and look for help in a distant kingdom.

Wisely, he was willing to do both.

> Naaman went in and told his master, saying, "Thus and thus spoke the girl who is from the land of Israel." Then the king of Aram said, "Go now, and I will send a letter to the king of Israel." He departed and took with him ten talents of silver and six thousand shekels of gold and ten changes of clothes. He brought the letter to the king of Israel, saying, "And now as this letter comes to you, behold, I have sent Naaman my servant to you, that you may cure him of his leprosy." When the king of Israel read the letter, he tore his clothes and said, "Am I God, to kill and to make alive, that this man is sending word to me to cure a man of his leprosy? But consider now, and see how he is seeking a quarrel against me." (2 Kings 5:4–7)

Because Naaman is a captain at arms and a man under orders, he goes first to his commander in chief to ask for sick leave. The king loves his servant and encourages him to go. He values him so highly in fact that the king goes one step better than just giving him time off. He decides to spare no expense to send him to "the best."

When you read the king's response, it is obvious that he never even considers the idea of Naaman going before some small-potatoes, backwoods prophet. If Israel is a place that offers hope and healing to his greatest knight, then Naaman will start at the top. He is given a personal letter from the king to go right to the chief of staff. No wasting time with interns or waiting in long lines for managed care. Naaman was worthy of royal treatment at home. This letter would demand nothing less from Israel's king and demand immediate results as well.

Before we go further, does this king's action bring to mind an earlier discussion we've had? Do you remember how the disciples misunderstood greatness and how Jesus sat them down and corrected them using a child? It seems this king suffered from a similar mind-set. He ignores the slave child's advice to go to the prophet for healing. Instead he goes right to the top, one king to another, for a miracle. Most kings find it impossible even to imagine that greatness could reside in a servant, even if that person was the servant of the Most High God. So this letter goes from one CEO to another CEO.

Along with the letter, Naaman travels with a host of fellow soldiers and servants and a fortune in gold and fine garments. It must have been an impressive procession, but it proceeded to the wrong change agent's doorstep. In fact, the king of Israel is so shocked and feels so inadequate with their unexpected visit that he tears his robes and cries out that he's been set up!

They were asking the impossible of him! In truth they were asking the impossible of anyone, royalty or not. The king of Israel feared his honest inability to help would generate anger and perhaps even war between these two nations. But then word reaches the one person with connections who could really bring change. "It happened when Elisha the man of God heard that the king of Israel had torn his clothes, that he sent word to the king, saying, 'Why have you torn your clothes? Now let him come to me, and he shall know that there is a prophet in Israel.' So Naaman came with his horses and his chariots and stood at the doorway of the house of Elisha" (2 Kings 5:8–9).

Can you imagine the step down from the king's palace to the bare-bones home of a prophet? It would be like leaving the Mayo Clinic, filled with its multi-million-dollar equipment and dozens of renowned physicians and specialists, all because a rural family doctor had called Mayo to tell Naaman he had misread the address on his appointment card. If Naaman was serious about change, then he had to walk down the palace steps, remount the whole procession, and ride down dusty roads to a tiny dwelling far outside the city.

To Naaman's credit, his need and motivation to change takes him those extra steps to Elisha's humble dwelling. But there Naaman's patience and perspective ends—especially when the prophet sends out a helper with an unexpected prescription for a cure:

Elisha sent a messenger to him, saying, "Go and wash in the Jordan seven times, and your flesh will be restored to you and you will be clean."

But Naaman was furious and went away and said, "Behold, I thought, 'He will surely come out to me and stand and call on the name of the LORD his God, and wave his hand over the place and cure the leper.'

"Are not Abanah and Pharpar, the rivers of Damascus,
better than all the waters of Israel? Could I not wash in
them and be clean?" So he turned and went away in a rage.
(2 Kings 5:10–12)

Emotionally, have you ever been there? Have you ever walked into a doctor's office feeling miserable, then walked out with only a "take two aspirins" speech and not even a decent prescription? Naaman was facing a huge, life-threatening crisis. He had come miles across the desert and even humbled himself to step down from the palace to the prophet's home.

Remember, this was a man of action who wasn't used to backing up for *anyone*. He was a valiant warrior, the second in command of a mighty kingdom.

Now he has to talk to a servant?

Not a prophet. A servant. And to make matters worse, Elisha's servant hands him a prescription that sounds like nonsense.

Go wash in the local river and he'd be cured.

Sure. Like something that small could cure a problem as big as leprosy. Imagine, the *nerve* of someone telling you that your health could change by making tiny changes. Or the nerve of someone saying that a marriage in deep trouble could be resurrected with small acts of kindness. Or the audacity of thinking that something as simple as a sentence prayer could start to restore someone's spiritual life. Or that washing seven times in a filthy river could really bring any change.

All of a sudden it hits Naaman, and you can almost see his eyes close and chin drop.

He's been duped.

That servant girl was wrong, and Israel's king was right. Only God could change what had happened to him, and that servant standing in front of him wasn't a god. In fact, now it made sense why this so-called prophet didn't come out in person.

He had nothing to offer, which meant there was no real hope.

Can't you just imagine that being the mind-set of Naaman? Can't you feel the tremendous anger that would have risen up if you suddenly realized you'd been swindled or "baited and switched"—anger toward both the perpetrators of the lie and yourself for being taken in? Naaman certainly felt that kind of anger.

The Scriptures tell us he became furious.

After all, Naaman was a skilled negotiator, a successful commander, and a counselor to the king. How could he of all people have fallen for the words of a servant girl? It's easy to think how ashamed he could have felt for being so desperate that he'd actually gone to his king for leave! And add to that the incredible inconvenience he'd caused so many friends who followed him on this long fool's errand.

Perhaps the anger started when he didn't even get to talk to the "head resident" but to some underling. And then that shock turned into disbelief and then a great anger when he'd handed such a silly prescription.

Go take a muddy bath?

That servant could go jump in a lake! Naaman would have seen the silt-filled, greenish-brown Jordan River in their journey from the palace to the prophet. If a simple washing would change anything at all, he could have done that in any of the crystal-clear mountain streams in his own country.

This is a man who had lived through hand-to-hand combat. Once his anger was roused at feeling that he'd been lied to and let down, such a man would die before stripping naked in a foreign land and washing in a dirty stream. And that's just what Naaman would have done. He would have died from a terrible sickness because of his pride—had not several people who loved him gathered up the courage to speak.

If you'll remember, it was a servant who Jesus said pictured "greatness." We've already seen how Elisha's servant shared the words that represented a cure. Now it is Naaman's own servants who will save his life—and at considerable risk.

With their master already furious, either out of fear or respect or simple cowardice, Naaman's servants could have just become bobble heads. The easy thing to do would have been just to nod in agreement at the rage this great man felt. Think of how easy and safe it would have been to say, "It wasn't your fault. How were you to know this guy was a fraud? How were you to know that little girl would lie to your wife? Just wait until we get home. She'll get hers. This guy is a sham. I wouldn't bath in that filthy river either! Let's go back home."

But eventhough they are servants, theirs is obviously a bond of love. Instead of addressing Naaman as master, they come up to him and address him as father. And then they point out what is the tipping point for so many of us when it comes to change.

THE TIPPING POINT FOR REAL CHANGE

As I've pointed out before, when we think of change, we think of wild cards and big things and dramatic events. But it's Naaman's servants who are so attuned to doing small things themselves that they point out the obvious thing Naaman has missed. "Then his servants came near and spoke to him and said, 'My father, had the prophet told you to do some great thing, would you not have done it? How much more then, when he says to you, "Wash and be clean"?'" (2 Kings 5:13).

It's easy to see where Naaman had gone wrong. After all, it's only natural for us to think that if there's a big rock to move, we need a big shovel. It's so foreign for successful people, or almost any person, to think that the little things count. The same thing is true for us living in a world where bigger is better and where our press blows almost everything out of proportion.

This servant's words were so *plain*. No drama. No shouting. No waving. No screaming. Holy men of Naaman's day often added emphasis to their incantations. There is none of that here.

For example, when the prophet Elisha faced off against the prophets of Baal on Mount Carmel, more than a hundred of them danced, and rocked, and screamed, and cut themselves with knives all day long. Elisha doesn't say a word, and his servant says little.

Just go bathe in the River Jordan.

Something inside us automatically says, "It can't be that easy."

Something deep within us warns us, "It's got to be a trick, a joke, some sort of scam."

But neither Elisha nor the God he served was about to humiliate a man of honor who was dying. And because of the courage of Naaman's servants to speak up, *because of his tremendous support system,* he finally gives it all up.

On the banks of the River Jordan, Naaman lays down every sword and weapon that had earned him his place in his kingdom. He strips off every symbol of success and authority and listens to the words of a servant who carried God's Word. "So he went down and dipped himself seven times in the Jordan, according to the word of the man of God; and his flesh was restored like the flesh of a little child and he was clean" (2 Kings 5:14).

To comment on the scale of such a miracle is unnecessary. God alone could affect such an incredible cure. So instead, let me go back to how we started this chapter, where I mentioned a HeartShift and a 2 Degree Change.

Had Naaman not made a HeartShift, one that required him to drop his anger and pride and admit he was on the wrong road, he never would have changed and certainly would have died of leprosy. And the first step he took in the right direction was to do something small. A 2 Degree step of bathing (baptizing) himself in that river. Seven times, going under the water and coming up—the number of completion— a picture of going from death to life.

Dipping himself in the river was such a small step that initially that fact alone held Naaman back from entering the river. He almost missed his chance for change by demanding, expecting, waiting for "some great thing" to effect change and demonstrate the great God of Israel's power.

Obviously, the purpose of Naaman's story in Scripture is to show God's power, not illustrate a point in a book. But as I mentioned in the first chapter, time and again in Scripture you'll see how a significant need was met by the requirement for an individual to make a HeartShift, to lay down his or her pride and pretext and to take that first small step.

Which is certainly something we'll see in our second Old Testament example.

Many People in Peril and the Small Step That Could Save Them

From one dramatic story of a leper who is given new skin and a new life, let's look at yet another life-and-death story. Only this time there were many people in peril, and the cure put before them was perhaps even smaller and more difficult to accept.

Then they set out from Mount Hor by the way of the Red Sea, to go around the land of Edom; and the people became impatient because of the journey.

The people spoke against God and Moses, "Why have you brought us up out of Egypt to die in the wilderness? For there is no food and no water, and we loathe this miserable food."

The LORD sent fiery serpents among the people and they bit the people, so that many people of Israel died.

So the people came to Moses and said, "We have sinned, because we have spoken against the LORD and you; intercede with the LORD, that He may remove the serpents from us." And Moses interceded for the people. (Num. 21:4–7)

The "they" in this story is the nation of Israel, fresh from their miraculous deliverance from Egypt. Yet on their way to where they would receive God's Ten Commandments, they had to go the long way through the wilderness.

This wasn't like going from Chicago to Phoenix in midwinter. A long journey for a welcome dose of desert warmth. The desert in that part of the world was an inhospitable place for a nation on foot. Thorns. Rocks. Little water. Even less shade from the constant heat. Yet in spite of the challenging terrain, you would think that God's people would be singing praises, not voicing complaints. After all, they had just been delivered from slavery in Egypt through the mighty works and miracles God had wrought through Moses and Aaron.

From the seven supernatural signs that had finally changed Pharaoh's heart long enough to set them free, to the unparalleled parting of the Red Sea that had sealed their escape and Pharaoh's doom, they had seen the greatness of God right before their eyes.

And it's not that God had left them on their own in the desert. To make their travel in the wilderness bearable, the Lord had already drawn water from rocks and laid out manna from heaven in similar miraculous fashion so that all would have enough to eat and drink.

Yet in spite of having had front-row seats to all these mighty miracles, there is little faith to be found in the crowd. Instead, the people grumble and question why they were ever led out into the desert in the first place. Their complaints grow so vicious, they even begin to call openly for a return to slavery in Egypt rather than accept God's leading them into a seemingly endless desert.

And so in response to all their complaints, Almighty God doesn't take his people back to the death he had just redeemed them from in Egypt. Instead, God brings the symbol of Egypt and death to them.

On the headpiece of Pharaoh was the symbol of the Egyptian nation, a fiery serpent. For all those who grumbled, Almighty God sent real-life serpents to burrow under the sand and lie hidden along the countless desert paths. As people complained, these fiery serpents— a living symbol of Egypt—began to strike. They were called "fiery serpents" because of the terrible way a person's skin would become red and inflamed where the venom went in, and as the poison moved toward their heart, they would die a terrible, unstoppable death.

Finally, linking the snakebites with their complaints, the people ran to Moses to beg for some kind of antidote. They implored Moses to ask God to call off his harsh discipline. Here is God's response: "Then the LORD said to Moses, 'Make a fiery serpent, and set it on a standard; and it shall come about, that everyone who is bitten, when he looks at it, he will live.' And Moses made a bronze serpent and set it on the standard; and it came about, that if a serpent bit any man, when he looked to the bronze serpent, he lived" (Num. 21:8–9).

There were twelve tribes that left Egypt and headed for the promised land. To keep these groups of families together, long poles with a crossbar attached were carried before each tribe, draped with that tribe's colors. Now Moses, under God's instructions, made a bronze cast of that same fiery serpent that was killing them and ordered it to be lashed upon a tribal standard. "And it shall come about, that everyone who is bitten, when he looks at it, he shall live."

Once again, a huge problem is met in Scriptures with the encouragement to do something incredibly small. It doesn't get much easier then just lifting our eyes. But can you imagine what went through these people's minds?

While the Scriptures are silent on this fact, I wouldn't be surprised if there were people who died instead of doing something so silly as looking up at a pretend snake. Perhaps some simply wouldn't believe it could be so easy. Perhaps some balked at the thought that all their pain could go away by doing something as small as shifting their gaze up to the long wooden pole and crossbeam and what was fastened to it.

Remember, the reason these people had been bitten in the first place was because of their vocal unbelief. They were up front in questioning God's direction for their lives and his provision for them on their journey. Now in order to live, they had to make a HeartShift. They had, at least internally, to admit that *they* were the ones on the wrong road by complaining and accept that the right road—the only road that led to life—was by believing God's word and his provision for them.

Once they'd made that HeartShift, then it still took a small 2 Degree step to stop their pain. They still had to look up to find hope and healing.

If you're not familiar with this Old Testament story, then you might not know that Jesus used this example to help picture for a doubting Pharisee his need to make a HeartShift.

WHEN JESUS HAD A PHARISEE LOOK UP

Early in Jesus' ministry, we read:

> Now there was a man of the Pharisees, named Nicodemus, a ruler of the Jews; this man came to Jesus by night and said to Him, "Rabbi, we know that You have come from God as a teacher; for no one can do these signs that You do unless God is with him." Jesus answered and said to him, "Truly, truly, I say to you, unless one is born again he cannot see the kingdom of God." Nicodemus said to Him, "How can a man be born when he is old? He cannot enter a second time into his mother's womb and be born, can he?" (John 3:1–4)

This Pharisee who comes at night is the first person in Scripture to hear that he must be "born again." But what does that mean? That seems like such a big, impossible task. Starting all over? Change from old to new? Being born *again*? How can that be? But watch how Jesus draws upon this story of the bronze serpent to give his answer and then links it with perhaps the most well-known statement in all the New Testament.

> Jesus answered, "Truly, truly, I say to you, unless one is born of water and the Spirit he cannot enter into the kingdom of God.
>
> "That which is born of the flesh is flesh, and that which is born of the Spirit is spirit.
>
> "Do not be amazed that I said to you, 'You must be born again.'
>
> "The wind blows where it wishes and you hear the sound of it, but do not know where it comes from and where it is going; so is everyone who is born of the Spirit."
>
> Nicodemus said to Him, "How can these things be?"
>
> Jesus answered and said to him, "Are you the teacher of Israel, and do not understand these things?" (John 3:5–10)

Jesus is talking to a biblical scholar of the first order. You didn't get to be a Pharisee by just getting a perfect attendance pin at synagogue. It took years of intense study. Nicodemus knew so much. Was respected so highly as a result. And yet here Jesus is telling him that he'd missed something.

"How can that be?" Nicodemus asks. And to help him understand, Jesus gives him this picture: "As Moses lifted up the serpent in the wilderness, even so must the Son of Man be lifted up; so that whoever believes will in Him have eternal life. For God so loved the world, that He gave His only begotten Son, that whoever believes in Him shall not perish, but have eternal life" (John 3:14–16).

John 3:16 is, without a doubt, one of the most quoted passages in all the Bible. Yet few know that just two verses before, Jesus himself gives a picture that illustrates it's meaning, drawn from that life-and-death time in the desert.

For those in the desert, bitten and dying with the venom of "fiery serpents," that small, insignificant act of looking up at a bronze serpent provided their only cure. For those in Nicodemus's day, and for all people since, only by "looking up" in faith—even the new or small faith of a fellow thief on the cross—it is possible to find the antidote to sin and the way to be "born again" into eternal life.

HOW, EXACTLY, DO THESE TWO STORIES OF FAITH AND SMALL ACTS HELP ME CHANGE?

I realize that some people may be growing impatient with all this discussion of "small things" and scriptural passages. After all, we're busy people. "What does this have to do with me dropping a dress size or restoring my marriage?" some might honestly ask.

Far from these passages being peripheral information on the change process, if pages permitted, I could write a hundred pages on their direct effect on those who need to make changes, even in their waistline. But let me share just three important applications that these Bible stories have on each of us who want or need to make a HeartShift.

1. In each story above, in order for someone in a serious situation to make a much-needed change, they first had to face up to the greatest sin.

According to Christian teachers throughout the ages, the greatest sin was the very thing responsible for Satan's fall. *Pride.* Through pride Satan lifted himself above God, and for that choice he was tossed down from heaven. Think of any sin or evil. Anger. Lust. Greed. Abuse. Neglect. In each of these, and all other vices and evils, you can extract trace elements of pride's DNA.

Pride always puts itself above change, above caring, above wanting another's best. Pride says, "I win (or deserve to win), and you lose." "I know the answer; you don't." "It's not my problem; it's yours." "It's what I want, not what you need." "God may say otherwise in his Bible, but I know best—and besides, he'll forgive me."

C. S. Lewis addresses the ultimate problem of pride bluntly: "As long as you are proud you cannot know God. A proud man is always looking down on things and people; and of course, as long as you are looking down, you cannot see something that is above you."[1]

That's why in the first chapter of this book we saw a church that was accused of a "Lucifer's fall." The church of Ephesus, who had done so many things so well, quit looking up when they felt they were on top! In lifting themselves up as being so grand, they lost their way and their first love.

Naaman would have died of leprosy had he not laid down his pride and looked up to the words of a servant.

The people in the wilderness had to drop the same pride that was behind their complaining about God's direction of their lives and humbly look up to a snake on a tribal standard if they wanted to live.

Jesus told Nicodemus that unless he put down the pride of being a Pharisee—including admitting that he couldn't explain everything about God any more than he could explain where the wind came from or where it went—and humbly looked up at him on the cross, he would never find the eternal life he sought.

And that's why we must admit we're a prideful people—and personally a prideful person—if we're ever to make a HeartShift.

Proud people don't feel the need to change any more than they realize they're off course. For proud people there's no need to see a counselor, or get a new direction, or even turn to the Savior. They're above all that. And so, little by little, they'll continue to drift toward darkness instead of light, and death instead of life.

It takes the opposite of pride—humility—to make a HeartShift.

2. Anger and a lack of forgiveness will also cut us off from any real change.

If pride is our ultimate enemy when it comes to change, then it's younger twin cousins are anger and lack of forgiveness.

Naaman's anger at Elisha and his servant almost kept him from accepting that small step toward change. For those who were dying in the wilderness, anger at Moses and even God led to their being bitten by snakes in the first place.

The more anger you carry as a person, the less likely you'll be able to see that small path toward change or accept it as real. Why? First, because anger always pushes us into darkness.

In 1 John 2:9–11 we read: "The one who says he is in the Light and yet hates his brother is in the darkness until now. The one who loves his brother abides in the Light and there is no cause for stumbling in him. But the one who hates his brother is in the darkness and walks in the darkness, and does not know where he is going because the darkness has blinded his eyes."

When Naaman was furious with Elisha's servant, he wasn't open to change. He was blind to the suggestion that something small, done in faith, could change his life. Those in the desert, who were so angry with Moses and their God for dragging them into the desert, were blind to the terrible consequence waiting for them until it struck.

If making a HeartShift requires facing our pride, it also demands that we be honest about the degree of anger we carry in our lives. That anger could be directed toward a parent who abandoned us, or a prodigal child who hurt us deeply, or an insensitive spouse who doesn't cooperate or seem to care, or an unfeeling boss who passed us over for promotion, or an unethical partner or corrupt financial planner who ruined us financially, or—and this is crucial—our anger could stem from a lack of forgiveness with ourselves.

For years mental health practitioners have been taught that depression equals "anger turned inward." Ask almost anyone who has been truly, deeply depressed, and you'll find they use all the imagery of a person lost in the darkness. Listen to them in counseling, and they commonly use metaphors such as, "I can't find my way" out of a situation, or "I don't see any light" at the end of the tunnel, or "I can't believe tomorrow will be a brighter day."

Anger turned inward or toward others pushes us into darkness and blinds us to something as small as a 2 Degree Change. And linked with anger is an unwillingness to forgiveness. Hand in hand with holding on to anger is an unwillingness to forgive.

The Greek word for *forgiveness* is often the first verb you learn when you begin the study of the original language of the New Testament. In biblical Greek, the word *luo,* translated "forgiveness" in

English, literally means "to untie the knots." Does that word picture give you an illustration of why so many of us fail to change?

Many of us who carry anger refuse to forgive the person or persons who hurt us, and so we remain tied up in knots as a result. If anger blinds us to a path that leads to love and life, then an unwillingness to forgive ties us up so that we never even take that first step toward change.

Anger demands payment before closing the book. It keeps us at odds with another (or ourselves) and says, "Whatever happened isn't finished yet. There's payback coming." And when anger mixes in with an unwillingness to forgive, people get tied up in knots and thrown in the dark!

So now can you see why those two biblical stories hold so much everyday application to our lives and why they also represent the starting point for being able to make a HeartShift?

A HeartShift requires that we first lay down our pride and admit we're on the wrong road. And hand in hand comes the understanding that unless we lay down our anger and untie the knot with forgiveness— for others and ourselves—we won't see or feel that we're making any positive movement at all.

Am I suggesting that the reason *some of us* struggle with our weight is because we're still tremendously angry with our parents and have yet to forgive them? *Absolutely.* (Not *excuse* their sinful behavior, which isn't forgiveness at all, but forgive them. Drop the anger and turn them over to God so that we aren't the ones tied up in emotional knots trying to eat away our negative feelings.)

Am I suggesting that the reason some are getting nowhere in their marriage is because they haven't forgiven their spouse for investing in that "can't miss venture" and losing much of your retirement funds? *Absolutely.*

Am I suggesting that some of us have seen our love for God grow cold because we're actually angry at him for sending us out in the desert? *Absolutely.*

Many of us must stop before going a step further toward change. If there are pockets (or deep wells) of anger, or if we're still tied up in knots from a lack of forgiveness, then now is the time to put down this book and go to the Lord in prayer.

Indeed, if we're serious about change and have been deeply hurt, then it might take days or weeks or months of clearing the deck each day of anger as the best way to begin to make a HeartShift.

Pulling Together a Definition
of a HeartShift

While examples always help, for those for whom it is helpful to have a definition apart from an illustration, it's time to pull together what we've seen in several chapters along with key passages and mold them into a few sentences. First, let's make sure we're clear on what is meant by a HeartShift.

A HeartShift is the conviction that we're on the wrong road and in need of making a turn back to better health, stronger relationships, or a deeper faith.

Let's also look at a brief definition of what is meant by 2 Degree Changes. Once we've made a HeartShift:

A 2 Degree Change is taking the smallest of positive steps, actions, or corrections to begin, sustain, or move us toward a needed change.

These simple definitions focus on the starting point of a change of heart and direction and are made real by the smallest of steps in that new direction.

Armed with these simple definitions, it should be easy to tackle our toughest, most stubborn problem area and find instant success, right? You know now that's not true if you've been reading from page 1.

While it is absolutely true that small steps can help you change your life in needed, even dramatic, ways, that doesn't mean insight erases effort. In fact, before we jump into the change process presented in this book, we need to see what stands between us and taking that first step toward change. As you'll discover, there are actually nine reasons you'll never change and one reason you must.

CHAPTER FOUR

Nine Reasons You'll Never Change—and the One Reason You Must, Part I

By the third chapter of a book exhorting you to make needed changes in your life and relationships, you're probably starting to hear voices. Actually, that's nothing to worry about. Even at this early stage of looking at the change process, it's common to hear whispered digs like . . .

"Are you *really* sure this is going to work?" or

"What about the *last* time you decided to change? *That* was a colossal failure, and you're in a lot worse shape now!" or even,

"There simply isn't enough *time* to do something small. He can talk all he wants about hitting singles. The only thing that's going to help you now is a home run."

Whatever the words, I'd be shocked if parasitic doubts like these haven't already begun to burrow themselves deep into your resolve, draining you of energy—*and that's just to keep reading this book!* We haven't even gotten to the good stuff yet, with all the applications and suggestions, and yet already some people will be fighting significant internal challenges that surface anytime we face up to making a life-altering change!

In the past three chapters I've made my best case for your and my need to make a HeartShift and to live out that decision by making small 2 Degree Changes. In this chapter, I'm going to try to make my best argument for why you'll never change.

OUR PROBLEM ISN'T THAT WE DON'T FEEL LIKE CHANGING

I truly believe our problem as people isn't that we don't *feel* like changing. We may feel terribly uncomfortable with the state of our person, faith, or relationships. But it's the *doing* that's so hard! So, before I present an entire change process, including an invitation and instructions on taking a powerful online strengths assessment that can help you pinpoint areas that cry out for needed adjustment, we've got to look at the barriers we face, beginning *the moment we decide to change.*

With our first steps toward change, it's like turning and walking into a brutal north headwind. Or to put it in more colorful terms, it's like my West Texas friend used to say whenever we'd start out on a trip, "We're off like a herd of turtles in a flood of peanut butter."

Welcome to a turtle and peanut butter chapter.

Before you read about how to make a HeartShift and live it out through small 2 Degree Changes, you must know what can slow you down and put changes on "turtle time." In Proverbs, it's the wise man who counts the cost before he builds, and it was our Lord who talked about closely considering the strength of the enemy before going to war. So it should be with you. And that's why in this chapter I'm going to throw at you my best and strongest case for why you'll *never* change.

We need to look at the major barriers facing us, beginning the moment we decide to change.

In presenting this case for why you'll never change, my goal is not to generate the kind of response that a certain cancer researcher recently evoked. Penelope Schofield, at the Peter MacCallum Cancer Centre in New Zealand, reported her results from a major study on lung cancer. Her conclusion was that optimism didn't help lung cancer patients live any longer than anyone else with the disease. As you might imagine, she has been *flooded* with thousands of e-mails and calls from physicians and cancer sufferers worldwide saying things like, "How dare you steal my hope!"[1]

My goal in sharing the sobering realities of the challenges facing us when we become serious about change isn't to steal anyone's hope or discourage anyone who's trying hard to do things differently. I certainly feel your pain when it comes to needing and wanting to make personal changes. Pick any area, from health to home to even my heart for God, and there have been times when I have needed to make a HeartShift. Yet as difficult as it may be, we have to take a hard look at what we are up against.

As a preface, I know this chapter and the next will be hard chapters to just breeze through. *Coming up are shorter, more applicational chapters.* But just forget the voices that say, "Just skip all this and get right to the good stuff." Please read and reflect on the challenges that follow. Not to do so would be like speeding off on a journey without knowing which roads ahead were closed.

I've tried to make what follows interactive; at the end of each challenge you'll have an opportunity to evaluate that barrier's impact on you personally when it comes to change. Go over these nine barriers with a loved one, small group, or close friend as a way of facing them and going around them as well. While it may not be fun to realize that what's up ahead may be extremely challenging, there's hope at the end. There may be nine reasons you'll never change, but there's that one reason you must.

Let's See What You Have in Common with Hercules

Making a HeartShift and then living that decision out in small, everyday actions is difficult from the moment you begin. In fact, it's every bit as daunting as the greatest challenge faced by that ancient superhero Hercules.

Unless you're a bodybuilder or professional baseball power hitter, I doubt if you ever thought you had much in common with this legendary strongman. However, you might be surprised. This ancient Greek superhero set out on a great journey, just like the one you're beginning. And from the beginning he knew it would be a challenge to get to his destination. In Hercules's case, he was given twelve impossible tasks. Actually, none of them proved impossible, and without question the most difficult of all the barriers he faced was the third. It's that third impossible task that we'll focus on as something you share in common with Hercules. That's because our hero's quest came to an abrupt halt when he met a giant, nine-headed serpentlike creature called the Hydra.

Obviously, a nine-headed serpent is myth. But in this chapter I'm going to point out nine real barriers you will face in making a HeartShift. Like a nine-headed Hydra, these factors can combine to create an imposing roadblock to anyone's courage or willpower. Each challenge is ready to spring and bite and claw and poison any real attempts you or I make to take even that first positive step.

Some of these challenges will come from deep within us—those little parasitic voices I mentioned earlier—while others reflect living in our unique time in history. Regardless, each one has the power to stop you in your tracks, and each one can emotionally push you back into the "pit of despond" or even into depression when things don't change.

Why even *try* to change if we're facing such a Hydra of challenges set before us? Why not just give up on having a stronger faith, or a closer marriage, or a more effective ministry, or better health? Because there is also that one reason you'll discover at the end of this chapter why you and I *must change*. It's a reason that will lead us into the next section of the book and present a change process where HeartShifts really are possible for everyday people every day.

NINE REASONS YOU'LL NEVER CHANGE

1. "I don't have time to change!"

During the age of the sundial, Sophocles wrote, "Time is a gentle deity."

While that may explain how people felt about time in 406 BC, for those living in AD 2004 and beyond, there's nothing remotely gentle about time. Time stands over us today and cracks a whip! Everything is moving faster, and almost everyone feels time-strapped. If there's a universal complaint I hear across the country as I talk to people about making changes, it is *"I don't have time!"* There's no time even to think about what we're *not* doing or failing at doing because we've got so much on our plate already! What's more, every single thing on our plate is an A item that demands our time and attention *right now*. We're fighting for every second, and today, seconds count.

For example, how many times have you punched the button for the door to close on an elevator? Ten seconds in an elevator without the door closing is *forever.* Or how long did it take you to go from dial-up to high-speed on your office computer? (Could you even imagine *not* having high-speed at work, and for that matter, at home?) Or take your cellular phone. Have you ever forgotten your home number, or the number of a family member or close friend, all because you couldn't push "speed dial" on your phone?

Who has time to punch in all the numbers, much less remember them?

In the jungles of New Guinea, a missionary friend of ours told us about a remote village they visited without a single mechanical clock of any kind. There, people measure their days by workdays and rest days. Meaning, you work one day, then you rest the next. Does that sound like *your* days? Can you even remember the last time you had a "day of rest"? Stores haven't been closed on Sunday for more then two decades in most places, and more and more are staying open all night.

As Americans, we lost the battle to slow down time long ago when railroads sped things up and forced us to first adopt standardized time. Before 1864, there were hundreds of time zones across the country. In essence, every major city had its own standard time. When clocks don't agree, there is a limit to how fast things can move. In short, a train might pull into a station and be on time if judged by the clock in the city where the journey began and be ahead of time somewhere else, requiring the train to wait before pulling out. In short, 150 years ago, time moved at a local pace, and that was slow. But once clocks agreed, time sped up.

As soon as the country went on standardized time, the accelerator hit the floor. When you don't have to wait, everything moves toward *now.* Once our entire country got on the clock, everything began to be measured by railroad time, which back then meant fast. But soon, railroad time wasn't nearly fast enough. We had automobiles that could speed past trains, and then airplanes, and now orbital reentry vehicles moving twice the speed of sound.

To keep pace, even our clocks have sped up as our technology and lives sped up. It used to be that atomic clocks were fast enough to measure time with their ability to measure milliseconds. Today, with space travel, supercomputers, and fiber-optic networks, things move much too fast for pokey atomic clocks. Now superclocks measure time in nanoseconds, *a billionth of a second.* A billionth of a second is now standard time, and every nanosecond counts.

For example, without billionth-of-a-second speed and precision, our worldwide television and communications systems would go down, including our Global Positioning System. For example, just be off a billionth of a second, and that means an error of roughly one foot in your positioning, the distance light travels in that time. Can you see how, if you're sending a signal via satellite from one point to another, being off just a *billionth* of a second can make you miss the receiver at the other end, and the signal goes down? Think about what it would mean to be just "one full second" off if you were flying a jetliner full of passengers and doing an instrument landing (or guiding a smart bomb heading toward its intended target). Everything has to be right now— on nanosecond time—or it is too slow. And even though we can't consciously comprehend a nanosecond, our lives have sped up to try to catch it anyway.

The average television commercial today is thirty seconds, not one minute like it was in 1970. Who has time to listen for an entire minute without tuning out? The average *counseling session* has dropped from one hour to half an hour. Who has more time than that to try and get better? And in case you're wondering, all that speed goes right to the bottom line when it comes to "change."

Just imagine what happens today when you say to people, "You need to make some changes."

"*When?*" comes back the answer in nanosecond time!

Two jobs. Night classes to get recertified. Church. Kids' programs. Choir practices. Soccer leagues. Helping with homework. In-laws. Bills to pay. Pets to look after. Repairmen to call. We're so overwhelmed with so much to do and all of it demanding to be done right now, who has time to change? And if we're married, that doesn't mean we have someone to share the load. Chances are excellent that our spouse is at least as overloaded as we are, if not more so.

What couple has time to have a leisurely talk about what they need to change?

While I'm at it, let me burst another bubble for married people, particularly those harried young couples with young children, who are just longing for those lazy days when "our kids grow up, leave home, and we have all that extra time." The fact is, by the time you get there, time will have sped up, not slowed down! In fact, here's an "equation" that none of us can escape as we get older.

Delta (t)(s)-Delta Exp/Total Exp.

That's an equation created by Dr. Germont M. R. Winkler, the director of time in charge of the master clock here in the United States. An undisputed expert on time, it represents his best thinking on why things seem to speed up as we get older. Have you ever noticed that sensation? Does it seem to you that everything seems to be moving faster now that you're older? In case math and science weren't your thing in high school, here's what his equation describes:

"The more we have experienced, the faster time flows."[2]

In short, the more experiences we collect, experiences now coming at us at incredible rates, the faster time seems to pass. Just talk to senior citizens today and ask them what it's like to "have all that free time" and then watch their eyes roll. If you're looking for a slower time in the future, it won't be there. *Time will continue to speed up with every passing year*—and with it the pace of our society.

So forget about changing.

There's no time.[3]

It's time to rate and discuss this barrier to change with a friend or group.

[ ] *Yes, lack of time is near the top of my list of barriers to change.*

[ ] *No, I'm with Sophocles and feel time's gentle movement on my days.*

---

2. *The barrier caused when technology squeezes out inefficiency.*

Hand in hand with the clock and our lives speeding up has come all the incredible advances in technology. For example, at the turn of the century it took an American steel factory roughly 22.4 man-hours to create one unit of steel. Today it takes *less* than two hours for a fully automated steel factory to create one unit of steel (and unfortunately, it's primarily done offshore).

How could technology so dramatically drop the number of man-hours? It's because *technology squeezes out inefficiency.* Unfortunately, that inefficiency has often meant getting rid of people and jobs that are now obsolete. The more machines, the greater the productivity, the fewer the people needed.

That fact doesn't just impact the manufacturing sector where technology has squeezed out inefficiency. Science journalist James Burke writes, "With the increasing pace in our society, the rate of change will be so high that for humans to be qualified in a single discipline—defining what they are and what they do throughout their life—will be as outdated as quill and parchment. Knowledge will be changing too fast for that. We will need to reskill ourselves constantly every decade just to keep a job."[4]

I'd beg to differ with this science writer.

With the pace of life today, if you wait an entire decade to retrain and reskill, I can almost guarantee you'll be making a change of occupation! We're in a race to keep up with technology as well as with time *just to try to stay employed!* Which is not to say there aren't tremendous benefits that come with increases in technology. (Just think how many medical breakthroughs there have been due to increases in technology alone.) But in addition to all the time that has to go into trying to keep pace with technology, technology also brings with it another huge barrier that directly impacts our need to make personal changes. Have you already seen it lurking in the shadows?

Because technology squeezes out inefficiency, with every advance the standard for acceptable defects in products keeps moving steadily toward zero. "Zero defects" used to be a dream of manufacturers. Now, for all practical purposes, it's the rule. (One friend of ours who runs a high-end plastic company that makes small surgical devices considers a .04 defect standard as *unacceptable.*) Between "just in time" inventories and automated processes, there are no margins left for excess, spillage, waste, or mess. Messes create returns, and errors cost money and time to fix—and remember, every nanosecond counts today.

So let me introduce you to the second head of the Hydra if you're serious about change. For not only do you have no time to change, *but your standard for error is now zero.* Think for a moment about the impact of that statement in your everyday life.

When was the last time you took in a broken blow-driver to have it fixed? If your computer is over a year old, the vast majority of people won't even bother taking it in to repair. Why not just toss out the old model and get a new version, guaranteed to have better features, be *faster,* and probably cost less money! (Or why not just lease it, since it's so disposable, and never actually invest in ownership?) And don't think that's not exactly what people are doing with their relationships.

For many people today there is simply no margin or patience for putting up with defects in another person. It's much easier just to trade him or her in on another updated model—one with fewer defects. Who has time to clean up messes? In fact, moving mainstream in our culture is the expectation that you won't even bother to try.

In the highly publicized book *The Starter Marriage and the Future of Matrimony,* author Pamela Paul *begins* with the assumption that your first marriage is just a "starter marriage." When it breaks (and it will), then just ditch it, learn what you can, and move on to a different one (or person) that has fewer defects.

Welcome to the second reason you'll never change.

Technology squeezes out inefficiency, and that means your standard for error has now become zero.[5]

**It's time to rate and discuss this barrier
to change with a friend or group.**

[ ] *Yes, in important areas of my life I do feel that my "standard
for error" is close to zero.*

[ ] *No, I'm in a grace-based environment with low expectations on me.*

---

3. The tremendous drain of past "open loops."

Let's pretend we can step off the conveyor belt of speed and technology, move twenty miles outside White Fish, Montana, and live a simple, slow-paced life. You're still not safe from the third head of the Hydra standing before us. For written on its ugly neck are the words *open loops.*

"Open Loops" isn't the name of a new breakfast cereal. "Open loops" refer to those past issues, still left unresolved in our hearts and minds (before we moved to White Fish), that can slow our ability to change to a grinding halt. Let's look again at a marriage relationship as an example.

"Some marriages have dozens of open loops. For example, couples may live in ongoing conflict over how to discipline their children, who is responsible for taking out the garbage, who balances the checkbook, how often they have sex . . . and some unresolved issues may be even more personal, such as wounds from criticism, insults, apathy, lack of love, etc."[6]

That's a quote from my good friends Gary and Barbara Rosberg in their outstanding book *Divorce-Proof Your Marriage.* Years ago Gary wrote an entire book, now out of print, on open loops in relationships. I've told him dozens of times if he had just called that book *Closing the Loop,* it would have stayed in print and sold a million copies! That's exactly what so many of us struggle with—energy-draining open loops.

It's not just a factor for marrieds to consider. Just think of the average life. Let's say, as we grow up, a grade-school teacher deeply hurts our feelings, but we never close the loop and instead just move on to another grade. Then there's that first love in junior high who rejects us, but we switch schools and never close the loop on all that hurt. Then after high school, we leave home angry with our parents and never take time to close the loop with them. And then there's that problem with our first boss where we lost our job, and we just move on to the next workplace, never closing the loop.

Having one open loop isn't fatal to our being able to make positive changes any more than putting one fist-sized rock in our backpack will keep us from completing a hike. But for many of us, we're not toting around a few rocks. We're carrying the added emotional weight of a seventy-pound pack every day, all from open loops from the past.

If you're not the hiking type, think about someone tying one ultra-thin strand of ten-pound monofilament fishing line to your belt. That one strand of fishing line won't stop you from breaking free and moving forward. But try breaking free from fifty small, thin, ten-pound strands of fishing line. However you picture it, open loops from the past can absolutely stop any movement in the present.

So forget about change, especially those of you with all those open loops. You're not going anywhere.

> **It's time to rate and discuss this barrier
> to change with a friend or group.**
>
> *[ ] If I'm honest, I've got a backpack full of past open loops
> that daily weigh me down.*
>
> *[ ] Unresolved past issues aren't anywhere near the top of my
> list of barriers to change.*

4. You've already accumulated way too many things to be able to change.

If you're not discouraged enough already, then how about this.

You already have too many things in your home to be able to make personal changes. Here's what I mean by that statement.

As a nation, we've been on a four-decade-long shopping spree. Consumer spending has fueled every boom. Consumption and dollars spent by everyday citizens have led us out of every bust. What's the result? Things and more things.

"Today, the American home is more spacious and luxurious than the dwellings of any other nation. Food is cheap and abundant. The typical family owns a fantastic array of household and consumer appliances: we have machines to wash our clothes and dishes, mow our lawns, and blow away our snow. On a per-person basis, the average American has sixty-five times the average income of the world's population."[7]

That's a graphic description of our power to consume. We have so much compared to so many. And there's just that one little problem that comes from buying so much (besides the credit card charges and personal bankruptcy). In order to purchase all those time-saving, space-saving things to put in our larger houses, we've taken the time saved by productivity and plowed it into more hours at work.

Productivity is defined by economists as the amount of goods or services that an average worker can create in one hour's time. While primarily linked with measuring those in the manufacturing sector, this really applies across the board. From 1948 until today, except for five of nearly sixty years, productivity has increased *substantially*. Meaning, if we were satisfied with the number of things we owned in 1948, we could create them in less than half the time it took back then. Forget the eight-hour workday; we could have the two-hour workday! Just think of all the free time we've gained by being so productive! But wait a minute; have you noticed a slight problem? Namely, we're not content with limiting our acquisition of things, and we haven't gained a single one-hour reduction in the amount of time worked, even with all those advances in productivity. In fact, just the opposite is true.

In order to purchase all those things we need today, "U.S. manufacturing employees currently work 320 more hours—the equivalent of over two months longer—than their counterparts in West Germany or France."[8] And it's not just manufacturing employees who are working longer and harder than their European counterparts. On average, men and women in all jobs and socioeconomic levels are working the equivalent of a month of hours *more* per year than they did in 1970!

Can you imagine that? Across every work setting, and for men and women, we're working longer and harder—a month more per year—just to buy and fix and maintain and upgrade the things we have!

You might as well give up right now. You've got five more heads ready to strike, and you'll never change.

It's time to rate and discuss this barrier
to change with a friend or group.

[ ] *The number of hours I'm having to work, inside and outside the house, is absolutely keeping me from having the time or energy to make changes.*

[ ] *I am working fewer hours for more money with less stress. (Please e-mail us your secret.)*

CHAPTER FIVE

Nine Reasons You'll Never Change—and the One Reason You Must, Part II

Let's start this chapter with a brief review of the heads of the Hydra we're battling so far when it comes to making needed changes. There's the one marked "speed," which keeps pushing us to go faster in every area, and then the second head that reflects all those advances in technology that lower our margin for error and patience with imperfection. Then there are all those pesky open loops from the past that rear their ugly head. And finally, that fourth head, swelled with a month's worth of extra hours that we're all working in order to own so many things.

And that's just four heads of the Hydra.

Here comes the terrible fifth.

5. How a crucial word, erased from our culture, crushes positive change.

While we've been so busy facing these first four challenges, we didn't even notice how the fifth head of the Hydra, cunning and merciless, broke into our culture and stole something priceless. If a police report were filed on this crime, it would read, "Stolen—a crucial word for our culture, our children, and our ability to change."

A missing word? With a dictionary filled with words, how bad can it be to lose just one word from our culture? The answer is it's really bad if that word is a secret. By that, I don't mean that what was stolen was a secret, but the word this fifth head of the Hydra has swallowed from our society is the word *secret* itself.

Tragically, we live in a time when secrets are now impossible to keep, even from the youngest in our society. Let me prove that to you by sharing two upsetting examples for those of us who are parents.

When President Clinton had his indiscretion with an intern just outside the Oval Office of the White House, how many parents had to have a talk with their child about a certain type of sexual behavior that was, before then, a secret to their young child? Until that particular type of sex became front-page news, third and fourth graders generally weren't coming home asking, "Mommy, what is oral sex?" With the explosion of twenty-four-hour news reporting and the unblinking eye that television and radio provides and demands, what once was a secret to young children has now become prime-time playground news.

If you think that's picking on politicians who make personal mistakes that unfairly get exploded onto television, then let's pick something safe, like sports. Certainly it's safe to turn on the TV and watch the half-time show of a football game with your young child, right? Did you actually sit in a room with a young child and watch the Super Bowl half-time show during prime time in 2004? How many children asked, "Daddy, why did he do that?" (meaning why did Justin Timberlake tear off Janet Jackson's clothing and expose her naked breast). Erase another secret once kept from young children.

With two daughters almost five years apart in age, I was forced to have both conversations. And what's terrible is that it will get worse, not better, no matter how high the FCC raises its fines. Why? Let's just take the clothing (or lack of it) issue and show how it affects children—and from there its impact on your making any genuine personal changes.

"For clothing is a means of keeping a secret, and if we are deprived of the means of keeping a secret, we are deprived of the secret."[1] So writes cultural observer Neil Postman in his chilling book *The Disappearance of Childhood*. He goes on to elaborate on what happens when there are no secrets for those of any age.

"Similarly, the shamefulness in incest, in violence, in homosexuality, in mental illness, disappears when the means to concealing them disappears, when their details become the content of public discourse, available for examination by everyone in a public arena. What was once shameful has now become a 'social problem' or a 'political issue' or a 'psychological phenomenon,' but in the process, it must lose its dark and fugitive character, as well as some of its moral force."[2]

Bingo. These words were penned long before President Clinton's impeachment hearings, or MTV halftime shows, or front-page pictures of hundreds of gay couples lining up to get marriage licenses. (*"Mommy, Daddy, why are those two men holding hands like that?"*) When everything is headline news, there are no longer any secrets and eventually no shame and no standard of right and wrong. Postman is exactly right.

While we have been so busy trying to keep up with changes at work just to be able to stay employed and purchase all those things, this fifth head of the serpent has cunningly struck and devoured the word *shame*. If nothing is shameful, then there's no need for any secrets. And if there are no secrets, then soon there is no childhood, which is exactly why kids are so at risk in our culture. Put every deviant behavior on public television that's available to everyone, at every age, at any time, and you erase any moral force to say, "This is wrong! Keep that off the airwaves!"

And what, exactly, does this loss of moral authority have to do with someone not being able to make a change in his or her life? Lots. First, now that there is no longer any shame in our society, why work so hard to change or conform your life to godliness? Take any stand on godliness, and you're automatically going to be branded intolerant. Stand up for any standard of decency, and watch yourself be shouted down with charges like "That's a private issue! You have no business talking about my behavior." (Of course, at the same time, watch these same people demand that public courts officially sanction their private behavior.)

So in a society where there's no longer any clear standard of right and wrong, just quit caring or trying to keep up with antiquated standards, particularly those that are intolerant and out of step with so many. And while you're at it, all the time you're having to spend trying to protect your child from a lack of shame (like working a second job to send them to private school) just robs you of more time that could have gone into your making personal changes for yourself.

Which is just one more reason you'll never really change.

*It's time to rate and discuss this barrier
to change with a friend or group.*

[ ] *I feel like I'm on a shrinking island and that it's getting more and
more difficult to keep up a high standard of right and wrong
for myself or my children.*

[ ] *I live in Mayberry, and things are actually getting better and
standards higher where I live.*

6. You must now be in fear for your financial future.

In building this case for why you'll never change, you've now seen
barriers like needing to be (or stay) perfect and defect free, even as you
watch moral standards in our culture fall off the table. You've seen how
our need for essential things has increased work hours dramatically and
erased any personal time left for change. Now you've got even more to
worry about in a world without shame that puts your children's future
at risk. Add together all these barriers, and mix in those nagging open
loops from the past that just won't go away, and you'd think things
couldn't get any worse. *Think again. You've still got to face the sixth
head of the Hydra.*

This sixth head of the Hydra can create incredible fear in our everyday lives. Not the Steven King kind of imaginary fear, where bad things
come back to life and chase you in a graveyard. But the real kind of fear
that can haunt you during broad daylight and was once only conceiv-
able in a nightmare.

What's so frightening?

Imagine waking up to find that Wall Street was actually just like
Old Tucson. For years the average person and even minor investor has
looked upon the towering Wall Street firms and markets as rock solid,
dependable, stable. Just the look of them gave you something you could
count on to be there now and for decades to come. Actually, we now
know that many of the biggest buildings on Wall Street were like the
houses in Old Tucson.

Old Tucson is the kind of place you visit on a vacation because
you've passed dozens of billboards, mile after mile along the interstate,

urging you when you finally go through Tucson to "stop and take the kids to Old Tucson!" If those billboards did break down your willpower and you actually stopped at Old Tucson, you would discover it's a replica Old West town, complete with a blacksmith shop, general store, jail, and row after row of wooden houses and buildings. Well over one hundred Western movies and countless television programs have been shot on its streets, and thousands of bad guys have been shot as well in the mock gun battles they stage every day.

And what does that have to do with Wall Street? Unfortunately, far too much!

If you walk down the middle of the dusty street running through town, all those wooden buildings look impressive. However, when you get closer to them on the wooden sidewalk and actually look through the windows of many of the buildings, you see that they're not real at all. Almost the entire town is a façade. Building after building is just a shell, propped up from behind with long poles to look from the front like the building has substance and depth, but all that is there is a false front. So now let's go back to Wall Street. Get ready to be afraid, really afraid.

Let's take just one building, from one Fortune Top 500 company. (To get in the top 500 companies in the entire nation, you've got to be the cream of the cream of the cream.) From outside their corporate headquarters, it certainly looks impressive. It's even more impressive when you walk into the huge open lobby. A feeling of success permeates the whole building, from top to bottom. From your view from the street, or even from the waiting room, it looks like the perfect place to put your hard-earned 401(k) or mutual fund investment. And just in case you had any doubts, you even get to hear the CEO of this company tell you what it's like to work throughout the rest of the building. Listen to his inside take on what's really happening with this company.

"You can't go through our building without seeing charts, which are revised every day, showing what people's stock options are worth. To be honest with you, this is the most satisfying part of my job. I could show you letter after letter from employees who write, 'If it had not been for the options, I never would have been able to send my child to college.' Or, 'I've never had the opportunity to own a home before, and now I can make a substantial down payment, thanks to what my options are worth.'"

Such a positive insider view of this company makes it look even better. In fact, this happy CEO concludes, "From a company point of view, we are pleased with the return we have produced for our shareholders and the participation that the board has allowed us to include for the people that work here. The results have been amazing."

Amazing is a humble understatement. Since the day this company went public, the *average* yearly increase in their stock went up 50 percent. *Which brings me to a question.* Wouldn't you just love to work for a company where you could walk down any hallway and see such excited, confident people? Wouldn't *you* want a significant portion of, or maybe all, your retirement account invested in a company whose future (on which stock options are based) brings so much happiness, trust, and fulfillment to so many people? The correct answer in this case would be *"Absolutely not!"*

That's because this Wall Street company was actually an Old Tucson firm.

The people working daily in this dream environment really *were* dreaming when they were at work. The CEO quoted above, bragging about his employees' stock options, was none other than Bernie Ebbers, the former founder and CEO of WorldCom. And in case you were onboard the Soviet Space Station during all of 2001–2002 and missed what happened to the financial markets on earth, WorldCom became the poster child for financial misdeeds and misstatements by corporations. How much of their business was real, and how much was a façade?

During a decade defined by spin and half-truths in the political arena, WorldCom conned the financial markets and its own employees and stockholders into thinking they were making those 50-percent increases. Yet subtract the spin and accounting fiction. Look behind the false front of their building, and in just two years (2000 and 2001), WorldCom actually posted more than *74 billion dollars* in *losses!* That's $48.9 billion in 2000 and $25.6 billion in losses in 2001—both years in which the company had proudly reported to its shareholders that it made a profit.[3]

So what difference does a measly 74 billion-dollar accounting lie make to small-potato people like you and me? Just ask that question to the thousands of laid-off WorldCom employees and subcontractors when the company imploded, or to the hundreds of thousands of blindsided stock and mutual fund investors who suffered as a result. To put 74 billion dollars into some type of perspective, during 2001 the entire total of all goods and services (GDP) for the *country* of Peru was only 60.9 billion dollars! That one lying façade of a supposedly trustworthy company lost more than all but a handful of countries earn on earth!

Can you see what's so genuinely fearful about this?

The everyday person didn't know and couldn't see the change coming. Talk about a wild card! Just when we thought all we had to worry about was trying to keep up with all the changes in our jobs and lives, or trying to fight back against all the moral erosion, or making time to close at least some of the open loops from the past, or perhaps making do with a few less things, here comes the fact that you can't trust Wall Street! You can't trust your financial future to anyone anymore. Not to WorldCom or mutual fund managers who allowed huge after-hours trading costs to eat away at your profits, or to Tyco tycoons who throw four-million-dollar birthday parties for their spouse, financed with money that could have gone to shareholders.

Anytime you even *think* you have time to work on personal or relational issues, you had better invest that time in watching your retirement funds instead. The costs of health and elder care are going up dramatically, and now you'd better be in fear of your financial future.[4]

**It's time to rate and discuss this barrier
to change with a friend or group.**

[ ] *Worries about my financial future, or hurt and anger from the emotional and financial losses I've already suffered in the past, drain me of any desire or confidence I have to change today.*

[ ] *I have a private trust fund, or I'm married to a multimillion-dollar heiress, so Old Tucson doesn't scare me.*

---

7. "Everyone looks better in a bathing suit than I do."

We're down to looking at the last three heads of the Hydra that strike their blows at a much more personal level. I'll also move through these three much more quickly since they don't require as much explanation or discussion of historical context. In fact, to understand why these heads of the Hydra are such fearful barriers to positive personal change, all you have to do is take one look in the mirror.

If you do, you'll notice that the seventh head of the Hydra is branded with a single word, *comparison*.

To the degree that you compare yourself with others, you'll find your desire or conviction to change *decrease*. Making constant comparisons with others is like drilling more and more holes in yourself. Just think about the unthinkable for many women—wearing that bathing suit. Certainly, for some women there's not a second thought about getting into a bathing suit for the first time at the beginning of summer and going to that swim party for the kids. (Mostly, that's young women ten and younger for whom this is a nonstressful event.) But once a young woman is in junior high, for a huge percentage of women there's that feeling:

"Not me! I'm not getting into that pool!"

And it's not because the water's cold.

You'll notice that I didn't mention the average guy when it comes to bathing suit issues. Unfortunately, most men will just slap on an old pair of cutoff jeans and do a cannonball as they jump in the pool, ultrawhite legs, extended love handles, and all! But where most guys may not care about physical comparisons as profoundly, don't think men are any less susceptible to comparison. One look at those ultrasuccessful men on the cover of any success magazine, and the average man feels demotivated, not motivated toward success. Guaranteed, there's someone at work or a brother or a relative who's doing better than they are, and they struggle with comparison. And when they and their wives and sons and daughters do fall prey to this word, the focus goes off any problems they have and onto the perceived gap between where they are and where they want to be. And whether it's gaps of inches around their waist for people concerned about their weight or cubic inches for people who envy someone with an expensive sports car they can't own, these gaps can seem like Grand Canyons when it comes to change.

"I'll never get from here to there, so why try," they say to themselves. For every person who goes home and starts that diet after seeing someone in better shape than they are, a hundred others will order an extra scoop of ice cream since they've already lost the comparison

battle. For every person who sees that lean, mean running machine on the cover of a running magazine, hundreds will be inspired to jog around the block in the morning and then kick the block back under the bed and go back to sleep. Comparison kills motivation for most people.

So just keep on comparing yourself with others. It's another great reason you'll never change.

It's time to rate and discuss this barrier to change with a friend or group.

[ ] *All those ads with success stories have done more to discourage me than help me believe I can make changes. I admit I struggle, sometimes even daily, with comparing myself to people who look or act better than I do or seem to have so much more than I do.*

[ ] *I'm a supermodel with a last name that's on millions of bottles of my father's product, and I get tired of everyone comparing themselves to me.*

---

8. There's got to be that magic pill.

We're almost done with all the negatives, and we're getting down to the very personal level of why we'll never change. Many of us won't take the hard steps needed to change, even if they're small steps. That's because we've become convinced that there's got to be an easier, quicker one-step way out of our problem.

For example, if you listen to talk radio, think of the thousands of times you've heard about some kind of pill that will instantly restore your memory, cause you to lose pounds and inches without taking time for exercise or diet, or that will restore your focus or desire with the snap of a finger (of course, that's after they have your credit card on file). Those ads for instant change make billions of dollars every year for their sponsors because that's our secret hope—that with all these barriers to change before us, there's got to be an easier way. There's got to be a way to change without really having to change anything. Did you know there's a wonderful biblical example of this everyday problem?

In Acts 24:24 we meet a Roman ruler named Felix. History tells us he was not a nice person. For example, he was so enchanted with his brother's wife, he made her a widow by having his own brother killed and then made Drusilla his wife! Now fast-forward to where the coura-geous apostle Paul is imprisoned in Felix's jail and brought before the great ruler. We're told that when Paul began to preach to him "right-eousness, self-control and the judgment to come, Felix became fright-ened and said, 'Go away for the present, and when I find time I will summon for you'" (v. 25).

That's a tremendous passage on why people procrastinate. We get convicted about being righteous, or needing to have more self-control, or even about where we'll spend eternity after we die; and we become afraid of what the answer might require. So we say, "Go away for now." Just like Felix. But it's what God's Word records *after* Felix sent Paul away that I want to focus on here. For even though this Roman ruler was afraid of making the major changes required, that didn't stop him from wanting to *hear* about them. That is why we read, "And Felix kept bringing Paul before him. And at the same time, Felix was hoping that Paul would give him money; but after two years, he was succeeded by Pontius Festus, and wishing to do the Jews a favor, he left Paul imprisoned."

Have you ever bought a book on change or bought yet another Day-Timer and thought that would get you organized? We like going to sem-inars on "let's get organized" or reading books about change, but when we realize what it really takes to change, many of us count the cost and get afraid. We hear a sermon that convicts us down to our socks. We don't quit going to church, or we even read a good Christian book on the subject. We want to keep hearing about the changes we need to make. But what we really want is reward without effort. Like Felix, we keep thinking there's got to be a payoff just for listening to all this change talk, even if we have no intention of really changing. There has got to be a way to gain all those insights into change but put in no effort into really changing and get rewarded for it.

Sorry. While there are people in this world who do absolutely no work and get overpaid for it, your chances of being elected to the United States Senate are slim. (Just joking, of course. I meant the House of Representatives.) Getting rewards without effort doesn't happen to real people except in rare cases. (For example, we all have a distant cousin or high school acquaintance who is lazy, unethical, and gets paid well for being that way.)

There's got to be some kind of pill or situation that will lift me above all the barriers and make needed changes for me. I just haven't ordered the right one that will provide that payoff.

Sorry, but that's just another reason you'll never change.

It's time to rate and discuss this barrier to change with a friend or group.

[ ] *If I counted up all the bottles of magic formulas I've bought over the years, they'd fill a closet. When I'm honest, I still like hearing about change more than doing it. I think there has to be an easy, quick way to change that I just haven't discovered yet.*

[ ] *I'll share my thoughts on this barrier right after that bottle of magic pills I just ordered off the infomercial comes in.*

9. The ninth head of the serpent.

Way back at the beginning of the previous chapter, I mentioned that Hercules's greatest challenge was in facing the Hydra that blocked his way. What I failed to mention to you then was something that our hero didn't realize either at the start of his battle. The missing insight for Hercules was that the ninth head of the Hydra was immortal. The other eight were terrible and dangerous as they could be. Combined, they were fearsome indeed. But when it came down to it, Hercules's greatest battle was with that ninth head, *as is ours.*

The Bible tells us, "For our struggle is not against flesh and blood, but against the rulers, against the powers, against the world forces of this darkness, against the spiritual forces of wickedness in the heavenly places" (Eph. 6:12). Beginning with our first ancestors, every generation and every person since has been at war with an unholy, ageless serpent. Of course, in the garden of Eden, Adam and Eve faced a single-headed serpent who twisted Scripture and became that first parasitic caster of doubts that led to their downfall.

Satan is called "the serpent of old who is called the devil and Satan, who deceives the whole world" (Rev. 12:9). And while a serpent is just one form Satan takes to defeat us (others pictured in Scripture are a "roaring lion" [1 Pet. 5:8] and an "angel of light" [2 Cor. 1:12]), the serpent is Satan's most chilling image.

Cunning. Patient. Deadly. Silent. Forever our adversary.

You could fill up a whole page with similar words that picture evil. And anytime any son of Adam comes up against Satan—from the beginning of time in the book of Genesis to the end of all things in the book of Revelation—Satan's strategy remains the same. That's because he tries to ruin our lives by using the same timeless trap that ruined his own.

Do you remember the church of Ephesus in the first chapter that had wandered off course? Do you remember how Jesus himself praised them seven times for doing so well? And can you see now what was at the heart of their waking up one day to find out they were so off course? In the words of *The Message,* you might remember, "Why have you fallen so far? A Lucifer's fall!"

If you're fairly new to reading Scripture, a "Lucifer's fall" may not make a lot of sense. In fact, if you're reading most modern translations of the Bible, you won't even find that word, *Lucifer,* anywhere in the Bible. That's because *Lucifer* is the Latin translation of the Hebrew word for "day star" in Isaiah 14:12 and was used in the old King James Version of the Bible. So *Lucifer* is another word for someone called the "day star," who we read in Scripture was at one time the brightest of all the angels.

> "How you have fallen from heaven,
> O star of the morning, son of the dawn!
> You have been cut down to the earth,
> You who have weakened the nations!
> But you said in your heart,
> 'I will ascend to heaven;
> I will raise my throne above the stars of God,
> And I will sit on the mount of assembly
> In the recesses of the north.
> I will ascend above the heights of the clouds;
> I will make myself like the Most High.'" (Isa. 14:12–14)

The ninth head of the Hydra takes us back to that terrible word we saw first in chapter 3—*pride*—which means putting ourselves above others, or even God, and as such, putting ourselves above and beyond any real need to change. Lucifer's fall from heaven came from thinking he could put himself above everything and everyone, including Almighty God. Can you begin to see now what tripped up that church that was doing so many good things? Over time pride crept in, and once you let pride begin gently to steer you away from an authentic first love, you're getting farther and farther off course. Let's look at this in a more personal way.

Prideful spouses don't need to make a HeartShift; it's their *spouse's* problem. Prideful parents don't need to read books on parenting or make 2 Degree Changes toward better understanding or loving their children. They just keep on doing things the right way, which is their way, even if it's only producing anger and rebellion in their child.

Adding pride to our church or small group leads us to think we can lean back for a while, take our hands off the wheel, and just let our outstanding worship or small-group study go on cruise control—before the crash. Pride can even be part of the reason our stomach is so big, if it is. Pride says, "I want what I want to eat when I want to eat it, and neither you nor any other overpaid, meddling doctor is going to tell me I can't!"

Pride, like that ninth head of the Hydra, is a timeless problem. Pride blinds us to our need for change. Pride keeps us from facing our problems. Pride stops us from asking for help with issues. Pride factors into all eight of the other reasons we don't change and into a hundred more I haven't mentioned.

Pride dulls our senses and ultimately leads us to those terrible wakeup calls talked about earlier. Pride blinds us to how we're hurting other people, stops us from forgiving or asking for forgiveness, and even causes us to look at Jesus, our Savior, as a good man, or even a great man, but someone whose death was unnecessary for us.

Pride is at ground zero of why we won't change because deep in our prideful hearts we know we don't really need to change. We're above all that. As long as we put ourselves above others or our Lord, we're headed toward that "Lucifer's fall" that tossed Satan down from heaven and will cause any of us to fall off course as well. Which is why we need to look at that one last thought about change.

In spite of all the barriers, a giant Hydra of them, there's still that one reason we must change.

It's time to rate and discuss this barrier to change with
a friend or group.

[ ] *It's hard to admit or even realize, but pride is one of my top reasons*
for not seeing or following through on change.

[ ] *But you've never met my spouse, kids, boss, parents! They're the ones*
who need to change.

THE ONE REASON WE MUST CHANGE

A dramatic event took place on the day before God's people crossed the Jordan River and took their first steps into the promised land. It's found in the book of Deuteronomy, which for most of us explains why we aren't familiar with this event.

On the day before God's people were to start a new life by walking out of the wilderness and into the promised land, God gave them a dramatic picture of the real choice set before them that day. After four decades of wishing things would change, now the opportunity to take steps into the land of "milk and honey" was at hand. So what does the Lord do?

Lying just outside the promised land are two side-by-side mountains with a small valley in between. Picture a huge, natural outdoor amphitheater with the slope of Mount Gerezim forming one natural grandstand and across the small valley another grandstand formed by the slope of Mount Ebal. To make a dramatic story short, Almighty God put half of the nation of Israel in one grandstand and the other half facing them on the other grandstand. Then, like players on the field between grandstands, he had Joshua and the priests walk down the middle of the valley, like they were walking onto a football field.

God's people were ready for change, but they also knew there were great challenges before them. For example, they had sent out twelve spies years before, and ten out of twelve had come back from looking at all the barriers going into the promised land and concluded, "We are grasshoppers in their eyes." In other words, the challenges to moving into the promised land were too great, and their ability or strength to fight past the barriers was not nearly enough.

Now, a new generation of God's people is given the same option: keep wandering around in the wilderness or take steps into the promised land, even with all the barriers. And here's what the Lord, through his servant Joshua, tells them that day:

"Behold I set before you a choice, life and death, the blessing and the curse" (Deut. 30:19 author's paraphrased).

Doesn't that remind you of those life-and-death choices of Naaman and the people of Israel we saw in chapter 3? There are those words again, *life and death*. And here again is the decision either to get moving and live or to isolate ourselves and start dying inside. Only now this decision is also linked with two other common biblical words, each with uncommon meaning.

To *bless* literally means to add weight or value to someone. In short-hand, to bless is to add to someone's life. And to *curse*? That means to subtract. Literally, the picture behind this word in the Scripture is someone having dammed up a stream so that those who wait for its life-giving water downstream end up with only a muddy, undrinkable trickle.

Let's go back to our place in the grandstands as that choice is laid before the nation of Israel and, I believe, before each of us today.

Before God's people were to take their first step forward, they knew all about the barriers to entering the promised land before them. (Ten out of twelve spies sent in said it would be impossible; only the two who trusted God knew it wasn't.) It would absolutely be a challenge, to say the least. And yet they had the God who parted the waters of the Red Sea with them, and soon he would part the waters of the Jordan for them to cross into his promised land.

And so the choice before them was to make a HeartShift.

It was time to decide.

Life or death.

The blessing or the curse.

In spite of all the barriers, it was time to get moving as well.

It's Our Time to Move from Theory to Practice

It's time now to finish all the lessons in theory that have gone on in the past several chapters and actually put our hands on the piano and start to play. If you're ready to get moving and start adding to your own and your loved ones' lives, then you'll love the rest of this book. From here on out, if you're a football fan, you're going to be moving from chalkboard talks to tossing the ball, taking snaps, and diving for passes.

In fact, you're going to notice a dramatic change to the tenor and presentation of the following pages. You'll notice that the chapters from here on out are shorter for the most part, and all are filled with more examples and everyday applications. That's because our focus will now be on practice not theory, on making that HeartShift in some important area of your life and seeing how to live it out by drafting your own 2 Degree Changes.

I wouldn't begin to think I could list every 2 Degree Change you could make in every area of your life. In fact, that's a big reason I'll be asking you soon to go online and join a community as people committed to change who will be posting their own successful 2 Degree suggestions and stories, a gold mine of everyday examples. Lord willing, *your suggestions* that you tried and that helped you move in a new direction will be posted there as well.

So let the changes begin.

Done is all the reasoning and looking at barriers. It's time to get out of those grandstands and start walking toward the promised land, giants in front of us and all. It's time to make that choice of life instead of death, blessing instead of curse. It's time to make a HeartShift and live it out with 2 Degree Changes. And in the process, it's my deepest prayer that this book will become a helpful, encouraging, even life-changing experience for you as you move closer to your loved ones and your Lord and find your way to better health and a stronger faith.

Part 2

The Five Things You'll Need Now That You're Ready for Real Change

Introduction to Part 2: The HeartShift Life-Change Process

A few years ago I had the great honor of flying the "best of the best" in fighter aircraft. Of course, that would be the Lockheed Martin F-16A Fighting Falcon, the unquestioned owner of the skies when it comes to elite fighter aircraft. Outside Phoenix, Arizona, at Luke Air Force Base, I lifted off at 9:42 a.m. on a beautiful spring morning. I noted the time because, in addition to all the ultra high-tech directional and weapons systems on the heads-up display in front of me, there was also a small digital clock readout.

After being cleared by the tower and giving power to the aircraft down the runway, I barely pulled back on the toggle mechanism that guided the plane and was instantly airborne. It was the flight of a lifetime—roaring over the desert, linking up with two other fighters and doing in-flight maneuvers, and then blasting away at targets and even "threats" that were thrown up in front of me.

The F-16A Fighting Falcon carries more than twenty-two thousand pounds of weapons, electronic countermeasures, sensor pods, and external fuel tanks in addition to its structural weight. But despite light crosswinds and warm weather thermals, it landed like a dream, and I rolled to a stop.

That's when I heard over the headset in my helmet, "OK, John, that was pretty good except for the landing. It's Laura's turn to fly it now."

The person speaking into my headset was Major Bo McGowan, a Desert Storm vet and close friend who at the time was a lead instructor pilot at Luke.

Laura is my youngest daughter, who was then roughly nine years old.

Did I forget to mention that I was in the famed *Hooded Falcon,* perhaps the world's most advanced flight *simulator?*

But it was so real.

The full-motion suspension that slammed you back in your seat on acceleration, the orange readouts on the heads-up displays (that turned to green when you were flying with night vision), the shuttered recoil in the plane when you blasted the 20mm cannon that spit out six thousand rounds a minute, the sight of an air-to-air missile streaking from your plane toward its target, the near sense of weightlessness when you dramatically pushed down its nose.

The only problem was, *it wasn't real.*

It was all fun and no real risk. As intense as it seemed inside that replica cockpit, I never left the ground. That was a good thing because later, when I crashed twice during landings, United States taxpayers weren't out the twenty-four million dollars it would have cost to replace each plane.

Which brings me to this second section of the book and the purpose of this story.

The past five chapters have been like going to ground school to learn to fly. You've already been introduced to the key systems in this book—a HeartShift and the idea of how small 2 Degree Changes can help your life lift off and reach new heights. The next four chapters will be like climbing into the simulator.

In the Hooded Falcon, you got a hands-on feel for the avionics, weapons systems, heads-up instrument readouts, and manual controls. In the next four chapters, you'll also get a feel for four crucial aspects of the HeartShift Life-Change Process.

Chapter 6 will briefly introduce the importance of setting up a "memorial marker" around the date and one area of life in which you decide to make a HeartShift. Included in that chapter will be an invitation to go to our Web site, www.HeartShift.com, and download a certificate similar to the one I received after flying the Hooded Falcon. You'll also see another biblical example, and why having such a tangible stake in the ground can be a crucial first step in the change process.

Chapter 7 is when you go online once again to www.HeartShift.com and take your online strengths assessment. I'll wait until that chapter to go into detail on the benefits of taking just five to seven minutes to receive your twenty-eight-page strengths assessment. Suffice it to say, among other things this tool will act as your Global Positioning System to help map out a successful change strategy.

Chapter 8 will introduce you to what I call a "33 Group." Like everything in this book, you'll find this to be a simple concept to grasp. However, the strength you gain from your own 33 Group as an essential support system in this change process will be instrumental in your success.

Chapter 9 will be your invitation to join a unique online community of people serious about making a HeartShift and 2 Degree Changes. For real F-16 pilots, like my friend Major Bo, there's a reason they build in time before and after every flight to hold briefings between pilots. In talking to (or in this case you'll be reading helpful posts from) others engaged in the same battles to change, in the same area as you, you will discover a tremendous source of updated (filtered), helpful, and practical information.

As you work through the change process outlined in these four chapters, the feeling that you're ready to solo will seem more and more real. However, so will the attacks described in chapters 4 and 5, and perhaps other fears of failure as well. Yet as you pick an area of your life that needs change (like your health, home, or heart for God), set up your own memorial marker, take your online report, recruit your own 33 Group, and sign up as a HeartShift member of a unique online community, change will seem more and more real. But remember, flight school and even sitting in a full-motion, full-color simulator isn't the same as walking out on the flight line and climbing into the real thing. That will come in part 3 of this book, where first with your faith, then with your family and friendships, and finally with your health, you'll be encouraged to create 2 Degree Changes that will help you gain altitude over procrastination and even long-held problems.

Yes, there is risk anytime you really go airborne. But remember, when you get to that point, you won't be alone in the cockpit. In fact, *you haven't been alone since the first moment you picked up this book.*

Without a doubt, the loving God who created you is even more desirous of your being successful in making changes that will make you more loving, or healthy, or committed, or caring! And even when we think he's been too busy or preoccupied or somehow out of the picture (hidden away), or that our rights have been violated (the justice due us escapes God's notice), he will never leave us or forsake us. You've got his word on that:

> Why do you say, O Jacob, and assert, O Israel,
> "My way is hidden from the LORD,
> And the justice due me escapes the notice of my God"?
> Do you not know? Have you not heard?
> The Everlasting God, the LORD, the Creator of the ends of
>   the earth
> Does not become weary or tired.
> His understanding is inscrutable.
> He gives strength to the weary,
> And to him who lacks might He increases power.
> Though youths grow weary and tired,
> And vigorous young men stumble badly,
> Yet those who wait for the LORD
> Will gain new strength;
> They will mount up with wings like eagles,
> They will run and not get tired,
> They will walk and not become weary." (Isa. 40:27–31)

"They will mount up with wings like eagles." What a promise! A promise that something, *actually Someone,* even bigger and stronger than a Fighting Falcon can lift you on eagles' wings to heights and places you may not have reached in years.

You've already walked through flight school in the first five chapters. I'm sure you'll run through these next chapters that lay out the change process. And then you'll be ready to "mount up with wings" and lift off when it comes to real life. And throughout it all, know that Almighty God will be both your wingman and the air under your wings.

CHAPTER SIX

Three Key Factors in Making Your HeartShift Real

It's annoying to hear some announcer at the end of a radio or television commercial talking at warp speed and trying to stuff into the last few seconds the most legal disclaimers possible. When it comes to your making a HeartShift, I haven't consulted a suite of lawyers to come up with disclaimers to announce. But I do feel strongly that there are three assumptions you, the reader, need to be aware of if what follows is really to take hold and become helpful and timely.

The first assumption is that there simply must have been a time in your life when you truly become real. Not as in "get real," as you might hear from an upset teenager.

But become real.

To explain what I mean, let me draw on a famous children's book as an analogy.

On the day when each of our precious daughters was born, I did the same thing with each child. With Cindy still in the hospital, and when the room was finally quiet and all the well-wishers gone, I pulled up a chair next to Cindy's hospital bed and started a tradition. As I held each precious brand-new gift from God, I read them a picture-book story, *The Velveteen Rabbit*.

Obviously, a tired and tiny newborn couldn't understand a word I read, but from that first day forward, their mother and I wanted them to know how much they would be loved. And in this wonderful children's tale of a stuffed rabbit who becomes *real* is a picture that highlights a great truth.

If you've never read *The Velveteen Rabbit,* then I envy you the opportunity of reading it for the first time. You can find it at any library or fine bookstore, and I urge you to read it as soon as possible. If you've already read it, then I suspect that, like me, every time you get to the ending of the book, it causes you to brush back tears. That's because it speaks of a favorite child's toy that had been lost and then was found. A well-worn, much-loved material bunny that ends up being left in the yard, all alone, until it is finally found and surrounded by real bunnies.

Because it's a children's story, that shabby child's toy, a pretend rabbit with most of its "fur" rubbed off through loving hugs, becomes a real bunny and is finally free to hop off and join the rest. And for me the tears always begin to flow when I try to read the words that explain the miraculous transformation,

"When you love something very, very much, it becomes real."

Of course, when I tell you an assumption I have for you if you're serious about making a HeartShift—that at some time in your life you must become real—I mean of course a real person. Someone who realizes he or she has been loved so much and has responded to that love in such a way that it literally and forever transforms that person into something real. That's not storybook talk. It's what the Scriptures call becoming a "new creation." You'll find a description of just such a transformation in 2 Corinthians 5:17. "Therefore if any man is in Christ, he is a new creature; the old things passed away; behold, new things have come."

Obviously, that doesn't mean that the moment we give in to God's transforming love and become "new creatures" we get a new nose for the old one we don't like, or wavy hair for strait, or smaller feet like our best friends. God's first focus has always been on the internal and eternal changes. His amazing love, shown most clearly by the sacrifice of his one and only Son, makes possible a newness of life that brings with it new attitudes, new behaviors, and new choices.

From a heart of stone, we are given a heart of flesh to care more deeply for others than we ever could have before. From the kingdom of darkness, we are transferred to the kingdom of light, where we finally have a light for our path. We are told by Jesus himself that coming to him gives us all the freshness, all the new potential, of being born again. In fact, that's a mark of a Christian, not an elective option. Once, we were people who were stuck with only old patterns and habits, causing life to become just a series of more of the same actions that ultimately lead to death (isolation). Becoming born again ushers in a new way of life; it lifts us out of the maze, frees us, and like that rabbit, gives us an entire field full of options we never had before. And that's not to mention the new family once we're adopted as a son or daughter and become real.

That's the good news of the gospel that I'm assuming you've heard and responded to at some specific point in your life. It's not that you became so wise or good or successful at some point that you earned the transformation. Even the most skilled surgeon cannot perform his or her own heart transplant. Nor that you somehow erased all the wrong you've done or deleted all the times you know you've failed yourself, or others, or especially God. Each honest person knows that the debt or errors we've piled up through selfishness and sin over the years is like an hourly worker trying to pay off a million dollars in credit card debt. We can't even make the minimum payments, much less ever catch up to the terrible interest being accrued, no matter how sincere or how hard or how many hours we work.

The good news is that Someone has paid that terrible debt for us! While the balance was all against us, "while we were yet sinners" (Rom. 5:8), Jesus died for us. In so doing, he redeemed us and wiped clean the slate. With the words "It is finished"(John 19:30), he stamped "paid in full" on your debt and mine and offers us that incredible freedom. For all those who look up in faith and accept that narrow way out of our debtor's prison, he gives us a new life without that crushing, unpaid burden.

Many of you have already made that decision, even if it was perhaps long ago or even if it doesn't seem as real as it once did. But we've already spoken about the secondary function of feelings. The reality is that if through long talks with a close Christian friend or roommate, or your parents, or your church, or even in reading this book, you have heard and responded to Jesus' offer that there is a way of escape from the old and a way to exchange it all for a new life, then you're ready to make a HeartShift. For new life in Jesus offers the best and only way to become real.

I love the way C. S. Lewis illustrates this amazing transformation in a chapter he wrote on "Making and Begetting." To him, this changing out of the old with the new "is precisely what Christianity is all about.

This world is a great sculptor's shop. We are the statues and there is a rumour going round the shop that some of us are some day going to come to life."[1]

FIRST-ORDER CHANGE VERSUS SECOND-ORDER CHANGE

I'm sure you can see why this newness of life is so important to making a HeartShift. It's the difference between "first-order change" and "second-order change." By these terms I'm referring to the two primary ways people approach making changes in their life. I'll describe "first-order change" shortly, but let me deal with the second first.

Second-order change is like having a nightmare where a bear or some other kind of monster is chasing you. If you've ever had a nightmare, it can be terribly vivid and real. Your dream may even be so real, you try anything to get away from the bear. But if you're dreaming, how much does it help just to run faster? That's second-order change. Just do more of the same, while you're dreaming, and think that somehow that will get you to a safer place.

That is exactly what I see far too often with couples and individuals in crisis who come into my counseling office. Over twenty-five years, I've literally heard dozens and dozens of people describe their situation during our first session by using the words, "It's like we're in a bad dream!" Indeed they are. And just doing more of the same in a dream, like running faster, *never brings change.* Perhaps you can understand now why couples who think, *We just need to talk more,* so infrequently talk their way out of their problems.

What *does* bring change, no matter how real that bad dream seems, is when something from the outside wakes us up and ushers in a new way of relating. In fact, it ushers in a way of relating that so substantially alters our situation that it forces us to wake up and discover the concept "real." And amazingly, that bad dream—even if it seemed so real—is shown to be all shadow and fear and unable to stay around once you're awake and the lights are on.

Bad dreams do have their own reality. Coming awake ushers in not only a way of escape from that bad dream but also a whole fresh world of real opportunities, not the least of which is a new way of relating to other real people. That's what first-order change is all about. It's allowing or having something from the outside break into our world, wake us up from what seems like our only reality when we're in the bad dream, and in the process usher in a whole new way of relating.

For dreamers it may be the alarm clock going off that wakes them up from the nightmare, or their spouse rolling over, or the kids calling out from down the hall. For people wanting to make a HeartShift, it's inviting the God of the universe to invade our lives, come into that bad dream, and wake us up.

Jesus is the ultimate first-order change agent. That's yet another reason it's so important that at some time in your life, you've come to Christ. The role of Jesus Christ and the Holy Spirit—who, for believers, is at work within us—is so important to making a HeartShift that I'll begin the third section of this book on making small 2 Degree Changes with ways to strengthen your spiritual life.

That great exchange or shift from life without Christ to having Jesus' life within us is the first assumption I'm making as we move forward. If you're still on the fence on this subject, then please talk to your pastor. If you don't have one, then talk to a pastor at an outstanding local church near you. (There are hundreds of outstanding churches in every part of our great country. Just drive around on a Sunday morning and look where lots of cars are congregating or talk to a friend or family member who is a Christian.) There are also outstanding books you can find on coming to faith if you'll visit your local Christian bookstore. (While Wal-Mart carries lots of Christian books, if you're an "on the fence" person, then I urge you to look up a Christian bookstore in your city and talk to the knowledgeable people there who can put a book in your hands.) Or talk to a friend you know is a Christian. Your Christian friends are not perfect, but they have a knowledge and newness within them that wakes them up every day with the truth of his word: "[Thy mercies] are new every morning: great is thy faithfulness" (Lam. 3:23).

That's the first assumption to all that follows. Feel free to take all the time you need to make sure you've made this first step before going a page further. Then once you do or have, here's another key assumption to making real changes.

I ASSUME THE PAIN LEVEL IN YOUR LIFE IS HIGH ENOUGH TO PROMPT CHANGE

It would be wonderful if every person who reads this book simply does so for fine-tuning purposes. But I know that's not the case. For many of us, making a HeartShift isn't an option but what seems like a last-chance necessity.

Believe it or not, being backed into such a corner can be a good thing!

If there is no conscious reality of the need to change in your life, then don't expect this book to have any real impact. If you're just doing this as part of a class or small group, or because you're afraid your spouse will be upset if you don't, then don't expect much from the pages that follow. You just won't see what's happening around you.

Here's an example of what I mean.

Years ago I had agreed to meet several of my friends to celebrate all of us making it through our first, grueling year at Dallas Theological Seminary. We were all language majors (meaning Greek or Hebrew majors), and at least for me, it had been an incredibly trying year. Not only had it been mentally taxing (I'd never had a foreign language before majoring in Greek in graduate school), but I was physically exhausted as well. Like most seminarians, I was working close to full-time, in my case at Interstate Battery company. I was also working close to full-time leading the Thomas Jefferson Young Life club in Dallas, Texas. And I was going to school full-time. That's not to mention the pressure that came from being flat broke due to trying to pay for school without taking on any student loans. I was so broke, in fact, that I almost called and canceled my golf and lunch outing with my friends. I was embarrassed to say anything to them, but I literally had no money to go to lunch, or to buy golf balls, and I didn't want to have to ask for a loan from a friend.

Struggling over that dilemma, I did two things that morning.

First, I prayed about whether I should go and if God might provide a way not to have to borrow any funds. Then I walked to my mailbox at the seminary.

As I did each weekday morning when I arrived at school, I walked to the small campus post office and opened the tiny bronze mail slot assigned to me to check for mail. That day there was a single envelope inside. I didn't recognize the handwritten name on the return address; however, when I opened the letter, there was thirty dollars in cash (six five-dollar bills). As I read the letter enclosed with the cash, it was from a young man I hadn't seen for more than a *year* and had only met one time. At a summer camp in Colorado, I had to loan a camper thirty dollars who had lost his wallet on the bus trip on the way to camp. That gave him some money for meals on the bus trip from Texas to Colorado and back, and he gave me his promise that he'd pay me back when he got home.

It was now fully a year later. He'd never paid me (and I'd never asked). Somehow God must have prompted his conscience while he was at school the week *before* I needed that money to place thirty dollars into an envelope and send it to me in the mail. As you might imagine, chills ran down my spine as I held those six bills. I couldn't believe the divine coincidence behind the money I held. But let's fast-forward from the post office to the end of the golf game that day and to sitting down with three first-year seminary friends.

"I'm quitting seminary," one of my good friends announced at the table that day. We had just played golf at Dallas Country Club, which was then and is now one of the most prestigious golf courses in Texas. The young man who was speaking was also the one who had gotten us on the course. His father was incredibly wealthy and held a membership at that club, among several others.

That day I paid for a sleeve of golf balls with a crisp five-dollar bill and still had plenty of money for a sandwich with the money I was convinced came to me as an amazing answer to prayer. Without any exaggeration, that same day my wealthy seminary friend gave the following as his reason for quitting seminary: "I'm quitting seminary because I just don't feel like God answers prayer."

That was literally his complaint. He had spent a year studying God's Word in depth, and his conclusion was that it simply didn't matter in real life. Even his prayer didn't seem to affect anything he did. He felt it was a waste of air.

Do you remember a time when Jesus told his disciples that it was harder for a wealthy man to come to faith than for a camel to go through the eye of a needle? When you're isolated from any real needs, it can be terribly difficult to feel there's any need to make a change in your life. It's also more difficult to see the small movements of God's hand if there is no real sense of need in your life. Hungry people struggle with looking at the buffet, not those who have just walked out of a seven-course meal.

My friend had great personal wealth from his portion of a family business, no need to work, a beautiful car, a loft apartment in arguably the best part of Dallas, and yes, a stop-traffic girlfriend. His conclusion: "God doesn't answer prayer."

I sat at that same table, living in a dilapidated garage apartment, driving an eleven-year-old car, having no girlfriend and no prospects, and having no money. But I'd been smiling all day about a God who cared so much about me that he'd mailed thirty dolloars for golf balls and lunch (and even gas for my car to get to the golf course!).

If I had had thousands of dollars in the bank, which in the 1970s was *real* money, I'm sure I would have thought that six five-dollar bills were nice but certainly not an answer to prayer. In other words, while I truly believe the change process that follows can help anyone move closer to others and to God's best, if you feel no real need to change, it's perfectly fine to put this book away until a time when you do. (And by the way, no matter how well you're doing today, a time will come when life brings you to a place where you will need to make a HeartShift in an important area of your life.)

Finally, I'm going to assume something of you that I require of every person I see in counseling.

I Assume You'll Actually Do Your Homework in Making Your HeartShift

I have a small counseling practice in Scottsdale, Arizona. Because I travel a good bit and don't have a large staff, I have to limit my counseling to a few people or couples at a time. For years I've had each person or couple I agree to work with sign a "therapeutic contract" before we take any serious steps forward.

Perhaps you've had a teacher in high school or college that made you do something similar. Let's say you were in an English class, and a professor handed out a syllabus. He or she then went down a list of class requirements, explaining assignments, when they were due, and what each meant to your grade if you didn't complete a particular assignment. While that can put dread into the heart of students who see all at once what's to be done over an entire semester, at least they know what's expected of them up front. In some cases the teacher may even ask students to sign and turn in a copy of the syllabus, thereby stating that they understand the requirements and agree to do the homework if they're to pass the course.

That's essentially what I do with counselees.

After an initial meeting where we both see if it's helpful to meet further, I then handed each person a therapeutic contract. This agreement says that I'll be honest with them and that they need to be honest with me in return. (I don't like surprises, like the person who came in with severe attachment problems and finally told me after our seventh session, "Well, I was adopted. I guess I forgot to tell you that.")

In addition to honesty, I also tell them that there will be homework that specifically links with every session. Not busywork like you get from a bored teacher, but specific things I'll ask them to do or discuss between sessions that needs to be done or else we'll need to end the counseling process.

In short, they have a choice. Complete the assignments so that our session can be as helpful as possible, or feel free to see someone else. I know that probably sounds harsh, but if a person or couple isn't serious about taking even small steps toward change by completing a few short assignments, they're wasting their time and mine.

I explain this to couples straight out, and only three times in twenty years of working with people have I had someone not sign their contract at the first session. (Those who refused, by the way, were involved in an ongoing affair they hadn't as yet admitted.)

I think the reason I get so little push-back on doing assignments is because they know in advance the importance of doing a few small things—like filling out a memorial marker, taking an online test, coming up with three other people who can become a 33 Support Group, or joining an online community of believers.

Obviously, I can't ask you to sign a therapeutic contract as you move forward in this book. But at least you know now how important I feel the homework process is in each chapter that follows. While I'm assuming you'll take each part of the process that follows seriously, I promise what follows isn't busywork; these are targeted assignments that have helped many others and can help you be successful at an area of change you want to make.

With those three assumptions in place, it's time to turn the page and start taking tangible steps toward change.

CHAPTER SEVEN

Setting Up a Memorial Marker to Celebrate the Day You Made a HeartShift

Change implies both an ending and a beginning. Certainly that's part of why change is so difficult. We can experience this by just walking out the door of a warm, dry home and over to our car blanketed with three inches of fresh snow from the night before. The moment we walk out our doorway, life is systemically different. If it's a bitter-cold day, that single step ends life in a snug, climate-controlled environment and launches many "can't miss" adjustments from our first breath of frigid air.

Changes in climate are often easy to feel.

That's not the case with many of the most important changes we make.

For example, a marriage ceremony signals a major change and marks both the end of life as a single (or at least it should) and the beginning of a legally, physically, and emotionally different way of life. I can remember clearly the late June afternoon when my wife, Cindy, and I were married some twenty-five years ago. When the ceremony ended and I walked with my wife of ten minutes to the reception at a small church in Tucson, I didn't suddenly feel married any more than you suddenly feel older when the clock turns 12:01 a.m. on your birthday.

In fact, what mattered wasn't the *feelings* we had that day, even though we were both thrilled and happy that the long-awaited day of our wedding had finally come. What counted was the *decision* we'd made at that time and place to commit our lives to each other.

Before the state and before God, it was our decision to marry—marked by a short ceremony and memorialized by the giving and receiving of rings—that initiated dramatic changes at multiple levels. An ongoing testament to what happened on June 30, 1979, are the rings Cindy and I received that day and have worn each day since.

Now, please, before you skip this chapter—especially if you're a confirmed single guy or if you've just gone through the hundreds of details of marrying off a daughter—you can *relax!* This first step in the change process won't require you to hire the equivalent of a full-time wedding planner to script a special event. What I'll be asking you to do is both simple and inexpensive, but that's not to downplay its importance. In fact, this first step which includes making a HeartShift and linking that decision with a tangible memorial marker, may be the very tool that pushes aside a challenging roadblock in the weeks to come. You may also find it provides the inspiration your children or a good friend needs in order to make a HeartShift in their life as well.

WHY A MEMORIAL MARKER IS THE FIRST STEP IN THIS CHANGE PROCESS

On our wedding day a few decades ago, the giving and receiving of rings memorialized our commitment and illustrated both an ending and a beginning. If you go back a few centuries, you'll see where a rock also became a memorial marker for an entire nation—the end of one season of life and the start of another. Actually, in their case this rock wasn't a diamond but twelve real stones—twelve river rocks.

Now when all the nation had finished crossing the Jordan, the LORD spoke to Joshua, saying, "Take for yourselves twelve men from the people, one man from each tribe, and command them, saying, 'Take up for yourselves twelve stones from here out of the middle of the Jordan, from the place where the priests' feet are standing firm, and carry them over with you and lay them down in the lodging place where you will lodge tonight.'" So Joshua called the twelve men whom he had appointed from the sons of Israel, one man from each tribe; and Joshua said to them, "Cross again to the ark of the LORD your God into the middle of the Jordan, and each of you take

up a stone on his shoulder, according to the number of the
tribes of the sons of Israel." (Josh. 4:1–5)

I realize we're dropping into the middle of this story, but this should
be both an easily remembered group and a recognizable setting. In chapter 3, we saw how Joshua, their new leader, had assembled the nation
on two neighboring mountains. As Joshua and the priests of Israel
walked down the field between those two natural grandstands, they
called out a choice that God had set before his people that day.

Life or death—the blessing or the curse.

To review, choosing life meant to move forward, while choosing
death meant to withdraw or isolate themselves. Those in the grandstands that day chose life and chose to get moving by taking that first,
challenging step into the promised land.

Their second choice was blessing or curse. Again, you'll remember
that to bless someone meant to add weight and value to their life, while
to curse someone meant to cut them off or subtract from their life.

Unlike their parents and grandparents, who chose poorly and as a
result perished in the wilderness, this new generation chose wisely. They
would trust that God would add his blessing to their lives and decision,
and they started moving into the land that would be their home.

We joined the story right after the entire nation of Israel had just
experienced something supernatural. In a dramatic replay of an earlier
miracle where the Lord had parted the Red Sea to save their parents and
grandparents, Almighty God now opened the door to the promised land
by pulling back the waters of the Jordan River at flood stage. The mere
memory of that miracle for those who had seen it could have been a
tremendous source of encouragement to those people. *Yet Almighty
God performed two miracles that day, not one.*

ONE WAY TO REMEMBER FIRST STEPS
TOWARD CHANGE

Getting an entire nation safely across a flooded river without a
single person getting the slightest bit wet was the first miracle that
happened that day. Here's the second:

And Joshua said to them, "Cross again to the ark of the
LORD your God into the middle of the Jordan, and each of
you take up a stone on his shoulder, according to the number
of the tribes of the sons of Israel.

"Let this be a sign among you, so that when your children ask later, saying, 'What do these stones mean to you?' then you shall say to them, 'Because the waters of the Jordan were cut off before the ark of the covenant of the LORD; when it crossed the Jordan, the waters of the Jordan were cut off.' So these stones shall become a memorial to the sons of Israel forever." (Josh. 4:5–7)

Twelve men, each one a chosen representative of one of the twelve tribes of Israel, were asked to walk back across the Jordan, stopping exactly halfway across the river. That's the spot where the priests, holding the ark of the covenant (a physical symbol of God's presence with his people), had stood during the dry-land crossing for thousands of people. Now, however, it's just the priests and a handpicked group of men who are left midstream, and each one has been given a special mission.

If you can imagine living near a large river like the Mississippi or Missouri, you would have grown up factoring in that natural obstacle to your daily life. Every time you had an appointment or meeting across the river, that meant going up or downstream to the closest bridge to cross.

Now imagine seeing something you may have dreamed about but never seen, particularly on those times when you were late to an appointment and stuck on a bridge. Suddenly, right in front of you, there is a wide dry-land walkway opening up.

As amazing as it would be to see the waters pile up above and below you, perhaps the most incredible sight of all would be just seeing the *bottom* of a huge section of the Mississippi or Missouri exposed to sunlight. Even skin divers today can get only a murky look at these great rivers' floors. Imagine acres of it now laid bare and bone-dry before your eyes.

That was what the nation of Israel saw and actually walked across, and now twelve men were getting a second chance to stand where only a day before the water would have been at its deepest and swiftest. From that halfway point they were told to reach down and pick up a rock to carry to their camp.

By *rock*, the Lord didn't mean to pick up a skipping stone that you could carry in the palm of your hand. These mighty men were asked to do some heavy lifting. Each one was to hoist a heavy river stone onto his shoulder and carry it to where the nation of Israel was already bedding down for the night. (It takes a lot of work to make new changes, not to mention getting an entire nation across a huge river!)

These stones had been covered in deep water for generations.

Now they would become a permanent display for generations.

But why make a memorial maker out of these stones at all?

There are many reasons, but let's begin by going back to the start of this chapter and to the way an internal decision of two people to join in marriage becomes a public, tangible, visible memorial to the day things changed in their life story. The genesis of a wedding ceremony can be traced back weeks, months, or even years to an internal heart decision. Even before the words "Do you?" from the pastor and "I will!" from the couple, it was their decision that had brought them to this place.

For the nation of Israel, their decision to choose life and blessing was what started them moving forward toward the promised land, a HeartShift. Now Almighty God makes sure their HeartShift and first steps are unforgettable. A river at flood stage is stopped in its tracks so that the people can make tracks into the promised land. And now twelve men are sent to pick up an outward, visible sign of each person's internal, courageous decision to get moving.

Those stones never could have been touched or seen unless God performed that miracle and God's people had stepped out in faith that day. Now those stones would become a constant reminder of God's greatness and love as well.

How significant would those rocks become?

From that day forward, once the rocks were piled up and the river started flowing again, there would be no other place you could see those deep-river rocks. In an age without photography, it provided a tangible reminder: "This was the place, and what God did was real!"

If you think about it, memorializing first steps is important in many settings. First steps of a beloved child are recorded in a baby book. A new proprietor often frames the first dollar bill he or she receives from a real customer. When you join the service, you stand with others and go through a swearing-in ceremony where you first sign and then repeat out loud an oath to protect and defend your country, even before you get the short haircut.

Those deep-water rocks would be a vivid word picture of how the Lord had gone in front of them. How he had piled back the waters before them so that not a drop touched them. Yet there are other important reasons shared in this passage for why Almighty God chose to have his people set up a memorial marker. This tangible touch-point would become both a tremendous help in the midst of later trials and a powerful teaching tool for their children.

The nation of Israel had made only the smallest of beachheads into the promised land at this point. They had crossed the Jordan and immediately bedded down. Battle after battle awaited them, starting with their taking on the mighty walled city of Jericho directly across from where they had just crossed.

It's not that these rocks were sacred or magical, like a good-luck charm that warriors could touch before going into battle. These stones weren't set up to be worshipped like a pagan god. But they were meant to be a tangible reminder that just as God had been with them from the moment they'd made their HeartShift decision to take those first steps into the promised land, he would be with them each step of the way until the land was theirs.

That's the kind of memorial marker worth having when times are tough and the outcome seems uncertain! A tangible reminder that points to the power *behind* the pile of rocks, not the rocks themselves. It also becomes a tremendous teaching tool for showing young minds the importance of unseen realities.

Each new generation seems to have a natural incredulity when it comes to what's important for its elders. For example, the kind of music one generation thinks is hip is almost guaranteed to be considered old school and out-of-date by the next. Let's not even talk about clothing or hairstyle differences between generations! What is taken for granted as "gospel" for one generation, you can expect to be questioned by the next—which is a stated reason God had them pile up those twelve stones.

If you have children, you know what incredible question-askers they can be. Can't you just picture a child, brought up on the promised land side of the Jordan, being taken to see a pile of stones and asking, "Dad, Mom, why are these stones such a big deal to you?"

With the open door, that mom or dad just had to point to that tangible reminder to have the best kind of object lesson. Those stones, once hidden and impossible to reach, reflected both the inner decision and HeartShift they'd made to move forward in faith and the dramatic way God had miraculously gone ahead of them to pave their way.

Setting up a memorial marker for the nation was an important way to note their HeartShift, to first steps, steel their resolve during future times of challenge, and even teach their children. Now it's time for you to follow in their footsteps.

IT'S TIME FOR YOU TO MAKE A HEARTSHIFT AND LINK IT WITH A MEMORIAL MARKER

I've spoken of wedding rings and river rocks as memorial markers. Let me give you one last example before I ask you to print off your own memorial marker.

I'm not going to say I was out of shape, but several years ago if I'd worn a bright blue suit, someone might have tried to mail a letter in me. The excuse I gave for not exercising or worrying about my diet was that I simply didn't have time. (Remember, that was the first reason given in chapter 4 for why we'll never change.) In a very sudden development, the ministry I was a part of for ten years decided to transplant its headquarters half a country away. With both my mother and father in failing health, moving cross-country simply wasn't an immediate option. So the first wake-up call I got was that I was suddenly on my own.

When we launched StrongFamilies.com, I had no office, no office volunteers, and no natural skills to manage the literally hundreds of details that go into booking and supporting the seminars I launched. The best part of that first year was taking myself out for National Secretaries Day. The worse part was that I was literally working every day and most nights as we got our ministry launched.

Then came that one night in San Antonio.

I was in the middle of a grueling five-day, four-city speaking trip, my longest of the year. In addition to eating poorly and skipping exercise (*Who has time to eat right and exercise on the road?* I rationalized), I was trying to manage all the details of upcoming seminars while working until late each night in the hotel to finish a book deadline. That's on top of trying to still be a good husband and father and finish my term well on the elder board at our home church.

I had just finished a three-hour miniseminar that evening and stayed around afterward until the last person's question was answered. That's when I remember being exhausted and walking out to my rental car in the dark, and then things got really dark. When next I awoke, I was lying in an emergency ward, sporting a beautiful, white hospital bracelet.

The emergency room physician ran tests all that night and gave me his diagnosis before he went off shift in the morning.

"Forced march syndrome."

You won't find that ailment listed in the *Doctor's Desk Reference* (which is actually in Palm Pilot editions now). It was more of an observation from his days in the military instead of a medical diagnosis. But it turned out to be accurate.

Many times he had seen relatively young men who had just dropped in their tracks. No heart attack. No stroke. No blocked arteries or seizures. His conclusion was that they had just come to the end of themselves on a forced march. Namely, a person pushes so hard for so long that suddenly they black out and hit the deck, or in my case the asphalt parking lot.

Needless to say, my wife and I and our ministry board had a long talk when I flew home the next day. Talk about a wake-up call! I thought I could push and push day and night without consequence. A deep gash and now purple bruises from when I'd done a face-plant in the asphalt were a graphic reminder that I didn't have unlimited energy and couldn't do it all alone.

Something had to change or, as several other doctors back home told me, the next wake-up call I'd get *would* be a heart attack, or worse.

It was time to make a HeartShift.

As I rested and prayed and thought about what had happened, I read through the same passage you read earlier in this chapter—Joshua leading the nation through the rivers at flood stage and then his being asked by the Lord to set up a memorial marker to remind them of what had happened. A reminder to them and a teaching object to their children that while tough battles may lay ahead, God would be there every step of the way.

That's why for years on my desk at work, and now even in my Day-Timer that I still carry every day, you can find a white hospital bracelet that I cut off my wrist in San Antonio. That wake-up call in Texas meant things needed to change—and right now. That small, plastic strip with my name and patient ID number stenciled in blurred, blue letters became my memorial marker to that decision. It became a tangible, physical reminder to the HeartShift decision I had made, even before I reinforced it with 2 Degree Changes that followed.

In an upcoming section on our health, I'll get much more specific on the 2 Degree physical changes I made after first making that HeartShift.

Yet the starting point, even before any diet or exercise changes, was to make that change of heart and then link it with a memorial marker—in my case, that small, white hospital bracelet.

Which leads me to your memorial marker and to the HeartShift you decide to make.

LINKING YOUR OWN HEARTSHIFT WITH A MEMORIAL MARKER

Enough talk and illustrations of other people and even nations who made a HeartShift and memorialized that decision in some tangible way. *It's your time now.*

I hope your decision to read this book and now to write down your own HeartShift decision hasn't come as a result of a hospital stay. But whatever the reason, I'm thrilled that you're standing at the edge of the Jordan, ready to take that first step toward a much better place.

It's time to pick that one area in which you've decided to make a HeartShift.

There may be more than one area where you feel you need to make changes. If that's how you feel, join the crowd. You might even be able to fill up a legal pad full of areas, from your health to your marriage to how you handle finances to your role as a parent to closing open loops with your own parents, and on and on. If that's the case, then I've been there in each area as well. But think back to what we've already seen about doing something significant. The issue isn't helping every child; it's helping just one. The issue isn't trying to list pages of problems, real or imagined; it's picking just one.

Put another way, if you approach change like you're walking down a buffet line, and pile up a plateful of changes, it's a lock you'll end up being sick. *Heartsick* that is, when frustration or fear or guilt sets in after you've failed again.

But by starting with just one HeartShift decision, you'll begin to see firsthand how that idea of "compound interest" presented in chapter 2 kicks in with every simple, positive, good step you take. For example, let's say your HeartShift decision is to get in better shape to protect your health. By slowly gaining some success in this one area, those positive actions can spill over into unexpected successes and disciplines in other areas of your life as well. If you've decided to make your marriage your HeartShift focus, then watch a slowly improving marital relationship make it easier to discipline your children or even to bless them.

"But I'm not a 'list' person, or creative, or I just don't feel this is the right time to start a change like this." Let me quickly answer those common last-minute arguments.

A HEARTSHIFT GIVES YOU SPECIFIC FOCUS FOR YOUR 2 DEGREE CHANGES

The goal in making a HeartShift isn't just to do more things. Most of us need another to-do list like we need a hole in the head. Rather, by having one specific, prayed-over area to focus our need for change, it's like loading a destination into MapQuest or some other online mapping site. Once you've pinpointed a destination, every small change and step from where you are toward your destination really does make a difference.

You can almost be certain that if the area you picked is a difficult one, you may *never* feel like going on record to make a change! But I'd take you back to that wedding ceremony and to facts, not situational feelings.

God-honoring change *always* begins at the heart level.

From the decisions we make in our heart flow our actions, good or bad. And from our actions flow our feelings. *Never the reverse.* In other words, if you're waiting for that *one fine day* when you feel like making a HeartShift, Halley's Comet will come around more often.

Decisions of the heart prompt actions, and actions dictate feelings. Or look at it the other way around. Positive feelings *follow* positive actions, and those actions flow from an initial willingness or decision to shift directions, to turn your heart. The time to go on record with your HeartShift is *today.*

Finally, it's important to be specific instead of just global in stating your HeartShift decision. For example, "I want to be a better person" may sound laudable and even bring a warm smile to your face, but it's about as helpful as being lost in the country and having a helpful farmer tell you, "Just go down the road a piece to where that big tree was that fell down last winter, then turn toward old Henry's barn, and that'll get you headed in the right direction to where you want to go."

Writing down "I need to make a HeartShift when I drive so that I don't yell at bad drivers" is a positive, specific, small, focused change of heart. (And again, it's one I've had to make.) "I want to be a better person" is like writing in a yearbook, "Stay as sweet as you are." Years later you still look at it and don't know exactly what it means.

Despite all the objections and excuses, it's now time for you to get specific about the HeartShift you need to make. It may be in an area I've already mentioned several times before, like your health or your home or your heart for God. Or it may be any one of a thousand other specific areas where you want to focus energy, prayer, and the encouragement of others to bring needed change.

Perhaps the HeartShift you need to make is to do better at closing sales or making cold calls at work or turning in homework on time at school so you don't needlessly lose points. Perhaps your HeartShift will focus on rebuilding a positive relationship with your in-laws or sharing your faith with others or finishing your senior year without giving up and quitting.

There are countless HeartShift targets, *but just pick one* with as specific, positive, tangible a focus as you can. And by the way, if you've come to this place in this book on change and you *still* can't think of a single area in your life that needs work, then pick lying; that would be a good target for you. (Either that or let me talk with your business partner or spouse or especially with your children for ten minutes without you standing there. You might be shocked how quickly those who know you well will come up with one thing you should work on.)

But what about all those other areas that are going untouched while I focus on just one?

For me, the first specific HeartShift I made was linked to that medical wake-up call I got in San Antonio. Three months later, bolstered by some success in the first, I made a second specific HeartShift when it came to the open loop of anger I had brought from my broken relationship with my own father into my parenting. I'll highlight how I tackled that HeartShift in the parenting section of this book. The third HeartShift I made came nearly a year later and was targeted at being a better husband, specifically doing a better job at sharing options with my wife and seeking her input *early* in a decision rather then just informing her of a decision I'd basically already made. (That HeartShift will also be explained in the section on marriage.)

It's my prayer that you'll be able to use this concept of making a HeartShift to tackle one specific area after another over the long haul. For me and for many with whom I've counseled, this has proved to be a doable, durable, helpful way to chip away at a host of issues and frustrations that may have been bothersome or even destructive for years.

If you're expecting Almighty God to part the waters of the nearest river to show you his support for your first step, he did much more than that for you. Today we have his eternal, unchanging word on the fact that he loves us despite any past failures or present doubts, and he not only wants us to change for the better, "He who began a work in you will complete it."

What follows is a place to write your target. You'll be asked the day's date on which you made your HeartShift decision, and a brief explanation of the change you've prayerfully chosen to tackle. (Only a few lines are provided because if it takes more room than those few lines, you've got more then one area or goal in mind.) Finally, you'll find a place to sign your certificate.

My First HeartShift Decision is simply, prayerfully stated below:

_____

_____

_____

On this _____ day of _____ (month), 20___,

I set my signature to this HeartShift.

_____

For me, this marks both an end and a beginning,
and my commitment to take the first step,
followed by small 2 Degree steps, toward God-honoring change.

You'll notice I didn't put any burden on you to be creative in coming up with a memorial marker. You don't have to come up with a hospital bracelet to frame, or scuba down and bring up a huge river rock to reflect the change you need to make. Just prayerfully, thoughtfully fill in the blanks. That's not to say you shouldn't come up with a personalized, creative memorial marker. For many people that's a helpful thing to do. However, if you're not the "creative type," then I don't want any creative blocks to stop you before you start.

Instead of writing in your book, if you'd like a large, colorful certificate to use as a memorial marker, then just visit www.HeartShift.com. There you'll find a community of people committed to making real, lasting changes in their home, their health, or their heart for God. (You'll learn more about this online community in chapter 9 and be able to join if you like.) You'll also get to click on "My HeartShift Memorial Marker" and download a colorful certificate that will print in either black-and-white or color if you have a color printer. (If you don't have a color printer or an Internet connection, then just use the earlier form in this book. Better yet, why not think of a friend right now who has both and get them to download your certificate and print it off for you in color!)

At that Web site you'll also be able to click on the tab "Share Your Memorial Marker" and see a number of memorial markers other people have come up with (shared with permission of course) that can give you lots of creative ideas in seeing what they found helpful for memorializing their first step toward change.

Your printable memorial marker is for you to frame, or put under the glass on your desk, or tape to a bathroom mirror, or fold up and put in your purse or wallet if that would be helpful. Feel free to download and print off a dozen certificates, stacking one on top of the other just like those twelve river rocks. Rather, and seriously, I encourage you to take the time to fill out at least the certificate in this book, show it to a loved one or friend (your 33 Group would be perfect to share this with as you'll see in chapter 8), and then use that HeartShift certificate as a starting point to change—a tangible reminder that you prayerfully, thoughtfully made a decision, on a specific day, to get back on track with a HeartShift and to start to live out that decision with 2 Degree Changes.

That's step one in the HeartShift change process.

Now comes a second step that involves taking one of the most insightful, helpful tools I think you'll ever experience. It's your chance to take a powerful online strengths assessment that can not only help you pinpoint potential areas where a HeartShift may be needed but can especially show you how incredibly valuable you are as a person.

CHAPTER EIGHT

Getting a Clear Starting Point for Change Today

With your HeartShift in writing and your memorial marker filled out or picked out, it's time to take a second step toward positive change. While this will involve a small investment of your time, it may well be the most helpful, encouraging few minutes you've ever spent learning about yourself and others. I'm going to ask you to take advantage of an incredibly gracious gift from a team of committed believers that can help you become even more serious about making successful changes.

Does being able to pinpoint areas of needed change and potential conflict and seeing clearly how unique and valuable you are as a person sound like too much to get out of five to seven minutes spent online? It won't after a short explanation and if you'll follow a few simple instructions to take your gift.

AN INCREDIBLY HELPFUL TOOL IN THE HEARTSHIFT PROCESS

Behind every book, and sometimes every chapter of every book, is a story. During the time when my father was dying, I wrote a book called *The Blessing*.[1] It was all about what it's like to gain or miss out on your parents' love and acceptance—what the Bible calls "the blessing." Seeing my own father's blessing slip away each day colored every chapter of that book.

Other books I've written have had much more happy and hopeful stories behind them. *Like this one!* To try to explain, let me give you an example that I hope captures some of the feelings I had in the early stages of writing this book.

Let's say, like my precious wife, Cindy, that you're a kindergarten teacher. If the idea of having twenty-four five- and six-year-olds wiggling, squirming, and just daring you to teach them makes your blood run cold, then you're like me! But let's say you're like Cindy. You've got a master's degree in early childhood education and loads of training beyond. You're convinced God wants you encouraging and equipping young children, and you're confident that you can make a positive difference in their little lives. It's the start of a new school year, and you're ready to give each bright, shining, five-year-old face the best foundation possible for a lifetime of learning.

Only there's one major problem.

In a technology-driven society, in the midst of an Internet world, kindergarten is the perfect starting point for kids and computers. Unfortunately, let's say you don't have a single desktop or laptop in your class. It doesn't do any good to blame it on the district or the system (or in an election year, whoever the sitting President happens to be). That's just the way it is in your classroom, but that doesn't stop you from seeing pictures of other kids and computers and knowing how valuable having even one would be.

So that's when you sit down to lunch with a few friends who are in the computer business. In fact, their company builds dream-machine computers with all the whistles and bells you could ever want. Let's say even their base machine has wireless Internet and loads of computer upgrades.

You build up your courage, buy their lunch, and then spend the whole time they're eating talking about your kids. How precious they are. How much they could benefit from having just one computer in the class. How well they'd share, how much they could learn. And then, at last, you build up the courage to ask if there is some way their company could provide your students, or at least some of them, with a chance to sit in front of one of their computers—for free. (Remember, you have no budget for computers for your classroom.)

Now it's finally your turn to take a bite of your sandwich, only to have it drop on your plate. That's because from across the table they tell you that instead of one, there will be twenty-four brand-new computers delivered to your class the first day of school—one for each child in your room.

What would you think about a computer company who saw the vision for helping people at a critical point in the learning curve by providing not one workstation but one for *each* child in your class? I think you'd feel just like I did when I had lunch with two good friends of mine more than a year ago at the beginning of writing this book.

The friends I sat down with are two men I have had the privilege of working with at a company called Insights International. Their names are Rodney Cox and Eric Tooker, and they're elders at their church, outstanding husbands and father, and the heart and soul of an Internet technology company. In this case it's not computers they create and deliver, but without question one of the most powerful, unique, online strengths assessments available anywhere.

No doubt you've taken some kind of personality test over the years. For example, there's the well-known Meyers-Briggs report, an excellent instrument that measures sixteen behavioral characteristics. Or at work you may have taken the DISC test, perhaps the most powerful and frequently used business instrument that measures twenty-eight behavioral characteristics (a CD version gets up to eighty-nine).

Insights International does something different. We've created an online look at who you are, called The Leading From Your Strengths™ report. It's only taken online, takes a mere five to seven minutes to complete, and then *instantly* e-mails you back a twenty-eight-page strengths assessment! Where other reports measure sixteen, twenty-eight, or even eighty-nine dimensions of behavior, this Internet-based tool is so complex in it's patented scoring and delivery methods, it actually measures *384 behavioral characteristics*! In other words, it's like taking the Meyers-Briggs on steroids when it comes to understanding who you are!

As I prayed and began work on this book geared to helping people make important HeartShifts, I thought early and often about how helpful and incredibly beneficial it would be if *each person* could take their own Leading From Your Strengths™ report. In order to make substantive changes, it's crucial to understand your own strengths and to be able to pinpoint predictable areas of conflict or adjustment. Having people sit down for just a few minutes and then come away with twenty-eight pages of personal insights into how God had uniquely created them would be a tremendous help to each person.

However, as you can imagine, a world-class tool like this isn't free. In fact, try talking your publisher into adding an additional twenty-seven dollars (the cost of this powerful online assessment) to the price of each book. While that's an outstanding price for a powerful, patented instrument like this (competitors charge more than eighty dollars for an online report that isn't nearly as detailed), would *you* have purchased this book if it cost nearly thirty dollars *more* than you paid for it?

Simply put, there was no way to build the cost of this unique tool into the price of this book, no matter how helpful it would be to each reader. So that's when I prayed and sat down at lunch with Rodney and Eric. These men know and love our ministry and family. But they're also businessmen. *Really good businessmen* who know you don't grow a company, much less stay in business, by giving thousands of your product away.

Rodney has trained Fortune 500 company executives for more than a dozen years and today works with high-level ministry teams across the country. Eric is a Michigan law school graduate and a past chief counsel for a huge company. But I knew they love the Lord and love to help people, and I knew I was buying lunch, so we sat down together.

At lunch I talked about you, the reader, and how incredibly helpful it would be in making a HeartShift if you could be armed with the insights the Leading From Your Strengths™ report could provide. They listened politely until I was finished. Then I would have dropped my sandwich (except I was eating a taco) when they said Insights International would provide a passcode for *each person* without cost to you or the publisher.

That's like someone giving Cindy a workstation for each child (which, by the way, would be a great help if you own a computer company). As a way to invest in your life and my ministry, they would absorb all the hard costs so that each person could take the full, twenty-eight-page online report, take off any masks, and see more clearly than ever their strengths and potential problem areas.

Needless to say, that was one of the best lunches of my life!

I am honored to be a part of a company led by believers like these two men who are committed to helping others change. I'll also say this: Insights International is a business, so if after taking your report you have friends or family or people in your place of ministry or workplace who need to understand their strengths, then please send them to the Web site, www.insightsinternational.com and tell them to order the Leading From Your Strengths™ report. But all you have to do is look on the unprinted side of the dustcover of your book to find your free single-use passcode.

What you're looking for in order to take your gift is a string of eight numbers, printed inside the back flap of your book jacket. Here are instructions on how to use it, and then after you've gone online and taken your report, I'll end this chapter by showing you how focusing on a specific section of your results is our second step in the HeartShift Life-Change Process.

USING YOUR EIGHT-DIGIT CODE TO DISCOVER YOUR STRENGTHS

I realize that anytime you purchase a child's toy with the words "easy assembly" on the box, you want to immediately drop it and step away from the box. If it says "easy" anywhere on the packaging, you can almost guarantee the instructions are in Mandarin Chinese or require roughly the same amount of steps as it takes to build a nuclear particle accelerator.

That's not the case here.

Taking this online tool really is easy, even if you're not the Internet type.

To take your strengths assessment, go online to www.HeartShift.com. Obviously, I'm assuming you already have a computer with Internet access or at least access to one. If you don't, then please visit your local public library or talk to your church. Even better, perhaps it's time to call a relative, neighbor, or close friend to ask for help in taking your report.

There is no paper-pencil version of this report and no way to take it other than by going online. The reason is that your answers are pushed through a mainframe computer and scored through a patented process that measures those 384 traits, meaning it's simply too complicated for any kind of hand-scoring process. But even if you have to call a friend or go out of your way to take your report, it is absolutely worth your time.

Getting your results instantly when you've finished taking the brief assessment and then seeing page after page of information can not only help you learn more about yourself and others, it is simply an indispensable tool for making your HeartShift. I'd go so far as to tell you to bake cookies for a friend if you have to in order to use their computer, or get them their own copy of this book with their own passcode (or order them a passcode online) so that they can take the report too. And of course, there's always the option of talking to the nearest teenager or college student who will not only have a computer but also a wireless laptop they can let you use!

Now that you've solved any computer problems and have gotten online, your first step is to go to www.HeartShift.com. Once the page comes up, you'll see a box at the top left-hand corner of the page. In this box will be the words "Book Code." All you have to do is take that eight-digit code printed on the inside of the back flap, type it into that small box, and then click "Take assessment."

How easy is that!

Each book comes with one code, good for one person to take their report. (If you're sharing a book, then just go to www.HeartShift.com where you can order additional codes for as many people as you'd like.) After typing in your code and making that one click of your mouse, then *if you put in your e-mail address when asked,* when you're finished choosing one "most" and one "least" in just twenty-four boxes, you'll instantly be e-mailed your own, unique, twenty-eight-page strengths assessment.

That's five to seven minutes tops if you just go by "first guess." *Don't dwell on each box.* Rather, just think about who you tend to be as a person, either in your family relationships or at work, and then click on *one* "most" and *one* "least" word or phrase in each of the twenty-four boxes. (If you do take too long and dwell on each box, this sophisticated Internet program will actually send you an error message, asking you to speed up!)

There will almost assuredly be some boxes where you say, "I'm not most *or* least like *any* of these choices!" or "I'm most or least like *all* of them!" Just force yourself to choose *one* most and *one* least response in each of the twenty-four boxes, first guess, and you'll be rewarded with an incredibly informative look at your unique, God-given strengths. In fact, it's so accurate, we constantly hear from people, "Did you follow me around the house? How did you know!" And even when people say, "That's doesn't sound like me at all!" often a spouse, good friend, or son or daughter nearby who has read their report will be nodding their head, saying, *"That's exactly what they're like!"*

So stop right now, take your eight-digit code, and take advantage of this awesome gift. Have fun with this instead of taking it with white knuckles. Remember, we created this tool to help you see how valuable you are, not to focus on your weaknesses. In fact, understanding your strengths is a key to dealing with weaknesses because for most of us, our weaknesses are our strengths, pushed to an extreme. And when you've finished, or when you get back home from your sister or computer friend's house with your report all printed out, then you'll be ready to jump right into the next section of this chapter.

Until then, may the Lord use your few minutes online to help you learn more about yourself and others and be successful at your HeartShift!

Now That You've Taken Your Report . . .

With your Leading From Your Strengths™ report in hand, let me give you a brief overview of the entire report, and then I'll ask you to focus on one key section that can be extremely helpful as you make your HeartShift.

One disclaimer before moving on.

While it's tremendously helpful to share your report with a spouse, close friend, loved one, or even your older children, ask them to please use this tool as a window, not a weapon. No saying, "I told you, you were like that!" or worse. Again, this should be a window to your heart, not a basis for a heart *attack* of the verbal or emotional kind.

Understanding Your Core Strengths

Now that you have your report printed, you'll see there are three key sections to this twenty-eight-page assessment. In this book we're going to focus our energy on looking at just a few pages of your report to help you make your HeartShift. However, let me give you another free gift. That's a free, downloadable, twenty-one-page workbook that can help you get the most out of every section and every page of your online report.

To get a self-paced workbook, filled with helpful questions that work you through every section and every page, just go to www.insights international.com. Once you're there, click on "Free Downloads" on the left-hand side of the page. When the page of free downloads opens, then click on the first free download, called "The Leading from Your Strengths Workbook." Click on those blue words (called a "link") and it will allow you to download a step-by-step free guidebook. How cool is that!

While I'd urge you to go through this workbook and your entire report with your spouse, close friend, or small group, we won't focus on the entire report here. Instead, I'll give you brief highlights of each of the three major sections of this report; then we'll focus on section 1 and your core strengths, applying what you see there most specifically to your decision to make a HeartShift.

An Overview of Section 1 of Your Report

Section 1 begins with several introductory pages, you'll come to your core graph, titled "Your Style Analysis Graph." This graph is followed by several pages of text. I'll give you an example of a "core graph" shortly. However, after your graph, you'll find at least two pages of line-by-line statements highlighting just how valuable you are as a person and explaining what your core graph shows.

That's one of the great things you'll discover about your Leading From Your Strengths™ report. It's designed to be read and understood by *real* people, not just Ph.D.-level psychologists. You don't have to be an expert graph reader; just read all about yourself! We've worked hard to put things into everyday English in the section titled "General Characteristics," and we think you'll find this look at who you are to be of significant help. In fact, we'll come back to this "core strengths" graph and these written statements shortly, as they'll be of particular importance in your HeartShift.

Once you read about your core strengths in the "General Characteristics" section, turn to the next page, titled "Value to the Team." This page gives you a bullet-point list highlighting why you're such a valuable and important part of your home team, your workplace, your ministry team, or any team.

Next comes a page titled "Checklist for Communicating," where you'll see a whole list of ways to communicate effectively with someone like you. This is a great section to highlight two or three statements that really resonate with you and then share those with your spouse or other family or team members. (This is something outlined in the free downloadable workbook if you'd like some coaching on discussing your report results.)

Turning the page, you'll come to "Don'ts in Communicating," where you'll find typical frustration points or roadblocks to communicating with someone with your particular strengths. It too is a tremendous discussion page for sharing with a spouse, a close friend, or even a work-place teammate. Again, your free downloadable workbook will give you guided questions and a process to talk through this page of your report with others in an honoring, helpful way.

A teaching section follows, called "Communicating with Others," with valuable information on connecting with others who have different strengths and communication styles from you. We'll talk more about this communication section of your report later in both the marriage and parenting chapters of this book.

You're still in section 1, and moving forward, you'll find a page titled "Ideal Environment," which I think you'll find very eye-opening in sharing with others. These insights are important to you, if you could create an environment that was ideal, and will also be referred to later in this book.

That page is followed by two pages titled "Keys to Motivating" and then "Keys to Leading." These highlight both information on what motivates you as a person and what someone should know if they're in a leadership position with you. Drawing on your free downloadable workbook for illustrations and guided questions, picking out two or three statements you really agree with on each page can provide outstanding discussion material for those you relate to often.

Finally, this first section ends with the one page in all the report that lists areas you need to work on, called "Areas for Improvement." This highlights how some of your strengths may be pushed out of balance, thus becoming potential problems in relating to others. (For example, you may be so good at taking "things" apart that you're also good at taking "yourself" apart—a strength that when pushed to an extreme becomes a weakness.)

You don't have to agree with each statement on this page, but see if two or three statements listed (if not more) do in fact hit a nerve. And I pray you'll have the nerve to share this page with others who love you and get their feedback. (Again, your workbook provides a set of guided questions to talk through this page in a helpful, honoring way.) A short section on "Perceptions" (meaning how others can tend to perceive you if your strengths are pushed out of balance) clarifies this "Areas for Improvement" page.

Can you see now why I thought this online report would be such an incredible tool for people wanting to make real changes in their life and their life story? Not every statement on every page will get that internal head nod, "Wow, that's me!" But many, many statement will hit close to home if you're honest and if you're willing to share your report with a close friend or spouse. (Or as we'll see in the next chapter, with your "band of brothers or sisters" support group, called your "33 Group.")

Before coming back to this first section of your report, and your "core graph" in particular, let's quickly get an overview of the remaining two sections of your report.

An Overview of Section 2 of Your Report

This section carries the title "Additional Insights," which does exactly what it says. As you will have already seen in your "core graph," you're going to score in one of four main characteristics, meaning you'll either be high or low in the Lion, Otter, Golden Retriever, or Beaver scales. Your core style pictures who you are when you're at home with your shoes off and feeling no need to act in any certain way. In this second section of your Leading From Your Strengths™ report, you'll get to see what other people most often see, namely, your "adapted graph." Here you'll find a second graph, set side-by-side with your core graph, that adds a picture of how you feel you're having to adapt to be successful in the environment you're in.

Let's take the following graphs as a brief example.

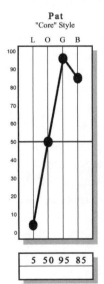

Pat
"Core" Style

These two graphs, shared with permission, are from a report taken by my good friend Patrick (a former 101st Airborne paratrooper who is a pastor today). In his core graph, you can see that he is very low in the L scale. In reading your report, you'll know that the L stands for Lion and represents those people who tend to take charge and be assertive individuals. For example, if you have a Lion child, they're the ones who are letting you live at home! They're the boss, and when they grow up, they're still the boss, or at least they think they are! In Patrick's case, he's low in this Lion scale in his core and adapted graphs, meaning his natural strengths aren't to have to feel like he has to take the lead in everything.

In the next scale, the O or Otter scale, you'll read how high Otters are fun loving, verbal, and spontaneous. If they're up near 100, they're the "party's waiting to happen" type of people who love people and love to yak, yak, yak. You can see that Pat is right at the mid-line or energy line on the O scale, meaning he can be talkative or not, depending on the situation. (The thick 50 percent line on each graph is called the "energy line," meaning if you score above that black line, you'll tend to see that behavior in everyday situations; if it's below the energy line, you'll tend not to see those characteristics in everyday actions. In Patrick's case, being right at 50 percent means he can go either way, based on the situation.)

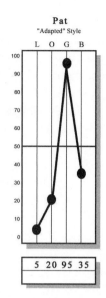

Pat
"Adapted" Style

| 5 | 20 | 95 | 35 |

For Patrick, you can see in his core graph that he's high on the next two scales, the G or Golden Retriever and the B or Beaver scale. That means (as you'll have seen in your report) that he's sensitive, caring, and compassionate (Golden Retriever traits) and that he is also detailed, precise, and likes to close loops and finish what he starts (all high Beaver and paratrooper traits).

Now remember, Pat would have been able to read all the "spelled out" details of his core graph in the general characteristics section of his report and wouldn't have to interpret his core graph at all. But now take a look at his adapted graph sitting next to his core graph.

In the Leading From Your Strengths™ tool, anytime a score on the L, O, G, or B scales moves from below the energy line (the 50-percent line) to above that midline, or moves from above the energy line to below it, that's significant.

That's because this second adapted graph highlights what a person feels he or she needs to do in order to succeed in the environment they're in.

For Pat, his core style is low Lion, fairly talkative in the Otter, highly sensitive in the Golden Retriever scale, and an organized Beaver. But look at his adapted graph.

Can you see any scores on the L, O, G, or B scales in his adapted graph that move *above* or *below* the energy line? Obviously, if you'll compare the two graphs, you'll see that his Lion score doesn't change at all, nor does his Golden Retriever score differ from one graph to the other. But both the Otter and the Beaver scales drop dramatically. Why? Because to succeed in the environment that Pat is in, he feels like he has to modify his core style to fit the demands placed upon him in ministry.

In short, Patrick's job day after day is to be the crisis counselor pastor at a large church. Every day he meets with grieving people who have lost a loved one, people who have lost a job or seen a marriage dissolve. He's the first person at the church to see someone in crisis, and as such, his goal is to be a great listener and encourager rather then being a Lion and telling them what to do.

In other words, to succeed as a crisis pastor, he feels he has to lower the Otter (fun-loving, verbal traits), and while he personally has high expectations and certain ways he likes doing things, he also feels he needs to lower his Beaver (detail) strengths as well. (People don't want a list or lecture when they're in crisis. What they want is what he does— build a warm, supportive relationship with them and then link them with the help they need.)

To succeed in his role of helping those who walk into the church and have lost a loved one, or a job, or have a prodigal child, or other serious issue or concern, Patrick has adapted his core strengths to do what he feels he needs to succeed. Most people will show a change of some sort (sometimes adapting in every scale) in their side-by-side graphs.

That's what you'll learn about yourself in this second section of your report. For some people, their core and adapted graphs will look like mirror images of each other. That just means that who you are in your core style and strengths, and who you feel like you need to be in order to succeed in the environment you're in, is a one-to-one match. Who I am when I get up in the morning is exactly who I feel like I need to be and do all during the day.

For most of the rest of us, however, there will be one or more areas that move above or below that energy line. Once again, don't worry about graph reading! Your online report will give you page after page in this section of your report that explain the areas you're choosing to adapt in. (And remember, there's your free workbook filled with guided discussion questions that can help you see just how you're adapting as well.)

While we won't focus a great deal on this section of your report, I think you can see how incredibly helpful just such a picture can be when you're thinking of making a HeartShift. For example, time and again we've had people say things like, "No wonder I'm so tired!" when they see how much they're having to "adapt" in their daily life. It's like writing all day with a pen in your nondominant hand. You can do it, but it takes more energy and thought than just signing your name with your dominant hand.

While major changes in the two graphs can signal high stress with all those changes, it's important to factor in God's calling and direction in your life as well. For example, I have another good friend here in Phoenix named Dan who is a police officer. His core graph looks just like Pat's— very low in the Lion, midline in the Otter, and off the charts high in the Golden Retriever and Beaver scales. Not surprising with all that sensitivity and high sense of right and wrong, Dan joined law enforcement twenty-two plus years ago because he wanted to "protect and serve."

While Dan is absolutely convinced that he's where God wants him to be, his adapted style graph shows he's having to make huge adaptations to succeed in what's demanded of him. As an "early response" team leader who has to rush to a trouble spot and take charge of a situation until help or specific backup arrives, his Lion score moves from 5 on his core to 95 on his adapted! Needless to say, that's a huge jump! Yet Dan feels he is exactly where God wants him to be, serving and protecting others in the police force. In short, while some people will find the reason they're so stressed in these areas of significant adaptation, just the fact you're adapting doesn't mean you're in the wrong place.

Armed with these kinds of helpful insights from this second section of your report and your own core and adapted graphs, let's look briefly at the next section of your report.

Section 3: The Leading from Your Strengths Wheel

The last page of your report is the highlight of the third section of your report called the Insights Wheel. This colorful wheel provides a helpful look at who you are as a person. What's more, it can help you get a picture of your whole family, small group, workplace, or ministry team as well!

As an example, while the Leading From Your Strengths™ report is of great help to anyone, from singles to wanting to have a close-knit small group, let's say you're a couple who has decided to make a HeartShift in your marriage. Here's an example of how this wheel can

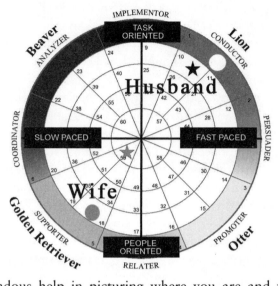

be a tremendous help in picturing where you are and what may be predictable areas of conflict or adjustment in making your HeartShift.

Above is a Leading From Your Strengths™ Wheel for a husband I'll call Brian. In this unique, patented, and helpful aspect of your online report, you'll notice both a circle (or large black dot) and a star in Brian's Insights Wheel. For Brian the dot represents his core strengths, and the star, how he's adapting. You'll also notice that at the top of his wheel (the north pole) is the word *task,* and at the bottom (south pole), is the word *people.* Over on the right (east side) side of the wheel, there's the word *fast,* and on the left side (west side) is the word *slow.*

As you look at Brian's wheel, you'll see both his dot and his star (his core and adapted scores) are almost side by side, and high on the northwest part of the wheel. In other words, Brian is a big-time Lion who is way up on the task side of things and likes for things to go fast instead of slow. Now take a look if we put his wife Brenda's scores on his wheel.

Brenda's dot or core style is on the bottom-left side of the circle, a high Golden Retriever/Beaver who wants time for gathering information, wants decisions to go more slowly, and is much more people oriented. Unlike her husband, Brenda's adapted score is almost in the center of the circle. That gap between the dot and star means she feels she's having to adapt in several areas in order to succeed. What's more, by being in the center of the circle instead of on the outside of the wheel, it means she's more of a blend of each of the L, O, G, B traits as well as fast/slow or task/people tendencies than someone on the far outside of the circle. (Remember, your free online workbook will go into detail on this wheel and give you examples and questions to talk through what this means in your specific graph.)

Now let's see where this couple's dots and stars are on the same Insights Wheel. While I'll talk more about this in the section on marriage later in the book, can you imagine some predictable issues or problems these two might have faced in their twenty-six years of marriage? How about the way they naturally approach disciplining their children? Or approach important decisions? And again, can you see why I felt this would be such a tremendous tool for you to take as you consider making a HeartShift in an important area of your life?

It's not just marriage where this wheel can be important. In the book I wrote with Rodney Cox and Eric Tooker, *Leading from Your Strengths for Ministry Teams,* I included the example of a wheel where I'd drawn in the core score for an entire church staff. Let me include it here as well.

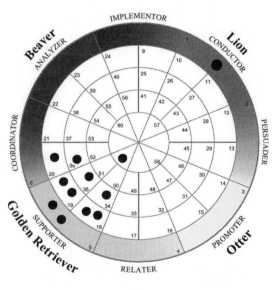

You'll see an Insights Wheel above with twelve dots, eleven within a few inches of one another and all on the bottom left quadrant of the circle and one at the top. In other words, eleven of the pastoral staff were high Golden Retrievers, slow in their preference for action and decision making and very people oriented.

Armed with just that insight, what kind of church do you think that would be to attend? If you guessed incredibly warm and friendly, you'd be right! They have greeters in the parking lot *before* you even get to the greeters inside the church foyer!

But did I forget to mention that there were *thirteen* pastors on staff?

While eleven of the pastors were all in the bottom left, you'll notice one dot all by itself at the top of the wheel!

That's right! You've got one high Lion on this pastoral team, and it's not the senior pastor, by the way. It's someone in an even more important position, the business administrator! With an entire pastoral staff of Golden Retrievers, he was the only one who was willing to take risks, push new changes, and say no, and he was good at it!

Can you imagine how helpful it was to this pastoral team, after the shock of seeing the elephant in the living room of eleven dots together and that one dot all by itself, to be able to talk through their relationship? What they saw that day, and finally faced in an honoring way, was that many of the pastors had looked at this one man as the enemy. And as we talked, they were amazed and touched at how lonely he'd felt for years, being the only one who said no to things.

Once they were able to see where they were, it made a tremendous difference in their relationship with one another, and it made their HeartShift to grow closer as a team and get more on the same page as pastors a two-foot putt.

So with that introduction to why your report can be so helpful to you as an individual, as a family member, or even as part of a team at work or in ministry, **let's focus on the first section of your report and apply it specifically to making a personal HeartShift.** While the entire report will prove helpful, I'd like briefly to go through four specific ways your core graph alone can help you pinpoint HeartShift areas and make successful change much more likely and positive.

PINPOINTING FOUR SPECIFIC HEARTSHIFT AREAS WITH YOUR CORE GRAPH

I don't have the advantage of knowing specifically what your HeartShift area was that you wrote down in the previous chapter, or the memorial marker you picked to go with it. But whatever it is, here's a crucial insight from the first section of your Leading From Your Strengths™ report that can help you follow through on the changes you want to make and even be aware of barriers that might trip you up.

SCORING HIGH OR LOW ON THE LION SCALE AND THE WAY YOU FACE PROBLEMS

Unlike other strengths assessments, we don't just measure highs when you take your Leading From Your Strengths™ report. What I mean by that is that in most tests you're asked, "What are you *most* like?" The feedback you receive is all then based on what you're most like. However, if you remember the twenty-four-block questionnaire you took, we asked you to click one most and one *least* in each box. In other words, unlike other reports—and the reason we're able to be so specific and detailed—we measure highs (what you're most like) and lows (what you feel you're least like) and even the correlation between the two! What difference does that make in making a HeartShift? Lots, as you'll see going back to just your core graph on page 4 of your online report.

For example, start with the Lion scale on the Leading From Your Strengths™ report. In that first L scale, we are measuring whether you're aggressive or passive when dealing with problems. In short, the higher you are on the Lion scale, the more aggressively you'll want to face and deal with problems. The lower you are on the Lion scale, the less likely you'll be to tackle and want to solve a problem immediately. ("Oh, it'll get better. Just give it a few days, weeks, years.")

Look at where you scored on the L scale of your core graph on page 4 of your online report. If you scored high on the L scale, you're ready to solve problems *right now* and in an aggressive manner. ("We've got an issue here. Let's jump on it and solve it!") If you scored low on the L scale (like Patrick did earlier in the chapter), your natural tendency when it comes to facing or dealing with problems is to give time for problems to work themselves out or more passively face issues or embrace needed changes. ("What problem!" Or, "If there is a problem, then for heaven's sake don't pick it up!")

While again, I'll come back to this in upcoming sections of the book (and it's addressed in your workbook as well), just think what this insight alone could mean to a couple. For example, my wife and I, who are sixty points apart on this scale, could finally see how different we were in approaching problems from our natural strengths.

It's not that Cindy and I hadn't gotten into heated discussion about this area of difference before, but we'd never *seen* this difference as an expression of our unique, God-given strengths. When we took this report as a couple and laid our core graphs side by side, it was not only eye-opening, but life-changing.

Suddenly, instead of my being frustrated that Cindy didn't want to stay up all night talking through something I felt we had to solve right now, or her feeling like I was going too fast and wanting to rush to make decisions without gathering all the facts, now we could see each of our strengths! *No wonder God has given me someone who approaches problems differently than I!* As someone who scores high on the L scale, I do tend to go too fast sometimes and can make a snap decision or choose a quick solution. That works if it's a fairly simple decision or problem, but snap judgments can actually cause more problems than they solve on complicated issues. On the other hand, it doesn't do any good to push off issues too long, and you can't gather every fact—one of Cindy's strengths—and so my strength of wanting to deal with issues now instead of later has become something Cindy greatly values.

So now tie this first issue of facing or fleeing from problems into the HeartShift you made. That insight alone can turn what was a possible major obstacle into a reason to draw closer! And such insights aren't just for married or engaged couples!

Let's say you're single, and the HeartShift area you picked was your health. Can you see how understanding your natural strength of either wanting to be aggressive or passive when faced with a problem can affect your HeartShift decision? If you're naturally a "do it now" person, perhaps you've jumped from one quick-fix trend, diet, or exercise fad to another. On the other hand, if you're low on the L and tend to avoid change and facing problems, this can provide great insight into why change has been so difficult, and why upcoming 2 Degree Changes will be so important to put into practice now.

That's just one insight this online report can give you into your HeartShift decision. Let's look briefly at the remaining three.

IN THE OTTER SCALE YOU CAN SEE WHERE YOU ARE ON BEING TRUSTING OR SKEPTICAL

Another incredible insight that comes through in your online report is whether you tend to be either trusting or skeptical when it comes to new people or information you receive. In other words, the higher you score on the Otter or O scale of your core graph, the more trusting you're going to be of new people and information. The lower you are on the Otter scale, the more skeptical you'll tend to be, both of people and information.

To again start with a marriage example, that alone is an insight I wish I had understood when I was first married. For example, it would have saved me from losing Cindy's entire teacher retirement savings that she had put away for six years!

While I'll go through this story in the upcoming marriage chapter, suffice it to say I'm on the high side of the Otter scale. As such, being skeptical of a new person I met who was a financial planner wasn't my natural strength. My precious wife, Cindy, is high on the Otter scale as well. In other words, who's the one in the family who is going to ask all the hard questions or be skeptical when it comes to new people or information? The answer in our home at that time was neither of us, which led to some real problems until we pinpointed where we were in terms of this Otter trait and realized that a HeartShift we needed to make was to not make an important decision without asking all the hard questions or being more skeptical of new people and information. Again, it's not just in a marriage where our response to new people and information is tremendously helpful.

Let's say, for example, your HeartShift was to be a better boss at work with those you supervise. If you work with lots of skeptical people (low Otters), how helpful do you think it will be to walk into work and announce with no discussion time for them, your new "can't miss" program for tripling sales that they're all going to love!

If your expectation is that people with natural skeptical strengths are going to welcome all your new ideas without asking hard questions, you'll not only get your feelings hurt, you'll see productivity go down, because the low Otters feel their natural skepticism isn't appreciated. (And if you're in a company, you'll know that someone who is willing to ask the hard questions is incredibly important once the high Otters realize their questions are an expression of a strength that can save time or money or sometimes even the company!)

I'm not talking about negative people who throw ice-cold water on every idea or someone who is hypercritical or mean in their critiques. That's never helpful at home or at work. But what if you approached your workplace or ministry team members who were naturally skeptical (low Otters) and instead of trying to sell your latest idea, asked them to use their strengths? For example, saying something like, "I've got this program that's a new direction, and I think it might be really helpful to us. How about if, after I explain it briefly, each of you reads this paper I've prepared, and then on Thursday, let's meet as a team and discuss its pros and cons, and I'd like to hear your ideas on how it might, or might not, make us a closer team."

By understanding where a person comes from who is naturally gifted at being trusting or skeptical, you can make huge headway in making a successful HeartShift. The same thing is true as an individual as you confront whether your being too trusting or skeptical might be a cause for problems or a roadblock to change.

Let's look at a third important insight that can directly apply to your heart that can be seen from the first section of your Leading From Your Strengths™ report.

MAKING A HEARTSHIFT WHEN IT COMES TO MOVING FAST OR SLOW

Since I've picked on Cindy and myself in the examples above, I may as well share about problems and insights we've gained in this third area as well! For while Cindy and I are different in the Lion (approaching problems) area and similar in the Otter (new people and information) area, here comes another area of difference, and a place where we've had to make a HeartShift to move closer together.

If you scored high on the Golden Retriever scale of your core graph, then you'll tend to be more slow when it comes to making decisions or taking on new projects. Being slow allows time for you to get all the facts you need, assessing what change might mean to the relationship and others. If you're at the bottom of the Golden Retriever scale, however, then who needs time to make a decision! Let's just do it now! Or, put another way, who needs to stop and gather facts; that's just something else to slow you down!

This G scale measures whether you want life and decisions to move fast or slow. With Cindy and me on opposite ends of the Golden Retriever scale with her at the top (slow) and me at the bottom (fast)—can you imagine any predictable issues we might have faced over the years? If you can't, just wait until the marriage chapter, or think about a close family or working relationship you've been in where one person wanted life and decisions to move slowly and the other person wanted everything fast.

As I've mentioned before, anytime you can make tangible the intangible, you gain ground in relationships. Here that insight on fast or slow is absolutely true. Just being able to see (by setting your graphs side by side) how you approach the pace of life or major decisions and then talking through any differences can be a tremendous road toward increased closeness. And as you might have guessed, in specific areas like parenting or marriage or friendships, small 2 Degree Changes *toward each other* spring out when you can see areas of difference like this.

There's one last area found in your core style graph that can help you with your HeartShift. That's whether you're the kind of person who needs a rule book or would rather go it alone or take risks.

In Making a HeartShift, Do You Want a Rule Book or Do You Like to Take Risks?

A final way your report can give you great insight on making a positive HeartShift is to pinpoint whether you're a standard procedure type of person or someone who wants to walk in all fresh snow instead of following in other's tracks.

I'll make some specific applications regarding where you are in this Beaver scale of your online report when it comes to your spiritual life. In short, you'll find here a key reason why for some people, reading their Bible every day is such a natural, easy process (high Beavers) and why it's so challenging for others—namely those very low in the Beaver scale.

Whether it's one parent who wants to know, "How have other parents we know and trust dealt with this issue?" or someone who just wants to take the risk and do something they've never tried, this can be another extremely helpful insight in moving closer to the Lord, your loved ones, or your children, not to mention being even more effective at your HeartShift.

We're at the end of this chapter, and you're now at the halfway point when it comes to understanding the HeartShift life-change process. You've gone on record by writing down and linking your

HeartShift with a memorial marker, and now you've taken your online report. Armed with that written commitment to change, and now loaded up with insights into your strengths and predictable areas of conflict or barriers to change, there's something else essential to being successful at your HeartShift decision.

Actually, it's not a something but someone who is crucial to your success—several someones, in fact, who make up your own "33 Support Group."

CHAPTER NINE

Why You Won't Succeed without a 33 Group

Have you ever noticed how a picture, phrase, or song has the power to push the instant rewind button on your memory? Even for those who claim to have poor memories, just play the first few bars of an oldies song and instantly they're singing right along to tunes they haven't heard since the sixties, seventies, or eighties. Just a few lines can nudge our memory and cause us to picture ourselves in our first car in the parking lot at school, or bouncing on those rock-hard green bus seats with our teammates on the way back from winning a game, or feeling again the intense loneliness after being dropped by that once special someone whom we haven't seen in thirty years!

That emotional rewind effect happens to me every time I see or hear a short phrase that you might know. It's the United States Army's newest recruiting slogan, "An Army of One."

Every time I hear this slogan, without fail, I have two immediate reactions.

First, while I couldn't be more appreciative and supportive of our brave men and women in the armed forces, my first thought is that the army needs to fire whatever ad agency sold them on that recruitment slogan (which, if you remember, replaced the popular "Be all you can be" slogan).

While I'm sure the ad writers would say back to me, "We're not aiming this slogan at a middle-aged guy. We're targeting seventeen- to twenty-one-year-olds who want to be empowered individuals." That might be true in their personal lives, but it absolutely won't work in the army. That's why to me that slogan is like someone dragging their fingernails slowly down a blackboard.

The reason I feel so strongly about this is because of the second reaction I have every time I hear this slogan. It pushes the rewind button and takes me back to a table at lunch with my father.

The year was 1969, and I was at a table at the then locally famous Green Gables restaurant. This used to be one of the finest dining establishments in Phoenix. Unfortunately, it was also located at a prime intersection that now sports a high-rise building. But at the time, it was such a fancy establishment that their trademark was a knight in shining armor on a white horse. Right next to the long, green canopy that covered the entranceway was a person costumed in knight's armor and sitting on a beautiful, white horse! (Needless to say, this knight only came out at night and never during the summer months in Phoenix, Arizona.) The knight wasn't on duty on an August day in 1969 when my twin brother, Jeff, and I walked from the intense sunlight outside into the cool darkness of Green Gables.

As our eyes adjusted, we could see thick dark-wood tables, every one filled, and the room filled with thick smoke as well. (There were no nonsmoking sections back in 1969.) This was a place where deals were made every day by the city fathers and high-rolling businessmen, and we'd just accepted what we thought was a great deal offered by our father. All we had to do was drive across town to Green Gables, and he would buy us whatever we wanted from the menu.

I should mention that such an invitation wasn't the norm. As it turned out, it was a once-in-a-lifetime event. That's because my father left our family when we were two months old and had only resurfaced in our high school years. This invitation to lunch marked the first time (and what turned out to be the only time) he ever called to ask me to lunch. As you might imagine, there was more than excellent food on the menu.

For the one and only time in my father's life, memories were being served up that day. Those memories were of his personal experiences as a combat infantryman during World War II.

As kids, we had seen an old, faded newspaper picture of our father being awarded a field decoration, a Bronze Star for something that had happened at Guadalcanal. We'd seen the picture, but we'd never heard a word about what earned him his medal, until that lunch. In fact, that day we not only heard about his carrying a severely wounded man back to safety under heavy fire, but we also heard story after story of his first-hand look at the horrors of war.

Actually, a few of his stories were funny, like the time he was bathing with a friend in a nearby river where they were bivouacked. As they took shelter on the riverbank, a mortar attack on their dug-in position scored a direct hit on their foxhole, shredding clothes and packs and making them walk back in a state of undress to the supply tent more than a mile behind their lines. (None of his friends would give him or his buddy a stitch of clothing to wear, which they thought was very funny.) Also humorous was how his squad would drop concussion grenades into small jungle ponds near their position. The blast would cause fish to float to the surface. The men would grab them, gut them with their bayonets, and then wrap them in banana leaves. They'd then dig a hole in the sandy ground, put the coals from the night's fire way down in the bottom, cover the coals with a layer of sand, put the fish wrapped in leaves on top, and then add another layer of sand. When they came back to their campsite after patrols that day, the homemade oven and banana leaves made the fish fall right off the bone and taste better than anything at Green Gables.

But besides those few positive stories, for two hours we heard one horror story after another of screaming enemies in night attacks that ended in hand-to-hand combat, and of snipers and limbs torn apart by booby traps during the day. He shared in detail the helpless, hopeless feeling of seeing artillery shells marching right toward his position. He spoke of how they began to take first-day replacements who snored loudly (giving away their position at night and thus requiring someone constantly to wake them up) and put them on point the next day and each day forward until they were killed or wounded. But most of all, he came back time and again to his most important bit of advice, the reason for replaying all those terrible memories before his two sons who faced the draft for the Vietnam War the next day.

The whole reason for his buying us lunch was to tell us:

"Always dig your foxhole two deep."

In a dozen ways and at least a dozen times he hammered this idea home. He knew both Jeff and I had dropped our student deferments, going 1-A for the draft if our country called. If that decision led into combat, he wanted us to know, *"Never, ever, be alone in a combat* zone." And now perhaps you can see why I react so negatively to the Army's newest recruiting slogan, "An Army of One."

You don't want to be an "Army of One" when the enemy floods toward you or the night is full of fear. You want a foxhole two deep, with someone or even a whole band of brothers beside you. You want people around you like our country saw in a recent, incredibly heart-wrenching picture on the front page of most newspapers. In a battle with terrorists in Iraq, a front-page picture was of a small group of Marines, sheltered behind a Humvee, praying in a circle around the body of one of their friends who had just been killed.

When the going gets tough, you don't want to be alone. You want a band of others around you. Which leads me to the battle you'll soon face in living out your HeartShift and why I truly believe you won't succeed if you try to do it all alone.

WHY A 33 GROUP CAN BE SUCH A CRUCIAL CHANGE AGENT

The famous evangelist of an earlier century, Charles Wesley, said, "The New Testament knows nothing of a solitary religion." What's true for warriors going into battle is also true for those of us facing spiritual and personal battles. You do not see "armies of one" anywhere when you look at God's Word. In fact, you see the opposite, "If one can overpower him who is alone, two can resist him. A cord of three strands is not quickly torn apart" (Eccl. 4:12).

You'd think "pulling together the troops" would be something natural for us to do as we seek to change. But we live in a solo world; we think people are too busy or preoccupied to help us bear our burdens. In fact, before I make a case for your forming a certain kind of small, supportive group to help in your quest for change (something I'll call a 33 Support Group), let me share two immense obstacles to your ever having such a personal support team.

First, there's a terrible lie we're constantly fed. Namely, we're told over and over again (particularly by politicians who don't want to have to be specific about their own religious beliefs or lack of them) that a person's faith is a personal thing and as such, shouldn't be openly discussed. That is supposed to mean that the best place to exercise our belief in God is alone, in private, and behind closed doors. Our faith shouldn't be equated with whether we're connected with a group of fellow believers or based to any degree on being with others who can see the presence or absence of our faith.

Nothing could be further from biblical truth.

We're *commanded* to be with God's people and not to forsake our gathering together. You do not see a single lone-eagle disciple anywhere in Scripture, particularly when the going gets tough. Instead, you see Jesus putting the disciples into small groups and sending them out to minister in his name. *Never alone.* You see his band of brothers all together when the Lord walked through the doors after his crucifixion. *They were never alone.* You even see a terribly discouraged Peter (after denying Christ) announcing to his friends that he is going back to what he is good at—fishing; and their response is, "We will also come with you" (John 21:2–3). Biblically, you don't leave hurting people to twist in the wind or to some "private" place.

The next time you hear, "Your religion ought to be a private thing," remember, that's counsel from hell, the one place where you are safe from any interaction with others and are truly all alone.

There's a second problem with our trying to isolate ourselves when we're hurting or in need of change. Not only is it not biblical, it's simply not *possible* in any real sense. That's because we have *never* been less alone than we are when we're alone today. Let me explain that statement.

When was the last time you were really, truly alone?

Recently I spoke at a men's retreat where a short time was set aside for each man to go off and be by himself. The camp was in a beautiful, secluded mountain setting, and each man was sent out for a half hour of solitude.

What I remember most about that quiet time was a man hurrying up to me after the bell had rung to bring us back together, his face beaming. He couldn't wait to turn his blackberry handheld PDA around to show me something he'd found during his time of solitude.

"I can't believe I got a signal out here!" he said excitedly. "I Googled in the word *solitude,* and look at this awesome quote I found. Maybe you can use it tonight in your talk!"

It was a good quote, and he was totally sincere and excited about what he'd found. But can you see what this says about solitude today? If we can use our handheld PDA/telephone to do an Internet search deep in the mountains during a time of solitude, we can almost forget about really being alone today. Even a cabin by our own Walden Pond today would come equipped with satellite reception.

I'm all for the personal responsibility you're showing in making the decision to make a HeartShift. But that doesn't mean you should, or even can, be alone in tackling such a challenge. But lest you think it's simply the presence of people that can be the most help, it's important to understand the difference between a crowd and a small group that can really make a difference in your life.

THE DIFFERENCE BETWEEN A CROWD AND A 33 GROUP

My office is roughly a ten-minute drive from my home—that is, it's ten minutes except on those days when it takes an hour and forty minutes just to get out of the parking lot.

That extra hour and a half I spent one day trying to get out of my office parking lot recently was courtesy of a crowd. One weekend day I went into my office early in the morning, thinking that with all the other offices closed, I could find a quiet place to write. What I didn't realize was that later that same morning the wide parkway directly in front of my office had been designated as the main parade route for hundreds and hundreds of motorcycle enthusiasts. Not just *any* motorcycle enthusiasts. Picture more than *two thousand* Harley-Davidson owners from across the Southwest, many with a passenger behind them, slowly roaring in front of my office on a sanctioned ride.

When most of us think about being part of a *group* today, it's really a *crowd* that comes to mind. We're connected because we all buy the same black leather jacket as hundreds of other people. We all ride only subtly different hogs with the same logo, Harley, because we can't get too far from the norm and be accused of not having a real Harley.

That's not to say that it isn't exciting to join a group of hundreds or even thousands of people headed in the same direction as you. For example, I stood in line for nine and a half hours to get tickets for game one of the 2001 World Series. I can't describe to you the excitement of being with my family and more than fifty-four thousand fans in Bank One Ballpark when Curt Shilling tossed the first pitch, a strike. I also happily joined twenty-one thousand runners when I ran the Rock & Roll Marathon in 2001. But whether it's fellow runners or fellow Diamondback fans or Harley enthusiasts, a crowd will never substitute for a handpicked group of friends. Crowds provide a short-term fix, like a shot in the arm or a dose of medicine, not a meal that can sustain you. Interaction with a crowd may convince us of the rightness of having spent all the money on our bike or on tickets to the game, but ultimately, we're standing with strangers when the event is over. If we're running, even if there are thousands of people surrounding us, we're still alone, running our own race.

The kind of group I'm talking about, which we see repeatedly in Scripture, is fundamentally different from a crowd and absolutely essential if you're serious about making a HeartShift. A 33 Group is a few people (I'd suggest two or three, but no more than six) who see you as an individual, not as a postage stamp. Our connection with crowds is based on our wearing the same colors or black jackets. (Go to a Yankees game in New York and see how you're treated if you wear blue pin-stripes or a Boston Red Sox shirt.)

A 33 Support Group can be made up of people all over the map. All they must have in common is being committed to you as an individual. That's the huge problem we face in a world that tells us, "We need a village," or there are no real sex differences, or that it's wrong for anyone to have more things than anyone else. There is a huge push toward sameness across our world; we're all one people, one giant country, one faith. We are the world. And in being forced to deny individuality, our individual needs and personalities become as unique as thousands of cola cans coming off a conveyor.

Deep inside we know sameness may keep us from being ridiculed in junior high, but it doesn't connect us on a deep level with others. It's OK to have your own unique strengths and struggles. For example, if you've ever tried out for any sport, you know everyone isn't equal in abilities. You quickly come to know that some people are bigger or stronger or faster than you are, or they have better balance or more potential to go to the next level than you ever will. There are and always will be people who live in bigger houses than you will, or who drive older, more dented cars than you'd ever drive.

The best answer secular society can come up with for solving our problems today is that we all need to become the same, and in that way no one feels bad or left out. But sameness actually breeds the thing they're trying to defeat! Dress us all alike and have us stand with thousands of others, and you have a crowd. That's great for a parade, but you want to go into battle with a squad, a person on your right or left, you know well, who will be there for you and who accepts you as an important individual.

We don't want to be swallowed up in a formless Brahman where, like Buddhism, our goal is to become nameless, faceless nothings. As Christians, we know Almighty God created and died for us as individuals, not as a class or crowd.

We are individual souls of infinite worth who will retain our personality for eternity. Who we are as a unique fingerprint of a person counts, and God even counts the hairs on our heads.

In fact, it's because we're so different as people—unique and designed for a specific purpose—that God never pictures us as a collective state where there are no differences. He pictures something that is the absolute *opposite* from the sameness of a crowd—a body.

Being Part of God's Body and Your 33 Support Group

Just read these verses below and what they have to say about how you're needed, important, and were designed and placed where you are by Almighty God to fill an important role in his body, even if you think being an ear isn't as important as being an eye!

For even as the body is one and yet has many members, and all the members of the body, though they are many, are one body, so also is Christ. For by one Spirit we were all baptized into one body, whether Jews or Greeks, whether slaves or free, and we were all made to drink of one Spirit. For the body is not one member, but many. If the foot says, "Because I am not a hand, I am not a part of the body," it is not for this reason any the less a part of the body. And if the ear says, "Because I am not an eye, I am not a part of the body," it is not for this reason any the less a part of the body. If the whole body were an eye, where would the hearing be? If the whole were hearing, where would the sense of smell be? But now God has placed the members, each one of them, in the body, just as He desired. If they were all one member, where would the body be? But now there are many members, but one body. And the eye cannot say to the hand, "I have no need of you"; or again the head to the feet, "I have no need of you." On the

contrary, it is much truer that the members of the body which
seem to be weaker are necessary; and those members of the
body which we deem less honorable, on these we bestow more
abundant honor, and our less presentable members become
much more presentable, whereas our presentable members
have no need of it. But God has so composed the body, giving
more abundant honor to that member which lacked.
(1 Cor. 12:12–24)

Our unity as believers comes because we are different from one
another, not because we all look or act the same. That's why we can genuinely need and value others who are different from us. In the same way
we need different parts of the body to support and surround us with
their unique gifts and strengths.

If you think about it, that's what is so special and challenging about
a family. Just think of a Thanksgiving dinner you've had with a large
group of family together. What binds you isn't sameness. For example,
you can be as different as night and day from your father, or a daughter can be the polar opposite personality of her mother. Seniors and
toddlers can make up a family, and no one would think of dressing
everyone in the family just like the junior high daughter. (Or at least
healthy families wouldn't think of such a thing!)

This is why God pictures us as a family and as members of his body.
This is why we can have unity even though we're made up of male and
female, slave and free, Jew and Gentile. Our unity is because we all
stand silent and awed at the foot of the cross.

IT's TIME TO TAP A FEW FRIENDS AND FAMILY TO BE YOUR OWN 33 GROUP

After all this discussion about avoiding being alone and our calling to
be part of a body not a crowd, it's time to put together some eyes and ears
and noses to help you reach your goals for change. I call such a small band
of brothers and/or sisters a 33 Support Group, a few people who will love
and support you as the unique individual you were created to be.

Your 33 Group are those few handpicked people who will get in
that foxhole with you because you shouldn't be an "army of one" if
you're serious about change.

In calling people to pull together two or three friends (or even a few
couples), I realize that many churches will already have in place many

versions of small groups, cell groups, or community groups. Some of these groups would be perfect for a short-term support group. But if you look at the average person in the pew (or the average person who feels the need to make a HeartShift), if asked the question "Are you closely connected with a small, supportive group of people?" most would say no.

Part of the reason it's easier to join a club or a crowd than a small group is there's nowhere to hide. And because this is such a new step for many people, I'm asking you to pick your own safe group of supportive friends or family to be your 33 Group.

Once a week for the next three months, starting as soon after the day you signed your HeartShift commitment as possible, I'd urge you to get together with your own 33 Group. They can be different from you in age, background, or vocation. They can be a subgroup of an existing group you're already in. If you're going through this book as a couple, then you can link up with two other couples (no more than six people in your 33 Group).

Yes, one person in your 33 Group can be your spouse if you're married, if he or she is open to doing so. (If you ask him or her and get turned down, then don't give up. Just grab two or three friends who love you and are willing for a short, focused time to help you make small 2 Degree Changes.

What do you do with such a small group of friends? You should actually hand each one a copy of the HeartShift commitment you signed in chapter 6. They are also people with whom you share your memorial marker, and each person should be given a photocopy of your Leading from Your Strengths Assessment. And most of all, they should be fellow members of the body of Christ—eyes and ears and noses—who once a week for three months will agree to support you as you seek to make small, positive changes in one specific area of your life. People who will pray for you, encourage you in any way they can, and most of all, people who will ask you three questions each week.

Because you're highly intelligent, I'm sure you've already guessed that the first part of the 33 Group means three people. The second part is three questions, discussed for 33 minutes. That's a 33 Group, and here are the three questions you give each person permission to ask you each week and that you answer honestly in talking with them.

Three Weekly Questions for Your 33 Group

1. On a 1 to 10 scale, how did you do this week at living out your HeartShift by making small 2 Degree Changes? Explain why you gave yourself that score.

2. What challenges or barriers came up that were hard to deal with or face?

3. What is one thing I could pray for you about between now and the time we talk next week?

As you might have noticed above, your 33 Group doesn't have to be all in the same city or meet physically each week for three months. For most busy people, we're spread so far from candidates for our 33 Group that it may be a phone call on Tuesday night with your brother who's out of state or sitting down for coffee before work with an in-town friend.

What's important is picking two or three foxhole buddies (or one or two faithful couples) who will pray for you, encourage you, watch your back, and offer support and ideas to stay in the battle.

You've already done the first step and put down in writing your decision to make a HeartShift, linked with a memorial marker. You've also taken your online report and looked at those four core issues that can pinpoint barriers to change. Now it's time to get a few people to support you in the change process.

Going on record with these friends, family, and loved ones about your desire to change can itself be life changing. In clinical studies, people feel better just by signing up to go to the doctor or counselor! But added together with the first two steps—and one more we'll look at right now—you'll be well on the road toward being successful at your HeartShift.

"But I don't have a single person in my life close enough to ask to do this!" Then join a church group and ask your pastor if he can help you find two other friends. Or pick up the phone and make yours a distance learning experience. But don't look for help from a crowd or try to do it all on your own. Isolation never leads to life. In a small, handpicked group of people who see great value in you, both the way you are now and in the way you want to change, you are starting with the ball on the ten-yard line, not facing the challenge of moving all the way across the field.

May the Lord bless and encourage you and your small 33 Support Group. Please read the next chapter and discover a place you can go to send your support group a special online thank-you note, as well as find encouragement to change from a much larger group of supportive friends in the body of Christ.

CHAPTER TEN

Your Opportunity to Join a Unique Online Community of Friends

Have you ever known something, but when asked a pointed question, the correct answer stayed right on the tip of your tongue? For example, think about the answers to the following questions that I'm sure you know.

Can you name the sport where neither the spectators nor the participants know the score of the leader until the contest ends?

Or which fruit has its seeds on the outside?

Or the only three words in standard English that begin with the letters "dw" (all three are commonly used)?

Or which famous North American landmark is constantly moving *backward*?

There are times we know something right *after* the answer has become obvious (as in boxing; strawberries; dwell, dwarf, and dwindle; and Niagara Falls, the rim of which erodes roughly two and a half feet each year from the millions of gallons of water that rush over it every minute).

Then again, there are times when some bit of information or truth seems suspect or even hidden until we actually see it or try it ourselves. To illustrate that kind of experiential confirmation, please indulge me by taking part in a quick experiment. I think you'll find the results surprising, if not amazing.

While you're sitting in a chair, lift your *right* foot off the ground. Now start making clockwise circles with your right foot. While you're making clockwise circles with your right foot, take your right index finger and start drawing the number "6" in the air with your right hand.

Feel free to try this a dozen or more times. You can even try concentrating as much as you want. But when your right hand starts drawing a number "6" watch your right foot switch directions and follow the movement of your hand. *Every time.*

What do brain teasers and unseen neurological pathways have to do with making a HeartShift and living out 2 Degree Changes? Actually, they highlight two things I hope you've already experienced by this point. (Neither of which is frustration over missing "boxing" in the brainteasers above or from failing to keep your foot moving in the opposite direction of your hand!)

First, I hope that in all the examples you've already seen in this book, both biblical and personal, the importance of making a HeartShift and living it out with small 2 Degree Changes are concepts you already knew inside but perhaps weren't at the front of your mind. If we're honest, we know deep inside that people simply do not wake up one day miles from where they want to be. We drift away by degrees. Nor do we get back on the right course by radically jerking the steering wheel 180 degrees. Again, it takes small 2 Degree steps.

Yet I also understand that while we may know the importance of small changes to be true and helpful, there is an element of that truth that lies hidden until we get our foot and hand moving! In other words, there are some things about making a HeartShift and making 2 Degree Changes that you will only know by taking small steps—in much the same way you can read about a sport or skiing, but it becomes real in the doing.

This chapter is an encouragement to do something—specifically, to join an online community of like-minded believers who, like you, have committed to make a HeartShift in a major area of their lives.

I'm sure that for some people it may come as news that there's anything redeemable to be found on the Internet. Yet, there's a great deal. For others, it may seem that joining such a community is like joining a health club—with all the depth of nodding to strangers between sets and looking at people whom you'll never look like even if you worked out day and night! Let me assure you that you'll find this group of friends more helpful and more in line with real issues you may be dealing with.

For example, you'll find creative examples of memorial markers and Bible studies for small groups, couples, and individuals. You'll be able to read about success stories and ongoing struggles from people wanting to make a similar HeartShift as you. And most of all, I think when you read others' stories and their 2 Degree Changes, you'll be encouraged to say, "I knew that!" and then, "I can do that!"

If you're the risk-taking type or you like to rush ahead, then feel free to jump right over the next few pages that follow and visit www.HeartShift.com. That's where you'll find how to add your name to a growing list of people who love the Lord and are committed to change, as well as find a great amount of tangible help for your journey.

However, if you're more comfortable with a map and a guide instead of just jumping online and going it alone, then by all means read the next several pages. What follows is like a highlight film of what you'll find on the Web site and why I feel it's such a positive step in the change process.

What You'll Find at HeartShift.com for You

When you visit www.HeartShift.com, the first thing you'll see is a welcome message to new visitors that highlights some of the key reasons to visit and points out the major places to visit on the Web site. While any good Web site will change its appearance or colors or certain content areas over time, anytime you go to www.HeartShift.com, you'll find eight major areas to visit.

At HeartShift.com you'll find a place to take your Leading From Your Strengths report.

As I mentioned in chapter 7, you can take your online report at www.HeartShift.com. At the top left-hand corner of this Web page, you'll find a small box that says, "Book code." That's where you type in the eight-digit code you find on the unprinted side of the back flap of your book.

After you've typed in your passcode, click on the button with the words "Take Assessment." From there, you're off and running to take the online report and find out your unique, God-given strengths. If you decide to purchase additional passcodes later by visiting the Resource Center on the Web site, then the eight-digit codes you purchase can go right here as well.

AT HEARTSHIFT.COM YOU'LL FIND A PLACE TO SIGN UP TO
JOIN THE HEARTSHIFT COMMUNITY.

As I mentioned in the last chapter, ours is not a solitary religion. We were made for fellowship, and we long to make a difference in the lives of others. You can absolutely join a group of like-minded and change-minded believers at this site just by clicking on the words "I want to join the HeartShift community of believers." Those blue words are a link, and clicking on them will take you to a sign-up page.

If you hate signing up for anything because your in-box is already full of unsolicited e-mails, neither my ministry—StrongFamilies.com—nor Insights International will ever sell our e-mail list or send you anything you haven't asked for, except for a welcome e-mail from me personally, letting you know we received your request to join and thanking you for making a commitment to move toward God's best.

Signing up to be a part of the HeartShift community is like carving your name on a monument. It's another tangible way for you to say, "I want to make a change in an important area of my life." Adding your name and HeartShift request to our wall of honor may be all you do on the Web site. However, there's much more there.

For example, I send out (only to those who ask) a free once-a-month e-zine—a short online newsletter that goes out to your e-mail address. Each e-zine has a short article or encouraging story and features one resource for change. Again, while we'd love for you to receive this monthly tip sheet on making a HeartShift, you have to sign up separately and specifically ask to receive it. (Look for the blue words "Sign up for Dr. Trent's Monthly HeartShift E-zine.") I'm sorry, but we don't allow you to sign up for someone else, so Grandma can't sign up her whole family, or an enthusiastic college student can't sign up his or her whole dorm floor. You have to sign up individually, and with every e-zine you receive, you have the opportunity to unsubscribe at any time.

YOU'LL FIND NUMEROUS SUGGESTIONS BY OTHER
HEARTSHIFT COMMUNITY MEMBERS AND BE ABLE TO SUBMIT
YOUR THOUGHTS, PRAYER REQUESTS, AND 2 DEGREE CHANGES
TO HELP SOMEONE ELSE.

If you've ever been on eBay, it's an incredible place to find everything! Though we're a growing community, you won't find everything at our site, but you will find loads of ideas you can use. In short, as a way of encouraging others and publicly thanking God for what he's done in your life, as a HeartShift member you can submit thoughts, prayer requests, and specific 2 Degree Changes to encourage others. All will be prayed over, and many will be posted online.

You'd be shocked how sharing a small 2 Degree step you made to repair a broken relationship with a high school friend or your spouse or a prodigal child becomes the very thing that means so much to someone else five states away. We all run out of creativity, particularly when we've been stuck in long-term trials. While it's easy to grow weary and run out of ideas when trying to make changes, suggestions by God's people can bring tremendous creativity and help for you.

AT HEARTSHIFT.COM YOU'LL NOTICE FIVE "TABS" ACROSS THE TOP OF THE PAGE.

The next five parts of the Web page that you can always find are at the top of the page. They look like five tabs on file folders. All you have to do is click on the words in the tab, and indeed, a folder will open (or a Web page actually) that contains specific things to help you in the change process. Here's the first of the five tabs that go across the page.

HeartShift Certificate

As mentioned in chapter 7 on memorial markers, by clicking on this tab you'll be able to download your free HeartShift decision certificate that can become a memorial marker for you. Even if you pick a more tangible memorial marker (like my white hospital bracelet), this certificate is also a great thing to download, print off, and hand to each member of your 33 Support Group. The certificate is in color and will only print in color if you have a color printer. (You'd be surprised how many e-mails we get informing us, "My certificate didn't come out in color!" from their black-and-white printer.)

Memorial Markers

Here's your chance to click on these words and find dozens of memorial markers from people in the HeartShift community (updated roughly once a month from the submissions we get from HeartShift community members).

Each memorial marker found here is shared with permission and has a short story that goes with why that person chose that particular memorial marker. Seeing other people's creativity and commitment to change can be a great source of creativity and encouragement for you as well.

33 Support Group

By clicking on this tab, you'll find information on creating, maintaining, and even thanking those who are in your 33 Support Group. Here you'll find helpful tools, encouragement, and stories from men and women in the HeartShift community about what helped or hindered their 33 Support Group.

2 Degree Changes

Part 3 of this book is all about small, positive things we can do to better our health, home, and heart for God. But I don't pretend to be able to come up with all the small things you could do in your unique setting in life. This folder is filled with examples from readers like you who submitted their small 2 Degree Change idea and saw God use it to help them gain traction or greater closeness. There are many outstanding people in the HeartShift community whose 2 Degree Change—and in some cases, the story behind it—can give you tremendous hope and creativity for your unique situation. Again, each posting is done only with permission, and we can't post every submission. Once a month we'll add new items that can give you a fresh look at small things you could do to improve your life or the lives of others.

For Pastors/Leaders

As I mentioned at the outset of this book, it's my prayer that not only individuals but also small groups, Sunday school classes, and even entire churches will adopt a three-month focus on challenging people to make a HeartShift. This section of the Web site will challenge pastors and leaders to set aside one or more meetings or Sundays to encourage their people to make a HeartShift in some important area.

In this section you'll find stories from church or ministry leaders describing what they did with their group that was successful. Also, for pastors or for those in men's, women's, or para-church ministry, you'll find several sermons and sermon outlines posted from HeartShift community teachers and pastors (with permission, of course). Yes, you'll be able to download or print these off as well. It gives great ideas for using the HeartShift concept in a small group, class, or church, and it's a great place to find insights on using HeartShift as a Sunday or midweek meeting.

Resources and Feedback

Finally, there will always be a place on the HeartShift Web site where you can go to find additional outstanding resources (like passcodes for the online report; books or book reports I've written; or reviews others from the HeartShift community have written to share a particular book or tool of great help in the change process). In addition to outstanding resources, there's a "Suggestion Submission" button that allows you to make suggestions to improve the site or even to add verses or stories to future editions of this book or workbooks.

I hope this chapter has provided a helpful and detailed road map of what you'll find at your online HeartShift meeting place. I'd like to ask you to consider prayerfully going to www.HeartShift.com, if you haven't already, and sign up to be part of the HeartShift family of friends. Doing so can become another "stake in the ground" for people who really want to change.

May the Lord bless, encourage, and embolden you to be, even more, the person he wants you to be. And, as you turn the page and after a brief introduction to this next applicational section, you'll find 2 Degree Change suggestions, beginning with strengthening your spiritual life.

Part 3

Putting 2 Degree Changes into Practice

Introduction to Part 3

In part 1 you learned basic concepts and terms like HeartShift and the 2 Degree Change.

In part 2 you filled out a written, dated HeartShift commitment to change in a specific area, linked with a tangible memorial marker. You then went online and took your Leading From Your Strengths™ report and prayerfully chose a small group of supportive friends and/or family to be your personal 33 Support Group. Finally, you were asked to become a member of the HeartShift online community as a way of finding new ideas, gaining ongoing encouragement, and strengthening your commitment.

Here in part 3 the focus is on examples of 2 Degree Changes you can make in specific life areas. We'll look first at what a 2 Degree Change might look like if you're wanting to strengthen your spiritual life, then at important friendships and family relationships, and finally how to use this concept to improve your overall health.

Whatever specific HeartShift area you choose, it's crucial to view change as a long walk, not a short sprint. To do otherwise is to fall into the performance trap.

THE DIFFERENCE BETWEEN A HEARTSHIFT AND THE PERFORMANCE TRAP

Making hurried, dramatic, or broad-brush changes is a great way to walk into the performance trap. For most people that's exactly the route they take when they become convicted enough to make a change. Bundled with fresh enthusiasm for change, they think if a little is good, then making lots of changes is better. As a result, it can seem ludicrous to set the bar at the lowest possible opening height and take all our warm-up jumps. Instead, we want to set the world record height, skip any practice or preliminary jumps, and go for a one-and-only attempt.

While we may not realize that's what we're doing, people who set out to make huge, immediate 90- or 180-degree shifts in habits or relationships often say things like "I'm going to be back in shape three weeks from right now, which will be right before my reunion, and I'm going to lose forty pounds doing it." Or, "This is the last time, *ever,* that I am blowing up and losing my temper at the kids. From now on, we're going to spend an hour together every night and the whole day on Saturday, just having fun together."

Guaranteed, those kinds of large-ticket changes come with a ticket to the performance trap. The performance trap is when a person ignores the counsel of Scripture ("He who is faithful in a little . . ." [Luke 16:10]) and sets inflated goals linked with unrealistic (if not impossible) time constraints. While that may sound a lot like your old boss or drill instructor, when it comes to making personal changes, huge changes meet major resistance in real life. And when we find our inflated goals blocked, blocked goals trigger anger.

For example, when our spouse isn't instantly supportive of all the dramatic changes we've decided to make "right now" after reading the latest best seller, we get angry. (Like if he or she slows us down by having the audacity to ask us if we've prayed or even thought seriously about what drinking wheat grass for a week will do to us!) If it's not our spouse blocking our new goals, then it's our boss who adds that extra project that erases our free time right at the very time we're ready to launch our new schedule. Or we get furious at our children for choosing now, of all times, to become high maintenance. Or we even get angry at God for not making the whole world get out of our way so we can change!

But life won't ever slow down or let you off the hook, as we saw in chapters 4 and 5. There is no little house on the prairie to escape to, even if you live on the prairie today. And when our exaggerated goals are blocked and lead to anger, that invariably leads to guilt when we fail. Guilt at letting ourselves or others down once again. Guilt that we have no willpower, even if our goal was immediately to start eating only low-fat celery between meals when we've been living on six packs of doughnuts for months.

Unrealistic goals + anger + guilt + more unrealistic goals = the performance trap so many experience. But that's not the kind of change process you've seen so far in this book, nor will you in the pages that follow. That's because your focus should be on taking small steps in the right direction, not on doing more, being more, having more, and ending up with less.

For the next three months it will be all about the small things, saints. It's starting slow and finishing well, not jumping out in front early and burning out before you reach the first turn. Even more, it's not going into the change process alone—ever. It's having the priceless prayers and support of your own 33 Group cheering you on for the next three months. It's going slow enough that you actually begin to see God working in small ways in your life again, and over time, it's waking up to find that you've become a slightly better person each day because you've focused on doing small things and making small choices each day.

The 2 Degree Difference lets you accrue that internal and eternal compound interest from making small steps toward faith, perseverance, sensitivity, self-control, love, respect, and courage. And it's time now to illustrate small ways you can do just that.

CHAPTER ELEVEN

It's Always Been the Small Things, Saints

You will say that these are very small sins; and doubtless, like all young tempers, you are anxious to be able to report spectacular wickedness. But do remember, the only thing that matters is the extent to which you separate the man from the Enemy.

It does not matter how small the sins are, provided that their cumulative effect is to edge the man away from the Light and out into the Nothing. Murder is no better than cards if cards can do the trick.

Indeed, the safest road to Hell is the gradual one—the gentle slope, soft underfoot, without sudden turnings, without milestones, without signposts.

–C. S. Lewis, *The Screwtape Letters*

So wrote a senior devil to a junior tempter in Lewis's classic work that sought to illustrate Satan's strategy against God's saints, meaning you and me. If your desire is to make a HeartShift in your spiritual life, then you're not alone. In chapter 1 we saw how the church of Ephesus fell prey to just such a subtle attack when they woke up one day to find themselves far from their first love. Slowly, gradually, unremarkably, they had left or drifted further and further away from Christ until his second-order-change wake-up call opened their eyes to both their problem and their need for change.

For Christians in every generation, it's easy to do the same thing— to start out strong and then wake up to find that our spiritual life has gone from rock solid to rice-paper thin. It's easy to see our prayer life become sporadic and then stagnate, to have reading God's Word become optional and then barely occasional. It's easy to see our fellowship with others become a challenge and then a bother and finally too much of a bother to get up on Sunday mornings to go to church at all. And finally, the more isolated you get from prayer and God's Word and his people, the greater the doubts about whether any of it is real in the first place.

If that sounds at all like you, then that's the slow, gradual slope toward hell, the place of ultimate isolation, that Lewis captures in the senior tempter's remarks above. It's like the second law of thermodynamics that rules our earthly world, leaning on our faith, slowing everything down, and draining us of any vitality, creativity, or energy until our faith is a pool of nothingness.

For those who have Christ's life within them and his Holy Spirit as their guide, the "newness of life" that Jesus brings breaks into a world that is spiraling down. God breaks into our world and renews our life from within and gives us a way of escape. And that escape route back to a first love for our Savior comes one small, sure step at a time.

So if your HeartShift is to regain that "first love" for your Savior, then let's look at several small, specific 2 Degree Changes you can make back toward God's best. We'll begin by looking at the Lord Jesus' words to that church that drifted away—three things, any and all of which can get you back on track to a "first love" for him.

A 2 DEGREE STEP BACK—"REMEMBER FROM WHERE YOU'VE FALLEN."

More than three hundred times in God's Word we're asked to remember. One of those times is the first of three challenges—three small steps if you will—that Jesus asked the church of Ephesus to take in order to get back on the right path and back to a first-love connection with him.

"I have this against you, that you have left your first love.

Therefore, remember from where you have fallen." (Rev. 2:4–5)

Why in the world should our first step forward be to look back?

At least in part, it's because where our eyes are pointed is always important. If you'll remember, those bitten by snakes in the wilderness had to look up to be saved. Jesus tells Nicodemus he must look up to him on the cross if he is to find new life. Here Jesus tells an off-course people that they need to take a small step back by looking back and remembering their first love for him.

An important distinction is that he asks them specifically to look back at the positive, not negative, memories and pictures. You do not fall from the low points of your life. Jesus challenges them to think back to a time (or times) when it was spring in their spiritual life, high points when things were going well.

Think about how Jesus differs from many leaders today.

He doesn't yell or threaten or shame or rub our nose in all our failures, even when we have failed and drifted away. Can't you just imagine your boss saying to you at the end of a negative evaluation, "Let's just forget how poorly you've done this past year. In fact, let's talk about everything you did right last year." That's probably not going to happen at work, but it is what Jesus asked that church to do in order to get back on track. They were to reflect on the high points of their faith, to think where they had fallen from, like when they first came to know and love Jesus. Let me give you a personal example of how such a look back can cause a helpful step forward.

THE DAY GOD SHOWED ME WHAT WAS MISSING

At times when I have woken up and realized that my relationship with Jesus isn't as strong or close or vibrant as it could or should be, I have taken this first small step—to think back on a spiritual high point in the past. Where do you come up with such high points?

If you'll slow down and think back to the time surrounding when you first came to Christ, there will certainly be a situation or example where you noticed God at work in your life. Not in dramatic ways necessarily, but in some small, unmistakable way nonetheless.

For example, the day you showed up at church soon after coming to Christ and you thought the pastor had followed you around the house that week because his message was so pointed toward exactly where you were. Or when you attended an Easter service (or saw *The Passion of the Christ*), and for the first time your heart was staggered at the price Jesus paid to redeem us. Perhaps it was when you actually found yourself spontaneously praying for a friend for the first time, or reaching for your Bible at night instead of the television remote, and realized you'd never done that before.

Or in my case, you might have noticed that something was missing.

I accepted Christ toward the end of high school. As a teenager, I had grown up in a single-parent home and was filled with anger. While that inner anger helped me gain success in contact sports where they reward you for expressing rage, it left my personal relationships in ruins. My life changed, however, through the influence of one family.

To draw on an earlier analogy, I met a family who was real in a way I had never seen before. At first, I couldn't understand what made them so different. It wasn't that they didn't quarrel at times or show frustration toward one another. But there was a love and acceptance, a valuing of each family member, that drew me like a magnet to their home.

That family was the Barram family, and the husband was our local Young Life leader. While Doug treated every club kid with great love and respect, his infectious smile, genuine warmth, and patient love toward my brothers and me was like pouring water on parched ground. We soaked up his affirmation and soon came to see its source, his faith in Jesus.

Doug's life was the first "Bible" I ever read. Where my own father had dammed up the stream and rejected us, Doug chose to open the floodgates, pour out his own love, and introduce us to the living water Christ offered. He treated us like his own children—something I discovered happens to everyone who comes to Christ and is adopted into God's family.

As a direct result of the investment of love and time the Barrams poured into my life, a night came when I trusted Christ. There were no audible whistles or bells when I made the decision to follow Jesus, yet I knew at the deepest level something had happened. Most of all, I knew my decision was real. And shortly thereafter I saw for the first time how real God was as he already was at work inside me in a small way that staggered me when I saw it.

It happened during a PE class less than a week after I came to Christ. At the time I had a hair-trigger temper and would lash out or strike out at the drop of a hat. In particular, I had tremendous pride that reflected itself in cursing or dramatic displays of anger if things didn't go my way, especially if I was losing at anything.

We were learning tennis. Near the end of the semester, the teacher had us play singles, tournament style. I was a football player and a wrestler, not a wimpy tennis player. But being a starting All-City linebacker didn't impress or intimidate a short, scrawny kid the coach assigned me to play. That scrawny kid used the strings on his tennis racket to strum me like a guitar. Usually the person who is running the most is losing a tennis match. He ran me from one side of the court to the other, and then he'd drop a lob shot that almost made me fall down, which made me feel stupid.

I was down forty love in the third set when it hit me. *I wasn't cursing.*

I was in the middle of being beaten like a drum, and I hadn't verbalized a single swear word. In fact, I wasn't even conscious of being angry with the other kid, even though several of my football friends, waiting their turn to play, had tossed in helpful barbs about what a pathetic tennis player I was.

It may not seem like a big thing to you, but I still remember standing on that sun-baked court and feeling a literal chill run the entire length of my spine.

God really is real, is what I thought. *Something did happen when I asked Jesus into my heart!*

That was the first small way I saw God invade my life, and it's still something I can go back to today for strength and encouragement when life throws in doubts or I'm tempted to become angry. If God could begin to tame my foul mouth and temper that day, he could do it again and again. He was real, and thinking of that small evidence of his presence in my life still can give me chills.

In part, that's why I think Jesus asks us to remember when our faith was real to us and our love for him was fresh and new. Memories bring back feelings, and feelings bring back more memories. Remembering times you were doing well in your faith, times when God seemed extraordinarily close or real, is like pulling open a window in a stuffy, sweltering room and drinking in cool, fresh air from outside. It reminds us that God does invade our life and can bring gusts of fresh air to our busy, fractured world, a tiny glimpse of the "fresh air" outside the world we live in now that we'll breathe in heaven with him forever.

That's the first, small step we're to take if we have way too much distance in our spiritual life. We're to *"remember from where you have fallen."*

For me, such a high point took place on a tennis court back in high school. What memory of a high point in your faith do you have?

Don't just push the "default" button and say, "There are no high points." Perhaps like me, you may have to go back decades, but if there was a time you became a new creature in Christ by a simple act of faith in accepting Jesus as your Lord and Savior, then tap your memory for a time when that truth showed itself real to you. In the lines below, or on a separate sheet if you need more room (or can't bear to write in a book), take a moment to go back to your first love for Jesus. If possible, reflect and write down a time when he seemed so present, so close—because he was.

_____

_____

_____

_____

_____

_____

A SECOND SMALL STEP IS TO POINT YOURSELF IN THE RIGHT DIRECTION—REPENT

I mentioned earlier that I was a Greek major at Dallas Seminary. That happened primarily because I got some bad advice! When I entered graduate school, I was told by a third-year friend that I should major in New Testament because of the outstanding professors in that area. That sounded good to me. I was a relatively new Christian, and the thought of reading the New Testament in detail sounded great! However, what I didn't realize was that majoring in New Testament at Dallas Seminary meant majoring in New Testament Greek! And not just learning an ancient language but translating the entire New Testament before you graduated (as a requirement to graduate), line by line and page by page.

The hundreds of hours spent learning and translating Greek did teach me a great deal about the word pictures behind many New Testament words. For example, the Greek word for *sin* is "to miss the mark." If you're serious about having *self-control,* then that biblical word literally means "to pull in the reigns."

What's the hidden Greek meaning of the word *repent*? Let's look at it in context first: "But I have this against you, that you have left your first love. Therefore, remember from where you have fallen, and repent" (Rev. 2:4–5).

The second step Jesus asks of the church of Ephesus is to turn around and get pointed in the right direction. For the word *repent* literally means "to turn around." Just because it's a "small step" to turn around doesn't mean it's an easy one, but what a tremendous HeartShift. Let me give you a counseling example of how just keeping this one small thought at the front of your mind over the course of three months changed one man's life and saved a marriage.

I have a friend who is fond of saying, "The first rule of holes is stop digging." In other words, if you're digging yourself a hole, the only way to keep the hole from getting deeper is to stop digging. Or in Jesus' words to the church at Ephesus, it's to stop heading in the wrong direction and get pointed in the right direction.

Several years ago I counseled with a man whose marriage was crumbling. He was a Christian, as was his wife, but he had gotten involved in an affair at work, and the marriage was hanging by a thread. While he had ended the physical part of the affair, his unwillingness to totally sever the relationship with this other woman acted like sulfuric acid, eating away any attempts to rebuild or restore the marriage.

Then this man went to a men's ministry retreat and came back convicted that he needed to "turn around," to repent. He wanted his relationship with Christ restored, and he sincerely asked his wife's forgiveness. But the emotional challenge of unplugging from this other woman was like trying to make it through Navy SEAL training. It seemed impossible.

I asked him to pick and make one small step over the next three months, a HeartShift back toward the Lord or his wife. And he chose this second statement of our Lord's to focus on to try to do both.

He would get up in the morning and commit to starting his day by "turning around," meaning he would ask God to help him turn away from this other woman and toward his wife. That was his prayer every single morning for three months, and the written HeartShift goal he shared with three men in his HeartShift support group.

Every time he was tempted to go back down the wrong road that had so nearly ruined his marriage and ended his relationship with his children, he thought of that small thing: *turn around*. There were some times he would literally turn around and not look at the phone instead of picking it up to call that person. Or he would internally "turn around" and force his thoughts away from her and toward his wife when temptation came.

It wasn't all turning *from* something; it meant taking small steps back toward his wife each day. But thinking consciously about his decision to get pointed in the right direction made small positive actions toward his wife more real and reachable. And over time his actions brought with them positive feelings toward his wife, and he saw the emotional hold this other woman had on him lessen and finally let go its iron grip. By that small step of pointing himself internally toward the Lord and toward his wife, he saw both relationships improve. Stepping toward one drew him closer to the other.

It doesn't take scoring a 1260 on the SAT test to realize that whether it's our marriage or our spiritual life (or both), getting pointed in the right direction is a crucial factor in making positive changes. In fact, just knowing we've made a turn away from sickness and toward better health makes people feel better—in the same way that people feel better just by calling a doctor and making an appointment before they even go in!

So now you've seen a second small step that can become a HeartShift toward a closer spiritual or personal life. And the question is: Is there an area in your life where you need to turn around? To get pointed in the right direction?

Perhaps you need to get pointed back toward your spouse, or away from hating the person who got the promotion over you, or toward that Sunday school class you quit attending at your church, or away from joining in the gossip mill at work.

A THIRD SMALL STEP IS TO "DO THE DEEDS YOU DID AT FIRST"

Let's finish the statement Jesus made to the church at Ephesus, "I have this against you, that you have left your first love. Therefore, remember from where you have fallen, and repent and do the deeds you did at first" (Rev. 2:4–5).

The legendary football coach Vince Lombardi was famous for taking his team back to basics. "Gentlemen," he said, "this is a football." The path back to closeness with Jesus is one that goes back to the basics—*doing the things that we did before.* Seeking to live your life for him every day. Spending time getting to know Jesus in prayer and through his Word. And then living out that love in our family, our church, our workplace, and community.

In the three chapters that follow, I'll give you more examples of small steps with such basics in building or restoring a stronger faith. And to do so, we'll begin by looking at two Old Testament heroes. Both chose to take small steps, one toward ruin and the other toward redemption.

Questions for Discussion with Your 33 Group, Close Friend, or Spouse

1. Dr. Trent feels that over time most Christians will wake up to find they need to make a HeartShift in their faith. Do you agree with that observation? Why or why not? If you do agree, what do you feel is a primary reason for believers drifting away?

2. You were encouraged to write down a specific time you remember God showing himself to be real to you. Was this an easy or difficult exercise? In what ways do you feel going back to such a memory can help you today? Can you think of a downside to looking back?

3. To *repent* was defined as needing to "turn around." Can you think of someone who was challenged to turn around—repent—and didn't? While Dr. Trent talked about this being a small step, do you feel it's a huge step for most people? Explain your answer.

4. "Do the deeds you did at first." Dr. Trent likened this to going back to the basics. Why is "going back to basics" so hard for many of us? What in our culture do you feel sets itself against doing things over or going back to basics?

CHAPTER TWELVE

Daniel and Samson through a 2 Degree Lens

Time and again you've read that small shifts have the power to move us toward or away from light and life. That is absolutely true when it comes to our spiritual life. One way to show this is to set side by side two biblical heroes. Samson was a hero in a military sense, and while a leader of God's people, he was hardly a man of great faith. Daniel wasn't a warrior, but he was a hero nonetheless because of his great faith. For one man 2 Degree Changes moved him further from God's best and closer to ruin. For the other, small 2 Degree shifts early in his life gave him confidence and courage to face much greater challenges in the trying days to come. Let's look at each through a 2 Degree lens.

SAMSON: TWO DEGREE CHANGES THAT TAKE US CLOSER TO THE EDGE

If you look at the military gifts and incredible strength God gave Samson, he was certainly a heroic figure. At a time when the Philistines were ruthless rulers over the Israelites, he burned their crops and killed thirty and then a thousand of their soldiers—not to mention thousands more at the dramatic end of his life. Yet in his personal and spiritual life, Samson started off strong but ended up a spiritual wreck. Not by running away from God but by consistently taking small steps in the wrong direction until it eventually led him off a cliff.

Early in his life, we're told of Samson that God's Spirit was upon him (see Judg. 13:25). Unfortunately, Samson was like King Saul, another leader of Israel upon whom God's Spirit was said to rest. While both started off with God's Spirit, neither man let that fact keep him from making incredibly poor choices. For example, when Samson decides it's time to marry, he orders his parents to set up a marriage with a Philistine woman. When they argue that he should marry a woman of faith from his own people, he tells them—and this is a quote—"Get her for me, for she looks good to me" (Judg. 14:3).

That ranks right up there with something a Hollywood actor or sports superstar would say in picking up a woman, not a spiritual leader picking his wife. If nothing else, it certainly reflected spiritual immaturity, even if he did have XXL-sized biceps.

That marriage would end in tragedy. (We won't go into detail here, but feel free to drop into the book of Judges to see the terrible tragedy that comes from his poor choices.) I want us to look at how Samson made a habit of making small 2 Degree steps *away* from God and toward a dangerous edge that would one day turn into a cliff.

After his wife's death, Samson first gets involved with a harlot he meets in Gaza and then has a relationship with another now infamous woman named Delilah. She too is a Philistine and uses her seductive beauty as a trap to destroy him. But it takes one to set the trap and another to fall for it.

When the Philistines offer Delilah a fortune to find out the source of Samson's incredible strength, she tries to entice him into telling her his secret. When first asked, he tells her that if he is bound with seven fresh cords that have not been dried, he can be captured and harmed. Of course, that is a lie, and he easily fights off the soldiers who come to get him when he is so bound.

He stays with Delilah for a *second* night, where her pouting and pleading bring another lie from Samson about his strength. This time it's new ropes, not cords, that can do the trick. Only the trick is on that group of Philistines who come to get him and are also destroyed. *Another* night passes, with her pleading with Samson yet again—this time more fervently than ever—to know his secret.

Now watch what happens.

Already Sampson has ignored God's Spirit time and again, chosen to pass his hand through the fire, thinking he can't be burned. But people who feel they are so strong (or rich, or smart, or well connected, or beautiful) face a major problem if they think they can't fail or be caught. The truth is, if you walk along the edge of a cliff long enough, you will fall. After three nights of Delilah's pleading, watch how he *almost* tells her the truth.

"If you weave the seven locks of my hair with the web and fasten it with a pin," he tells her, "then I will become weak and be like any other man"(Judg. 16:13). Of course this wasn't true either, but can you see how his lies are slowly moving him toward the edge?

I've used that word *edge* a number of times. Let me explain what I mean by that term, and how Samson and so many people today err in creeping toward it.

There is in each of us a push/pull when it comes to danger. We hate the slow climb of the roller coaster (and for me the entire ride), but when it's over, there are smiles and excitement and even an exaggerated sense of achievement—after all, all we did was sit in a metal tube and scream! If nothing else, there is tremendous relief that we've dodged the bullet and somehow, despite the double loops, we're still alive! Here's another way of looking at what I mean.

Winston Churchill once said of his experience as a young solider, "There is nothing as exhilarating as being shot at without effect." It's frightening to be in battle, but danger brings with it a certain kind of exhilaration as well. So, too, does dangerous behavior like speeding or extreme skiing—or in Samson's case, going in to a harlot and slowly inching your way toward sharing with her a secret that if exposed could literally lead to your death.

Can you see what a common, if terrible, problem that is for the X Games generation we live in? No wonder people take illegal drugs thinking they won't get addicted or die. For some it's just part of walking on the edge. No wonder so many inch closer and closer to an emotional and then a physical affair with a neighbor or coworker with a warm, listening ear. Walking so close to the edge is exciting! Solomon, the wisest man who ever lived, knew this, saying, "All sin is pleasurable for a season." The problem is that the short season of pleasure passes quickly (if it ever comes); then we're often left with decades of a winter reality in its aftermath.

And by the way, I'm talking about believers here!

Certainly it's worse in the world, but every week in my counseling practice I see the terrible fallout of people who inched closer and closer to the edge and still couldn't believe it when they finally fell off the cliff!

It's the same kind of logic that rationalizes they can take a few drinks before they drive because they got home safely the night before. Tragically, and predictably, the next time they drink they'll take a *few more* drinks before the drive home until without realizing it they cross a line and ruin (or kill) themselves or others.

With that picture in mind, let's go back to Samson. He's already stayed day after day in the danger zone. Now he's actually inched his way into telling her that the secret of his strength has to do with his hair.

Granted, tying up his hair into seven locks with a hairpin isn't true, but it's close! And Samson *still* doesn't admit the danger of his situation and stays with her yet *another* night.

And now the mighty Samson finally gets so close to the edge that he falls in, like so many people ever since who have thought they were too strong or smart to fall (like the people C. S. Lewis described as following the wide, downhill road in *The Screwtape Letters*).

One last time Delilah pouts and even pulls out the "if you really loved me" line. And thinking he might lose her (even though losing her would be the best thing that ever happened to him!), he gives in. He kids himself into thinking she's in it for love, while she knows she's in for the money. And so when he finally does reveal to her his heart and secret— namely, that his strength is linked with his uncut hair (a part of his Nazirite vow to serve God)—she takes him to the bank. She gets word to her countrymen that the minute she is finished cutting his hair he will lose his extraordinary strength, which is exactly what happens.

Judas betrayed Jesus for twenty pieces of silver. Delilah does much better and gets several *thousand* silver coins for Samson. But while the end of Samson's life story is well chronicled in both the Scriptures and numerous movies, let's keep our focus here on how his life fell apart in the first place. Or actually, let's look at a modern-day Samson—a man of incredible spiritual strength and vision who, like Samson, kept pushing the edge.

I'll call this man Cliff.

Several years ago Cliff was an outstanding pastor, speaker, and ministry leader. He was cutting edge with technology in his sermons long before it was fashionable to be cutting edge. He also was one of the first to push and push to make his congregation relevant to the many in his community who didn't know Christ.

In fact, Cliff pushed so hard to be relevant that the last time I saw him, he gave a talk at a Christian conference on why we should *never* use a "4 Spiritual Laws" booklet with non-Christians. ("The 4 Spiritual Laws" is a small tract used in the millions by Campus Crusade to lead people to Christ.) Cliff felt handing out a tract for evangelism was so old school that it was guaranteed to turn off a seeking someone, not lead them to Christ. Instead, he shared *his* latest tool for reaching the unchurched in their upscale community—that was to have a keg of beer brought into the church gym on Monday nights to draw in non-Christians after their pickup basketball games.

Having a keg of beer after basketball was explained to show non-believers that you were "with them." So instead of praying before the game, have some suds with the sinners afterwards. That, not sharing the four spiritual laws, was how to reach this generation from his perspective. Unfortunately, instead of people looking at him like he had lost his mind, I could see several people in the room were actually buying what he was selling.

Which leads me to this question.

When you take a white glove and put it in the mud, does the mud become "glovie"? Or does the glove become muddy? I simply couldn't believe an evangelical elder board in our country would let their senior pastor get away with that, but they did. After all, he had tripled church attendance.

Things looked great at his congregation until the day he stepped one inch closer to the edge and fell off the cliff. Less than six months after his "bring a keg of beer to church basketball" talk, in addition to making church functions more alcohol friendly, he had inched his way into being so "friendly" with a woman in his church that their uncovered affair imploded his ministry and marriage.

Like Samson, this man's life became so focused on the edge—how far he could go from biblical standards and still not fall off the cliff—that a 2 Degree step finally led him off the edge.

Which brings me to yet another question.

Has the focus of your life been on the "out of bounds" line lately? Inching ever closer, without actually stepping over the line? That is far too easy to do. Even good people from great spiritual backgrounds inch their way into sin and ruin every day.

Perhaps now you can see why Satan doesn't want you to think about small things or that small sins really count. For a climber trying to scale Mount Everest, there are no warning signs to keep you from walking over a crevice that has been covered with snow. It's only when your feet drop out from under you that you know you've gone one step too far.

That's the dark, terrible side of letting small 2 Degree Changes ruin our witness, ministry, family, and life. But there's another road to take. There's another way to make small changes that lead us down Christ's narrow way, and we can see this by looking at our second biblical hero.

Daniel was someone who, like Samson, consistently pushed the envelope—only in his case, that was a good thing! As we'll see in Daniel's life, while he lived in a dangerous, secular, antifaith environment, he kept pushing the edge toward godliness. Inch by inch he brought himself and his countrymen closer than ever to the Lord.

DANIEL PUSHES THE EDGE SPIRITUALLY BY MAKING 2 DEGREE CHANGES

When ancient Israel was overrun by King Nebuchadnezzar's forces, they brought back to Babylon a number of the finest young men to be slaves and servants in the king's court. These young men were royalty and the privileged youth in Israel, and they were expected to do things the king's way now that they lived in Babylon. That included living on foods that Israelites were forbidden to eat.

From the start Daniel, like Samson, pushed the edge. He could have just gone along and not made waves with a diet that God's Word forbade him to eat. After all, he was a POW and couldn't be expected to fight back. But as even prisoners know, there are small ways to fight back, and so Daniel made a bold request.

At the front end of his imprisonment, he asked if he and his friends could eat healthy food instead of the king's food. Daniel gently pushed the envelope with his request, risking the wrath of his captor so that he could bring as much godliness into his godless situation as possible. His courage to ask for a change of diet was rewarded, and Daniel and his friends ended up being the healthiest captives of all.

That kind of courage to take steps gently and quietly to bring godly beliefs into a workplace hostile to his faith led to positive things in his health—and downstream, in his faith. That was true not only for Daniel but also for his friends, who were influenced by his life. And the result?

What started off as the courage to ask for God-honoring food gave him a strong footing to make several later stands for the Lord as well. Of course, Daniel being tossed into the lion's den or his friends being tossed into a blazing fire are much better known than his first, small step. But the little victory of a godly diet became the launching pad for later, greater acts of courage and faith—the kind of courage a modern-day Daniel (or the following story), a Donna, showed in taking small, consistent steps toward godliness in a situation patently unfriendly to faith.

Donna is the name I'll give a grade-school teacher my wife and I know. She's a tremendous example of someone who takes small steps to advance God's kingdom, even if at times it means she puts her job at risk. For example, when several Christian students wanted to start a Bible club on campus, she volunteered to be their faculty advisor. Initially, the club was turned down to meet on campus. But Donna stayed patient and positive and didn't give up, and a year later a student-led Bible club began at her public school.

Then Donna carefully and with honor talked to her principal about having a student-led "rally 'round the flag" day. It took another year after first introducing the idea *and* first being turned down before more than fifty students and parents showed up early before school one day to surround the flagpole at her school and pray for God's blessing on our country and on each student's life.

Time and again Donna has been the one at her school to gently move spiritual opportunities forward for students. And she's done it by taking small courageous steps toward God-honoring goals.

What's the difference between Cliff and Donna and between Samson and Daniel? I hope you can see clearly in the contrast between them that small steps toward danger led Samson and Cliff to catastrophe and finally resulted in their forfeiting their place on God's front lines. However, for Daniel and Donna, small steps of faith, in spite of possible consequences, led to later acts of courage and faith.

Which brings me to you and your spiritual life.

Are you more like Samson and the beer-keg pastor, taking small 2 Degree steps toward a cliff? Or are you more like Daniel and Donna, who are consistently committed to looking for ways, small ways, to keep moving toward God's best?

I pray I will be more like Daniel and that you will as well. And I pray this next chapter encourages your heart. Up next are ten short 2 Degree Difference devotionals, one for each of the next ten days, that can teach you more about small things in Scripture and help strengthen your spiritual life as well.

CHAPTER THIRTEEN

The 2 Degree Difference
Quiet Time

I passed by the field of the sluggard
And by the vineyard of the man lacking sense,
And behold, it was completely overgrown with thistles,
Its surface was covered with nettles,
And its stone wall was broken down.
When I saw, I reflected upon it;
I looked, and received instruction.
"A little sleep, a little slumber,
A little folding of the hands to rest,"
Then your poverty will come as a robber
And your want like an armed man. (Prov. 24:30–34)

I had the great honor of attending Dallas Theological Seminary. In particular, that honor came in getting to sit under some of the nation's finest linguists, theologians, and teachers. Right at the top of that list was Dr. Howard Hendricks.

At seminary, everyone called Dr. Hendricks "Prof." Today he's in his eighties, still going strong, and still encouraging men and women to be godly leaders. But one of my most vivid memories of Prof was an assignment he gave us on the first day of my first Bible class at Dallas.

That class was Bible Study Methods, and the assignment was to write down *forty* observations that jumped out at us from the five verses you read above. That's more than three dozen things that stand out, like principles, lessons, words, phrases, sentence construction, tenses, or whatever you felt was important. As you might imagine, about five observations jumped out immediately, and then thirty-five took lots of work to pull out of only five verses. At least that was true for me as it took me the whole weekend to accomplish the assignment.

I finally did finish, and patting myself on the back, I showed up at my second Bible class with my forty observations all typed out. What I didn't expect was the second assignment Prof gave us. You might have already guessed it; our assignment for next class was to come up with *forty additional* observations from these same five verses.

Prof is a master teacher who used those assignments to open our eyes to how deep, rich, and inexhaustible is God's Word. But at the start of our graduate school training, there was a second reason for his picking these verses. He knew that if we spent hours looking at these five verses, we'd never forget them. He also knew that even slow students like me couldn't miss this story's message that had particular relevance for incoming freshmen.

Graduate school would be extremely demanding.

Our ministries would be equally demanding when we got out.

Keeping our spiritual lives and families strong day after day, year after year, would be a huge challenge. And Prof wanted us to remember, *always,* "a little sleep, a little slumber" was all it took to ruin them all.

That doesn't mean you should be a workaholic and never rest. It does mean that you can't ignore the small things, the daily 2 Degree maintenance steps that keep fences strong and weeds out of the garden. It's the little things that led to the ruin of that vineyard pictured in these verses, and it would be the little things, if neglected, that would ruin our spiritual lives, or grades, or families, or future ministries.

But those five verses aren't just a warning. They bring hope as well.

"When I saw, I reflected upon it; I looked and received instruction."

The fact is, it's someone *else's* vineyard we're looking at that has fallen into disrepair. We're walking past a tragedy caused by small acts of neglect, but it doesn't have to be our story. Not if we'll commit to looking and learning and then doing the small things consistently that can keep our vineyards in bloom.

Dear Lord,

Thank you so much for the insights that come from your Word and the warnings as well. Like that sluggard, I've seen people whose lives, and marriages, and friendships, and ministries, and jobs have fallen apart from not doing the small things. Lord, I don't want that to be my life. I pray for your protection and even more that you would open my eyes and help me see and do the little things that can make all the difference. I love you, Lord Jesus. Amen.

What you've just read is day one of ten 2 Degree Difference quiet times that make up this chapter. They're all short. They're all focused on just a few verses in Scripture, and each one seeks to encourage or point us toward a life of deeper faith, hope, and love by doing the little things. What's more, they're also a model for the kind of 2 Degree Difference quiet times I encourage people to build into their daily lives.

If you're already reading five chapters of the Bible a day, every day, then keep going! But for the other 117 million across our country who claim to know the Lord and don't read five chapters a day, I'd suggest starting with just three minutes. In three minutes you can read a few verses, digest a short commentary on God's Word, and then echo a prayer out loud or to yourself. Small doses of God's Word, none of which "return void," can act as little spiritual multivitamins that strengthen our spiritual lives.

I'd like to ask that for the next nine days you take the time to read one a day. In less than two weeks you'll have spent enough time looking at a 2 Degree Difference quiet time to be able to pattern one on your own.

For example, on day eleven I'd encourage you to pick out a New Testament book (I'd suggest starting with Colossians, then James, then 1 John, then the Gospel of John) and read just two or three verses a day. Then think about what's written there for a few minutes (*I saw . . . I reflected*) and finally close your time with an applicable prayer, like the ones you'll find at the end of each sample devotional.

That's it. A few verses. A few moments to reflect on what the Lord wants to teach you about loving him and others, and then a short prayer asking the Lord of Lords who loves you to help you live out what you've learned.

One more thing if you're an aspiring author. If you'll go to our Web site at www.HeartShift.com, on the home page you'll find instructions on how you can send us your own 2 Degree Difference quiet time devotional that may be picked to post online. We must have your permission in writing to consider posting your devotional. It can't be any longer than those you find here, and we can't post every devotional. (There are only 365 days in a year.) Each day on the Web site we'll have another 2 Degree Difference quiet time posted from people just like you who made a small observation or insight on God's Word that encouraged them to grow and that can encourage others as well.

As people walk by your home, may your walls and vineyard always be in *Home and Garden,* front cover condition, as you live out those little things that make our faith strong.

GOD IS SERIOUS ABOUT US USING OUR STRENGTHS, EVEN IN SMALL WAYS

"And the one also who had received the one talent came up and said, 'Master, I knew you to be a hard man, reaping where you did not sow and gathering where you scattered no seed. And I was afraid, and went away and hid your talent in the ground. See, you have what is yours.' But his master answered and said to him, 'You wicked, lazy slave, you knew that I reap where I did not sow and gather where I scattered no seed. Then you ought to have put my money in the bank, and on my arrival I would have received my money back with interest.'" (Matt. 25:24–27)

Do you remember the story of the woman caught in adultery? At no time when Jesus spoke with her or with any other sinner we see in Scripture does he call them names like "wicked" or "lazy," even when they'd committed serious sins. But did you notice the strong language Jesus uses here in the parable of the talents?

The one who buries his talent is called both wicked and lazy. What's more, at the end of this parable, the amount he was given is taken away and given to others who will invest it. Those are strong words and serious consequences, but it shows Almighty God's tremendous displeasure with those who *could* make an investment—people who could give love, or help, or encouragement, or hope to others, even in the smallest of ways— but instead bury their strengths or gifts and don't use them at all.

God has given us so much. All that we are, all that we have, and all that we will be. It's his expectation that we will at least give back "bank interest" when we stand before him and he asks for an accounting. To do nothing isn't just sad; it's wicked and lazy, and those are Jesus' words.

So how do we accrue at least "bank interest" on his investment in our lives? Just think about a small 2 Degree Change for the better you can make in someone else's life today. Perhaps it's your spouse, and you could take three minutes to make the bed for her before you head to work. Or your child, and you put a note in his lunch that tells him he's the coolest kid God could have ever given you. Or you buy a huge card and send it to a friend who is hurting, giving your friend a "can't miss" picture of how valuable the friendship is to you. Or you pay for the toll for your car and for the person *behind* you on the toll road when you stop at the toll booth.

God is serious about us making investments that gain interest each day. May we make life just 2 Degrees better for each person we meet today.

> *Dear Lord,*
> *I admit it is so easy to take the gifts and strengths you've given me and just bury them in the backyard of my busy life. It's so easy simply not to want to get involved because I already feel so overwhelmed. But Lord, I'm not asked to help the whole world—just one, starting with the one person you've put in front of me. So help me look for those small investments I can make in someone else's life today, to gain interest on your investment in my life. Amen.*

A NOBODY, NOBODY NOTICED

But the LORD said to Samuel, "Do not look at his appearance or at the height of his stature, because I have rejected him; for God sees not as man sees, for man looks at the outward appearance, but the LORD looks at the heart. . . ."

And Samuel said to Jesse, "Are these all the children?" And he said, "There remains yet the youngest, and behold, he is tending the sheep." Then Samuel said to Jesse, "Send and bring him; for we will not sit down until he comes here."

So he sent and brought him in. Now he was ruddy, with beautiful eyes and a handsome appearance. And the LORD said, "Arise, anoint him; for this is he." (1 Sam. 16:7, 11–12)

It was time for the nation of Israel to pick a new leader. Samuel is picked to be the executive headhunter, and God himself points him toward a family that unknowingly was raising the next king of Israel.

The father brings one son after the other before Samuel, from the oldest and strongest on down. But none pass the test. And then the prophet Samuel asked, "Are these all your children?"

Jesse's answer should be a great encouragement to all of us who think life has passed us by or that what we're doing right now doesn't count. For guess who God chose to lead his people? A nobody, nobody noticed. The one who had been sent out to the sheep. The one doing all the small things it takes to care for a small flock, like take care of tiny newborn lambs, in a place where no one sees and no one notices except Almighty God.

My encouragement to you today is to stay faithful to doing the small things, wherever God has you. Protecting the flock, finding the best grazing area, making sure those under your care get water and rest. The small things David did each day ended up preparing him for much greater responsibilities. Small daily investments in being faithful to a small flock were the very things God built into his life to make him a great leader of an entire nation. And that lesson isn't just for royalty.

I love the way when you ask any Marine what his or her job is, you'll hear, "I'm a rifleman." Then they may tell you they're also an artilleryman, or pilot, or cook, or mission specialist, or intelligence officer, or expeditionary force commander; but they all start off by training to do the small but important things like carrying a rifle before they go on to other duties.

Faithful in a little becomes the basis for being given greater responsibilities or even command positions down the road—in every walk of life. Even if we think that we're a nobody, today, doing a job that nobody notices.

> Dear Lord who sees our efforts and knows our hearts,
> Thank you, Jesus, that I'm not a nobody that nobody notices. I may be doing small things in a job that few people see, but I know I'm not forgotten. Lord, teach me the lessons of faithfulness and patience and nurturing and courage that come from being a good "shepherd" of whatever situation you've put me in. And as I learn to be faithful, then make me ready for great things you may call me to do. Amen.

MAKE ME A LITTLE CAKE

So he arose and went to Zarephath, and when he came to the gate of the city, behold, a widow was there gathering sticks; and he called to her and said, "Please get me a little water in a jar, that I may drink."

As she was going to get it, he called to her and said, "Please bring me a piece of bread in your hand."

But she said, "As the LORD your God lives, I have no bread, only a handful of flour in the bowl and a little oil in the jar; and behold, I am gathering a few sticks that I may go in and prepare for me and my son, that we may eat it and die."

Then Elijah said to her, "Do not fear; go, do as you have said, but make me a little bread cake from it first and bring it out to me, and afterward you may make one for yourself and for your son." (1 Kings 17:10–13)

It isn't easy to give to others when we feel we have only a little to give ourselves. For example, I can't tell you how many times I've had people in counseling say to me, "I'm just too wounded to serve anyone else." My question back to them is always, "Is there anyone who lives near you, anyone you know, who is in worse shape than you either physically, emotionally, or financially?" I've yet to find someone who can't answer the question with a name, and that is a person they could help.

Even if we have only a little to give—like that single parent with only a little flour and oil—remember that "compound interest" factor that shows up again here in Scripture. Here a starving prophet asks for a small glass of water and then for a small piece of bread to eat. But to meet the needs of this stranger, a poor widow has to make a choice. Take from what meager resources she has and give part of that little away, or keep it all for a last meal.

This widow chose wisely because there was a promise attached to her act of faith. "For thus says the LORD God of Israel, 'The bowl of flour shall not be exhausted, nor shall the jar of oil be empty, until the day that the LORD sends rain on the face of the earth'" (v. 14).

Give a little, and God will give back enough and more. Which is a wonderful principle for each of us to realize and apply to our lives today and every day.

When my wife and I were first married and I was a youth pastor making all that "good money," even with both of us working, we could barely pay the bills. That's why we started tithing from the first day of our marriage, out of our first, very meager paychecks. God owns it all after all, which isn't at question. But it is truly hard to let go of even a small amount when all we have is a little. Yet God rewards that kind of faith.

I know people today with great resources who have never given of their time, or talents, or finances to love or serve the Lord or others, and 99.9 percent of the time, there's a reason. They never started giving, being generous, when they had little, so they don't give today when they have much. Perhaps they didn't know that if they had given even a little when all they had was a little, they would have found gratefulness, which leads to wholeness, which leads to generosity, and all of which lead away from greed. Lord, make me a giver today, even if I don't have much to give.

> *Dear Lord of our "little,"*
>
> *I'll admit I'm greedy, oh Lord. I like to hold on to what I have, and it makes no sense to give up a little when I only have a little. But whether it's a little time, or talent, or money, or whatever you have given us, it makes spiritual sense to share. And Lord, in the process, may you make me more grateful, more whole, and even more generous because I'm giving from a heart and life filled up to fullness with you. Amen.*

FAITHFUL IN A LITTLE

"He who is faithful in a very little thing is faithful also in much; and he who is unrighteous in a very little thing is unrighteous also in much." (Luke 16:10)

Jesus never set out to win a popularity contest. That's particularly true with the Pharisees who were the ones who first heard these words. In part it's because he doesn't hesitate to point right to where it hurts or right to where people were hurting others.

The Pharisees were experts in the law, and like lawyers today, they knew that if there were laws, there were loopholes. For example, they took the command to "honor your father and mother" to mean that if they just said those words verbally, then they were free from having to provide financially for their aging parents. "I honor you, now get out of my house" could have been a Pharisee saying. However, Jesus slams them for such nitpicking when it comes to trying to get out of loving and serving their parents, and he slams them here by pointing out another important spiritual truth.

Being faithful in the small things leads to being faithful with much, while cheating or being unfaithful with small things leads to larger acts of faithlessness. There's that "compound interest" equation again, this time from the Lord Jesus; and if you read the Gospel of Luke, you'll see that Jesus' words infuriated the Pharisees. They were experts at cutting corners, making a little on the side here and a little more on the side there.

Jesus says be faithful in a little and the same thing will be true when you have a lot. You can't miss it. It's the small things again that count—or will count against us.

Dear God of faithfulness,

Lord, we all have a faithful friend who followed through on something for us. We love that person more, appreciate him or her more, because they followed through, finished the task, helped us in small or large ways. Lord, we want to be faithful. Faithful in doing the small things, not just the big things. And ever aware that small acts of cheating or cutting corners link us with the Pharisees who opposed you—not with you. Amen.

It Doesn't Take Much to Ruin It All

A little leaven leavens the whole lump of dough. (Gal. 5:9)

It's so easy to think that just one small act, one small decision, one small choice won't lead to major problems. Like when I skipped reading the instructions before doing my first oil change. I was newly married and wanting to show Cindy that I could be "Tim the tool man." So I went next door to borrow some tools and changed the oil myself for the first time.

If I do say so myself, I thought I did a great job. I crawled under the engine, unscrewed the large bolt I saw on the bottom, and then drained out all that red oil. Of course since I'd drained out all that "oil," I was sure I needed to add another seven or eight quarts to the engine. Probably few of you are surprised that the next morning on our way to church I burned out first the transmission and then the engine (which you probably already guessed was inevitable since I had drained out all the red transmission fluid and put in twice the recommended amount of oil).

In my case, a small step of stupidity on my part ruined the whole engine. In our spiritual life, Galatians tells us a small choice to sin can have great consequences. It can act like leaven and affect the whole lump. Like Brian's choice to celebrate his graduation from college by getting high with his friends—for the first time. What Brian didn't know was that "one time" caused a severe drug reaction that led to a stroke. Four days later his grieving parents made the heart-wrenching decision to turn off the life-support machine.

It doesn't take much leaven to permeate the whole loaf—or for small things to lead us forward or backward. May we pick the positive small things that lead to life.

Dear Jesus,

It's been nearly a week, and here I am again, praying about the small things. But it's so hard to think that one cigarette really shortens life or one stupid choice to cheat or steal can really affect everything. But it can, and it does, and it's something we ask you to remind us about often. Lord, may the "leaven" in our life be the small acts of kindness and love and faith, not the small acts of evil or anger or lust that can ruin everything. Amen.

Imagine if Joseph Hadn't Been Kind to Those in Jail with Him

When Joseph came to them in the morning and observed them, behold, they were dejected.

He asked Pharaoh's officials who were with him in confinement in his master's house, "Why are your faces so sad today?" (Gen. 40:6–7)

Can you imagine what would have happened if Joseph hadn't taken an interest in those he was serving time with in prison? If he had focused all his energy on hating his brothers who unjustly sold him into slavery, or on hating Potipher's wife for unjustly having him thrown in the jail, he wouldn't have noticed or cared about two discouraged cell mates. But Joseph doesn't waste his time on hating, or revenge, or bitterness, or the past. He's present when he sees his cell mates, and he can see that they're down and discouraged.

It was Joseph's interpretation of the cup bearer's dream that would lead to that man's mentioning what happened to Pharaoh, and from there, finally to freedom for him and a place of refuge for the nation. But Joseph standing before Pharaoh actually started with such a small thing. Noticing someone else who was hurting, even when Joseph is in prison himself. What a model for being alert and aware and for noticing the small things around us.

Dear Lord of the busy,

Lord, that old booklet "Tyranny of the Urgent" has such a powerful message for us today. We're so busy, so consumed, so much in a rush. And Lord, on top of that, we carry so many hurts, and so many of us aren't where we want to be. But remind us of Joseph. He had tasks and chores to do in a place he didn't want to be, but he still noticed the small things like a friend's fallen countenance. Lord, make us like you— sensitive to the needs of others around us. For your name's sake and purposes. Amen.

WHEN PEOPLE REACH OUT TO US IN SMALL WAYS

And a woman who had been suffering from a hemorrhage for twelve years, came up behind Him and touched the fringe of His cloak;

for she was saying to herself, "If I only touch His garment, I will get well."

But Jesus turning and seeing her said, "Daughter, take courage; your faith has made you well." At once the woman was made well. (Matt. 9:20–22)

We saw how Joseph noticed something small, the downcast glance of two cell mates. Today we can look at Jesus, who took sensitivity to another level. Here's a poor woman, afflicted for years with a bleeding problem, and she reaches out to him—just to touch the hem of his garment. She's afraid, so she waits until Jesus is in a crowd of people before reaching out, but Jesus notices and feels her gentle touch immediately.

I hope that encourages you today in a tremendous way. While we can and should be like Jesus in looking for small ways to help and care for others, when *we* need help, Jesus notices even the smallest cry of our heart or smallest move toward him.

Jesus never chooses the crowd over individual needs and is there to meet them. What a tremendous truth to chew on today!

Dear Lord who sees our needs and hurts,

We don't need many words to describe what took place with that poor, hurting woman. She was scared, and hurting, and embarrassed to come to Jesus for help. She certainly wasn't the "come down front" type. But she did have the faith to reach out, and he knew it—felt it—in the midst of a crowd. Lord, thank you that you're never too busy, too rushed or "crowded" by other needs, not to notice when we reach out for help. Even the small touch you sense, and we thank you and love you for that. Amen.

It's Not Just Big Things That Bring Down Giants

He took his stick in his hand and chose for himself five smooth stones from the brook, and put them in the shepherd's bag which he had, even in his pouch, and his sling was in his hand; and he approached the Philistine. (1 Sam. 17:40)

I don't know about you, but if I were going up against a giant, I'd want as much armor and artillery as I could get my hands on. (Plus lots of other people!) David had to fight this giant alone, and that's why Saul piled on layers of metal and leather armor. But David opted for another way to bring down the Philistine. He chose small things—five small, smooth stones—and ultimately only one of the five, as his weapon of choice against Goliath.

Size can be deceiving. We've all seen pictures of the mushroom clouds that swallowed up Hiroshima and Nagasaki. That devastating blow came by splitting a minute atom. In the same way, energy focused down to a laser beam is used to bring down a speeding missile. David used one small stone to bring down a giant. And there's an application here for the giants we face as well.

A book like this isn't written in one day. It's finished in small steps, one paragraph at a time. Getting out of debt doesn't happen overnight for most people, but with small steps and small choices to cut spending and start saving. And when it comes to facing whatever "giant" we're up against—anger, lust, broken relationships, spiritual lethargy—the best way to ensure victory is to choose small things, like five smooth stones.

Dear Lord of all courage and strengths,

Thank you, Lord, that you can help us topple giants of anger, or lust, or debt, or indifference, or sloth, or guilt, or whatever Goliath we're facing. There were certainly doubters that day when David stepped out against Goliath, but it didn't take a hundred pounds of armor, only one small stone. Lord, help me take the small steps each day that can bring down that giant. And I'll be careful to give you all the glory when it one day falls. Amen.

FAITH LETS US SEE SMALL THINGS THAT SIGNAL GREAT CHANGES

It came about at the seventh time, that he said, "Behold, a cloud as small as a man's hand is coming up from the sea." And he [Elijah] said, "Go up, say to Ahab, 'Prepare your chariot and go down, so that the heavy shower does not stop you.'"

In a little while the sky grew black with clouds and wind, and there was a heavy shower. (1 Kings 18:44–45)

Elijah the prophet had just finished defeating the prophets of Baal on Mount Carmel in a dramatic display of the God of Israel's strength, power, and presence. Now God will do something else to show his presence to his people. He will send rain clouds to a parched land.

That's what you see here. Almighty God had already told Elijah that once he showed himself to the wicked King Ahab, he would bring rain back to the land. Elijah had God's word on it. So Elijah shows himself to Ahab, and the dramatic confrontation with the king and 450 of his prophets of Baal takes place on Mount Carmel. The score at the end of that great challenge: God and Elijah, one; Baal, zero.

Now Elijah buries his head in his knees on that same Mount Carmel and prays that God will open up the heavens. Remember, he already has God's word on it, and he has seen God work in miraculous ways on that mountaintop. So while he prays, seven times he sends his servant to go face toward the ocean and look for rain clouds.

If you live in Seattle, spotting a cloud would be a slam dunk almost any time of year. But in ancient Israel, God had locked up the heavens for *years*. Severe drought conditions were everywhere, and rain clouds were on the endangered species list. But God has already spoken, so

Elijah takes his word to the bank. Six times he sends his servant to look for evidence of a storm while he prays, and you read what happened the seventh time. His servant sees a single cloud "as small as a man's hand" coming toward him. What is Elijah's response?

There's no waiting to see if it's real, but instead he sends his servant to Ahab to tell him that a downpour is coming. And what, exactly, does that have to do with making 2 Degree Changes?

Elijah didn't see God's hand just in big things, like when fire fell out of the sky earlier as he stood on Mount Carmel. He's able, in faith, to believe the small evidences of God's presence and promises—like seeing a small cloud, far away, and believing in full faith that the rain Almighty God promised is on its way.

In the book of Hebrews, we're told, "Now faith is the assurance of things hoped for, the assurance of things not seen" (11:1). It's hard to wait for anything, especially when life gets dry and dusty. But when Elijah sees that small cloud, he doesn't have to wait until he's soaked to believe God delivers on his promises. He gets moving when he sees the first small cloud that announces a storm he can't yet see.

Dear God whose Word I can trust,

Thank you, Lord, for giving us so many promises in your Word. That you will never leave us or forsake us. That you'll guide our paths and forgive us of our sins. That you'll make us a new creature. So help us to have the kind of trust that sees the small clouds of change on the horizon, thanks you for them even before the rain pours down, and believes what you've said will happen and is true, including the small changes you make in our life. "For I am confident of this very thing, that He who began a good work in you will perfect it until the day of Christ Jesus" (Phil. 1:6). Amen.

CHAPTER FOURTEEN

The 2 Degree Difference Church and Small Group

A great multitude gathered that day. More than five thousand men alone by biblical accounts. And when Jesus saw them, we're told, he felt compassion for them. He healed their sick, but then he did something else. When the disciples wanted to send them all away to go buy food, Jesus gave them a huge challenge.

"They do not need to go away; you give them something to eat!" (Matt. 14:16).

It's one thing to say that as a solution and quite another for the disciples to pull it off. To provide dinner for this huge crowd would bankrupt the disciples's meager savings account, not to mention the logistical nightmare of going by foot to nearby villages and trying to bring back enough food for such a crowd.

But then the disciples made a wise choice.

Instead of taking out a loan or rushing to various towns for food-stuffs, they went to Jesus with what little they had. It was not much. "We have here only five loaves and two fish"(Matt. 14:17). That's meager rations if it was meant only to feed twelve disciples and Jesus. A few loaves and fish are certainly no match for the appetite of a great multitude. But Jesus stepped into the picture when asked.

He had the disciples gather the crowd into small groups, and then he took their little and made it more than enough. In fact, twelve full baskets of leftovers more than enough, and that's after every man, woman, and child had eaten until they were full.

It's that picture of bringing a little to Jesus and watching what he can do with it to meet needs that I want to camp on in this chapter.

Specifically, I'd like to challenge you to take this idea of making a HeartShift and the 2 Degree Difference and link it with a fellowship you're a part of. Perhaps it's your church, your Sunday school class, a small group you're a part of, or a men's or women's study.

For three weeks I'd like to urge you to give your large or small group some teaching and training on what it means to make a HeartShift. Then ask them to pick one area in their life that needs work, and for thirty days commit to making small 2 Degree Changes in that specific area. Then on a forth and final week, it's time to call for a celebration to share what God has done with the little we've brought before him.

Sound interesting?

You can contact us directly at the StrongFamilies office to find out more information about involving your church, ministry, or small group or class (StrongFamilies.com, 4718 E. Cactus Road, #208, Phoenix, AZ 85032, 480-922-8640) or visit www.HeartShift.com.

Here are some suggestions to help you get started.

A HeartShift Church

Imagine a three-week teaching or preaching series based on this book. Actually, you don't have to imagine. All you have to do is look at the end of the book and in appendix B find three outlines for three sermons based on chapters in this book.

You can certainly do your own messages and weave in your own stories, thoughts, and favorite verses, but feel free to use these sermons or teaching session outlines as a jump-start in the process.

You'll notice these three sermons follow three key teaching points in this book. The first message talks about waking up one day, miles from where we want to be, and how even God's people can get off course. The second sermon explains that now, perhaps more than ever, we need to make a HeartShift, turn around, and get pointed in the right direction. And the third talk is about how the small things and small steps toward God's best in whatever area—2 Degree Changes—will help us succeed in the change process. It's giving them a highlight film of the things you've learned so far.

That's three messages, given to a congregation or large or small group, that end with a challenge. On that third worship or teaching time, hand out to them a HeartShift memorial marker certificate.

(Yes, you have permission to go online at www.HeartShift.com, download the certificate, and print as many as you need of that one page for your congregation or group.) Ask them prayerfully to fill out one area in their life they need to work on. (Remember to tell them that if they can't think of a single area to work on in their life or most important relationships, then they need to pick lying!) With that one focal point picked out, urge them to think about one, two, or three small things they could do to move them closer to the Lord, or their family, or even better health, over the next thirty days. And then have a time of prayerful commitment, praying in faith in advance that the changes we can't see today will be changes that do happen when God takes our little and does his work over the next month.

And how will you know what's happened in people's lives?

Four Sundays or meeting times from that commitment date, I think you're going to be shocked with some of the testimonies. On that morning (or afternoon or evening), if you'll let people share, I wouldn't be surprised that in lives of those who "sat down in small groups" (33 Groups) and made small changes, you'll pick up twelve baskets full of blessings that God has accomplished in their lives. Perhaps you'll hear of a marriage that's stronger today because of the small things done and what God has done as a result. Or a friendship or relationship with a child is repaired or closer because of 2 Degree Changes and what God has done. Or someone will share how in their spiritual life, in only a month of small 2 Degree Difference quiet times or sentence prayers, they moved from distance to closeness with the Lord because they've given Jesus their little and discovered he can do much.

Whatever the area of change, let the people know that there will be a time to thank the Lord for even small victories. I know setting up a celebration time ahead of anyone living out their HeartShift or 2 Degree Changes may sound premature, but it's like Elijah seeing that small cloud on the horizon. Faith always involves the unseen. We're told, "Draw near to God and He will draw near to you" (James 4:8). And while certainly some will be like the sluggard who neglected his fence and vineyard and did not take part, most people will take this seriously, as they should.

And on that day when you hear from those who have seen God work in their life in small ways, then just use music or prayer or praise to thank him for what he can do with our little because of who he is.

And if you would, a few days after your celebration, I'd love it if you would jot a quick e-mail or send a letter letting us know what God has done in your life or the lives of God's people. If you'll do that, we'll thank the Lord with you and pray for those represented by every letter that is sent.

A HEARTSHIFT SMALL GROUP, WOMEN'S MINISTRY, OR SUNDAY SCHOOL CLASS

While you can build a HeartShift challenge into a congregational meeting, it's also a great way to see God work in a smaller group. Just as I suggested above, you can use the messages in appendix B to teach some of the principles of this book, or if you do book studies, then obviously I'd suggest working through *HeartShift* as a group. You can even find a small group study at www.HeartShift.com that takes you through each chapter of the book, or just use the questions at the end of most chapters of this book to form your discussion time. Teach your smaller group the basic principles, then call for a time of personal commitment. And in particular, urge them to do what Jesus did and have the people sit down in small groups, what we've called 33 Groups in this book. Then come up with doable 2 Degree Changes toward one specific HeartShift area that needs change. And thirty days later, make your meeting time an opportunity to see what God has done with your little.

One more encouragement for small groups, or for large groups that break into small groups, is to read appendix A. There you'll find some additional pointers on having a successful small group time.

We've looked at small ways of strengthening your spiritual life, including starting a 2 Degree Difference quiet time and getting your church or small group to join you in making a HeartShift. Now it's time to look at specific ways to strengthen your friendships, or marriage, or parenting, or grandparenting. Small things can gain for us the compound interest that can begin to change outcomes and move us ever closer to our loved ones.

CHAPTER FIFTEEN

The 2 Degree Difference and a Stronger Marriage

Imagine you're a medical missionary living near the jungles outside Papua, New Guinea. Each day you see people who are in need and hurting, and you offer them the best help you can with the limited equipment you have. Then a small delegation shows up from the States with a gift from your home church—a state-of-the-art X-ray machine.

Imagine the difference in the level of care you could provide hurting people with that single tool. No matter how skilled you are at guessing the injury beneath the surface, it's not hard to picture the tremendous difference it could make to be able to pinpoint a break or stress fracture or tell a strain from a tear.

While it's easy to picture how technology can improve patient care, what does an X-ray machine have to do with building a stronger, closer, more caring marriage?

Actually, you've already taken a relational X-ray!

You already have in hand a powerful way to look beneath the surface and pinpoint positives as well as issues and concerns in your marriage, areas that can predictably block or build closeness. If you haven't guessed by now, you took that relational X-ray when you went online and took your Leading From Your Strengths™ report.

Back in chapter 8, as part of the HeartShift change process, I asked you to go to the Internet, take five to seven minutes to take a short assessment, and then you'd be instantly e-mailed back your own twenty-eight page personalized strengths assessment. (If you borrowed this book from a friend, then one passcode comes with each book. You can, however, either purchase your own book with a passcode, or simply order additional passcodes at www.HeartShift.com.)

How important is it to take your report?

If I were to sit down with you and your spouse for a counseling or relationship coaching session, I'd require you to take this report *before* your first session. That's because it's the best relational X-ray I know of to quickly and accurately help you understand your own and your spouse's God-given strengths. The level of detail and technology behind this "look beneath the surface" tool didn't even exist a few years ago.

Today, thanks to the power of supercomputers and the Internet, it's available 24-7, and it can help you get an extremely valuable picture of yourself and your spouse whether you're in the United States, Europe, or Papua, New Guinea.

TAKING ADVANTAGE OF YOUR RELATIONAL X-RAY

Your online report is invaluable in pinpointing an area to make a HeartShift that scratches right where it itches. Instead of guessing at what will work to bring you closer to your spouse, you can actually see predictable problems as well as reasons for praise. What's more, it provides a tangible, positive discussion tool that can bring healing and wisdom to bear *before* significant differences become a major problem in a relationship. In fact, for my wife Cindy and me, the insights we gained from just such a look became a major turning point in our marriage.

IN MANY WAYS, WE ALL MARRY OPPOSITES

Perhaps the primary reason for mate attraction is that we're so *different* from the other person. Obviously, I'm not talking about gender differences, which can and should attract. Rather, it's the way God so often draws opposites together to complete us.

In emotional, personal, and relational ways, once we can see differences as helpful and complimentary instead of competitive or combative, it's incredible how much ground we gain in our marriage. In many cases, those opposite strengths can be the thing that protects us from mistakes or stops us from making poor decisions.

In every marriage, no matter how compatible we are in our courtship, areas of difference in attitude or approach will surface. When we bump up against these differences, there is a natural push away from our spouse, like two people floating in inner tubes who bump together and then rebound apart.

For wise couples the gap that results when we drift apart should signal the need to make 2 Degree adjustments *back* toward the other person by renewing our commitment and better understanding why we moved apart. That's why seeing our loved one's strengths all tangibly written out in their report and looking at these four predictable areas of conflict becomes such a powerful force for coming back together closer and stronger than ever.

Your online strengths assessment gives you statement after statement that highlights how valuable your loved one is, a great reminder of who they are and what attracted you to them in the first place—particularly if you've begun to see their "strengths" as a weakness. And by understanding those four predictable areas that push most couples apart at times, you can learn how to stay closer or come back together more quickly.

If that all sounds like theory, here's how it applied to my wife Cindy and me, and changed our marriage dramatically for the better.

Cindy and I are different in a number of ways. She's left-handed; I'm right-handed. She's a morning person; I'm a night person. She's a saver; I'm more of a spender. She makes lists; I lose lists. She wants the toilet paper to go off the top of the roll; I just want it to be there!

In short, even though we both shared many things in common when we first met—from our love for the Lord to a lifetime commitment to serving him—what attracted us initially was how different we were. I am good at starting things; Cindy's great at finishing them. I like large groups; Cindy wants to go deeper with a few.

We saw the iceberg tips of these and other differences when we courted and married. But over the years, you begin to realize that these differences are often much wider and more deeply set than you ever thought. In fact, they're often deeply rooted in who we are as a person.

A key insight to building a stronger, more fulfilling marriage is to realize that *time highlights the depth of our differences.*

As these differences push above the surface over time and become more real, then there also comes the potential for increased frustration when our strengths bump up against our spouse's different ways of doing things or making decisions. Those are the same strengths that initially drew us together, yet over time they can become the things that frustrate or irritate us the most!

Wise couples, when pushed apart by differences, look for small 2 Degree ways to continue to value, affirm, understand, and appreciate their loved one. But just do nothing—let a frustrating difference in one area push you 2 Degrees apart from each other—and even the best of couples can easily drift apart.

In fact, it's common for couples who are deeply in love when first married to move from appreciation to frustration, to serious irritation, to major misunderstanding, to separation emotionally if not physically *in a single year*. I see that progression every week in my counseling office. And invariably, as you follow the bread-crumb trail back to where their problems began, it's because they were pushed apart by their natural, God-given strengths, and they never knew how to move back together in a positive way!

But what if you could pinpoint important areas of difference that predictably push two people apart? Differences that, if not worked on and appreciated, can gently lead you further away from each other, down that soft path of indifference to isolation? (And remember, isolation means death—in this case, death of a marriage.)

There is a way to look beneath the surface and see what pushed us apart—and more clearly, how to come back together. When you take your Leading From Your Strengths™ report, it's like two doctors looking *together* at an X-ray, getting an objective (instead of emotionally charged) picture of why you should thank God for your and your spouse's strengths and similarities.

That's because you'll see more clearly why you need that other person who's so different from you to come alongside you and shore up your differences. And if there have been previous hurts, then taking your report helps you see *where* the break occurred and helps you better formulate a 2 Degree Change plan to begin a targeted move closer together.

Isolate the hurt or difference and then put in place a 2 Degree plan to move closer together. That's a great advantage to couples serious about closeness and positive change and who want to have a positive response the next time their differences bump into each other.

Enough promise, let's move to practical application as we dive into those four predictable areas of adjustment.

Pinpointing Four Specific Areas of Difference or Agreement

If you've already read chapter 8, you'll remember that your Leading From Your Strengths™ report highlights four major areas of adjustment. Set aside your adapted graph for right now (which can be a great discussion topic for later) and just focus on your and your spouse's core graph.

Let's begin with the Lion scale.

The Lion scale or continuum deals with how we face the inevitable problems that surface in life and relationships. The higher you score on the Lion scale, the more *aggressively* you'll tend to deal with issues or problems that come up. The lower you score on the Lion scale (i.e., the further below the midline or what we called the "energy line"), the more *passive* or even hesitant you tend to be in dealing with issues and problems that surface.

Think about the incredible benefit of getting to see where the two of you are in this area, not to mention being able to talk about how your natural reaction to problems can cause predictable stress or misunderstanding. If you're a high Lion, you'll tend to see a problem and want to pick it up and solve it now! If your spouse is a low Lion, then when a problem surfaces, you'll see them backing or even running away from it!

If you and your spouse are forty or more points apart from each other on the Lion scale, that's a significant difference. At the end of this chapter, you'll have a chance to talk through this area of predictable conflict in an honoring, helpful way, just as my wife and I did.

How Do You Look at People?

Then there's the Otter scale on your core graph. What your report pinpoints here is how you typically tend to interact with people, *in particular with new people or new information brought by those people.* The higher you score on the Otter scale, the more trusting you naturally tend to be of new people and information. The lower you score on the Otter scale, the more skeptical you'll tend to be of new people or information.

Let me give you a picture of how important just the ability to pinpoint where you and your spouse are on the Lion and Otter scales can be by looking at an example from my marriage. It's actually a costly mistake I made several years ago that was a direct result of me using my strengths to an extreme and, unfortunately, not taking into account my wife's God-given strengths.

Before I share the story, as a point of reference, here's my wife and my core scores on the Lion and Otter scales, overlaid with each other.

As you can see, going back to the Lion scale, I'm pretty high up on that continuum, meaning I tend to deal with problems aggressively instead of passively. On top of that, I'm at 100 on the Otter scale. (My wife says I'm probably higher, but the report only goes up to 100!) In short, I'm a party waiting to happen, and new people are just friends I haven't met yet!

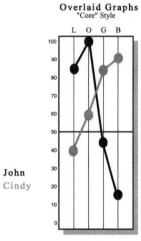

Overlaid Graphs
"Core" Style

John
Cindy

Put those two characteristics together (high Lion and high Otter), and I'm aggressively *trusting* as well, which proved to be a terrible problem when, without Cindy, I sat down with an ex-FBI agent who was now a fledgling financial planner.

This man and I met for the first time at a breakfast at a local restaurant where it seemed like half our church went for breakfast meetings every morning. In other words, I felt safe there and was impressed that he claimed to know the Lord and had years of service in the FBI. What I didn't know and didn't ask about was his skill level in picking safe investments. Failing to do so would soon prove extremely costly.

I met with this man because Cindy had given me an assignment. We needed to transfer one of her IRA accounts from Arizona to Texas now that we'd moved, and we didn't know any financial advisors in Texas. That was a problem. I'm good at aggressively jumping on problems, so I quickly surfaced a name from a new friend, set up a breakfast meeting with the ex-FBI agent, and before the check came that morning, I'd not only heard about a "can't miss" growth opportunity for Cindy, I'd signed the papers!

My natural Lion strengths to "solve this problem now" linked with my Otter "This guy must be trustworthy; he worked for the government!" trusting strengths and led me to sign up right then for his can't-miss offering. *Boy, will Cindy be proud of me!* I thought as I left the table.

Did I ask the hard questions at that breakfast? Did I insist on seeing a detailed prospectus to read carefully before investing any money? Did I spend time with Cindy talking through all the pros and cons of such an investment and how it fit with our short- and long-term goals? Did I tell this man that Cindy and I always pray before making any kind of major investment in anything? If I had done any of those things, then I wouldn't have made such a colossal mess of things. I spontaneously invested her entire IRA into a natural gas and oil partnership and lost every cent of Cindy's money *in less than six months.*

Think about that. She had given me six *years* of weekly paycheck deductions from her long hours as a teacher to invest wisely, and I'd erased every cent in a few months. At that breakfast it would have been more redeeming if I had just left Cindy's money on the table for the waiter rather then throwing it into that "can't miss" investment/boondoggle!

As Cindy and I talked and worked through the emotional aftermath of my losing several thousand dollars, something instantly became apparent. I had used my strengths to get connected to a new person and deal quickly with a problem, but by not factoring in Cindy's strengths of slowing things down, asking hard questions, and being skeptical about financial promises, I'd gone in with my right flank unprotected! Think about how her natural strengths would have protected my weaknesses!

I'm ashamed to say that it wasn't until *after* we'd lost the funds that it dawned on me what a treasure I had in my own house! In solving a complicated problem in a simple, quick, unprocessed way (typical of Lions), I *caused* more problems than I solved. And yet as bad as things were, that loss led to a major breakthrough in our marriage.

After that traumatic event, Cindy and I took the first draft of the instrument you've taken that is now the Leading From Your Strengths™ report. That was the first time we saw objectively and clearly each other's strengths and had a safe platform for talking about our differences.

In spite of all the emotion that surrounded my losing her IRA funds, that early-generation relational X-ray actually provided a way for us to go beneath the surface, to see and understand and value each other more than ever, and to talk about what we could do as a couple to keep something like that from ever happening again.

While it's obvious to us now, before we took that test, we were beginning to wonder why the Lord had put the two of us together. Not that there were any thoughts of separation, but we were so different. After only one year of marriage, it seemed like all we were doing was bumping up against each other's differences.

For us, a breakthrough in our marriage happened after taking the report and being able objectively to see each other's natural, God-given strengths. All of a sudden, it was obvious why Cindy was my helpmate (someone who makes up or helps come alongside what is missing). And she needed my strengths as well and saw them more clearly.

Like scales or blinders falling off, I could see that if Cindy had been at that table with me that morning, her low Lion reluctance to signing any papers that morning would have saved us a terrible loss. Her more naturally skeptical, lower Otter strengths would have led her to say at breakfast something like, "I'm not so sure. Who are some people you've worked with for more than five years that we can talk to about your financial advice?"

Cindy and I learned so much from the early paper-and-pencil version of the online assessment you took, it changed our marriage dramatically. Today, we still take the Leading From Your Strengths™ report every year as a way to remind us of why God brought us together and to see areas in which we've changed or grown.

If you haven't taken your relational X-ray yet, then put down the book, go online, and do it right now. You won't regret going deeper, seeing both the healthy connection points and predictable areas of frustration in your marriage—like those that come from the third predictable area of adjustment.

Facing Up to the Pace You'd Like Life to Go

We've looked at the Lion and Otter scales. The higher you scored on the Golden Retriever scale of your online report, the more you'd prefer life and decisions to go slowly. That doesn't mean that your *life* is slow (we're all busy today) but that you would prefer time for gathering facts, thinking through the ramification of decisions or actions, and interacting with other.

The lower you are on the Golden Retriever scale, the faster you prefer the pace of life to go. These are the kinds of people who don't need to go slow to get all the facts. They just say, "There's water down there. It's got to be deep enough. I'm jumping!" If you'll think of my investing and losing Cindy's retirement funds, it's no wonder I acted the way I did with my aggressive (high Lion) trusting (high Otter) and fast (low Golden Retriever) strengths.

At the end of this chapter, you'll be able to talk through this area in a helpful, positive way. Just like facing problems or being trusting or skeptical with people, this area of the pace of life has huge ramifications. For example, just think of the average weekend with a couple at either extreme. He's worked all week so that in his mind he can stay home and do nothing with just the two of them. She's worked all week so she can invite four couples over for a game night without telling him, and the next day she's already scheduled a day hike with four other couples she forgot to tell him about!

Getting on the same page when it comes to pace can be crucial for long-term commitment and compatibility. It's not that we have to *be* the other person. It's not God's design that we marry ourselves. But out of love and honor and respect for the other person, we can make small changes, 2 Degree shifts, that move us closer to our loved one's natural pace. In our marriage I'm learning to slow down, and Cindy is speeding up.

That's the third of four areas your online report highlights. The forth is tied in with the Beaver scale, and it also provides crucial insights for those serious about closeness.

Do You Prefer Rules or Risk?

The fourth area of predictable adjustments that can push us apart in a marriage is highlighted in the Beaver continuum. If you're at the top of the Beaver scale, then your natural strengths would want to ask things like, "How has someone else done this?" or "Is there a manual for this?" In short, it's our natural desire to want predictable procedures. For high Beavers, life simply works better if there's a rule book to follow, and better still if we can ask someone how they've done it. Having standard procedures for a high Beaver person is like having a safe base to run to in a game of tag. People and things may be whizzing around, but those rules give a sense of rest in the rush that Beavers relish.

In short, high Beavers don't have to be the first one to drive their car out on the lake to prove the ice is thick enough to hold the weight. However, if the ice is certified by the state as thick enough, they just might do it—if they see a semi-truck go across before them!

Of course, other people are low on the Beaver scale. These people are the risk takers in life. If they're low enough on this Beaver scale, they don't need a state inspection before driving out on the lake. They just need gas in their car! And here again, it's patently obvious that understanding where you and your spouse fall on this scale can highlight both positives and predictable negatives. Talking through a difference in rules versus risk, and slowly getting on the same page, can be a huge breakthrough for many couples.

As you might guess, my wife and I are opposites in this area as well. She's an off-the-chart Beaver, while I'm off the chart in the other direction! While taking risks may be beneficial in many settings, it can also combine with your other strengths to lose your wife's entire teacher retirement. And while rules are important, Cindy has learned more and more about God's grace and his unmerited favor that free us from perfectionism or a fear of making mistakes. (High Beavers often have that tendency and fear.)

Those are the four areas of agreement or difference that are highlighted in your online report. With each in mind, here's a discussion exercise for you to complete. At the end, I'll share with you more about small specific 2 Degree Changes that help you move closer together if differences in these areas naturally push you apart.

Marriage Discussion Exercise

Very soon (today or tonight if possible), talk through these four predictable areas of difference, and walk through the questions below. They, along with reading together each other's online report, can be a tremendous help in pinpointing one specific HeartShift area in which to make small 2 Degree Changes over the next three months—before you tackle the next.

Discussion Questions with Your Spouse

1. When it comes to being *aggressive* or *passive* with **problems** . . .
   - On a scale of 1 to 10 (with 10 a great deal and 1 a little or none), how significant a difference and a potential problem do you see this area in our marriage? (Each person answers and gives a reason for the score he or she chose.)
   - If you scored high on the Lion scale on your core graph, complete the following statement and share it out loud with your spouse: "When I see a problem and don't try to solve or 'pick it up' right now, it makes me feel . . ."

- If you scored low on the Lion scale, complete this statement: "When I see a problem and move away from it, it's because . . ."
- Both of you ask this question, beginning with the one who's birthday is closest to Christmas (on either side of the calendar): "Is there something I've done in this area that has pushed you away from me? And if there is, what is one small way I could move us closer together in this area in the future?"

2. When it comes to being *trusting* or *skeptical* of **people** . . .
   - Each of you answer this question: "On a scale of 1 to 10, how significant a difference and a problem is this area for our marriage?"
   - If you scored high on the Otter scale, complete this statement: "I think being trusting of others comes naturally to me because . . ."
   - If you scored low on the Otter scale, complete this statement: "I think being skeptical of others comes naturally to me because . . ."
   - Both of you ask this question, beginning with the one who was born the closest to the Empire State Building in New York City: "Is there something I've done in this specific area that has pushed you away from me? And if there is, what is one small way I could move us closer together in this area in the future?"

3. When it comes to wanting the **pace** of life to be *fast* or *slow* . . .
   - Each person answers this question: "On a scale of 1 to 10, how significant a difference and a potential problem is this area for our marriage?"
   - If you scored high on the Golden Retriever scale, describe to your spouse what it feels like inside to have the time to go slow and gather enough facts or information before moving forward on something. (The other person, be a positive, active listener.)
   - If you scored low on the Golden Retriever scale, describe to your spouse why you like things to go fast and what it feels like to have to slow down.
   - Realize that out of the four predictable areas of difference and adjustment, this one can bring incredible relationship rewards when you slowly get on the same page.
   - Both of you ask this question, beginning with the one who had the most siblings (if it's a tie, then the one with the oldest

sibling begins): "Is there something I've done in this area that has pushed you away from me? And if there is, what is one small way I could move us closer together in this area?"

4. When it comes to **procedures** and wanting *rules* or taking *risks* . . .

- Each person answers this question: "On a scale of 1 to 10, how significant a difference and a potential problem is this area for our marriage?"
- If you scored high on the Beaver scale, describe to your spouse how having a rule or instruction book is important in relaxing or freeing you. (Feel free to use your own words. The other person, be a positive, active listener.)
- If you scored low on the Beaver scale, describe to your spouse why you think taking risks, or feeling comfortable without having to follow footsteps in the snow, is such a part of who you are?
- Both of you answer this question, beginning with the youngest of the two of you: "Is there something I've done in this area that has pushed you away from me? And if there is, what is one small way I could move us closer together in this area?"

Using your report to work through these four areas in your marriage can move you closer together and form the basis for making small 2 Degree Changes. Which leads me to a list you may have been waiting for, namely, how *small* are small 2 Degree Changes? Here's a list of a dozen small things couples just like you did in light of what they learned from their online report. Each husband or wife picked an area of concern and then did a small thing that moved them closer to each other.

A DOZEN 2 DEGREE CHANGES FOR COUPLES

1. A fast-paced husband stops his car at a park around the corner from his house. For five minutes he stops and thinks about all the details of his day and then prays specifically that the Lord will "slow him down" before he walks in the door. For thirty days, that daily five-minute cool-down period and time of prayer before he comes in the door at a less hectic pace blesses his slower paced wife.

2. For thirty days a very rule-oriented wife works at saying yes to one thing a day that is not on her list, such as going out to dinner if it wasn't on the calendar or going on an early morning walk with her husband *before* making the bed.

3. A husband who also likes procedures in place decided to use his detail strengths to do something spontaneous. He decided to call his wife at random times once a day for thirty days. Sometimes he'd call right after he got to work, other times after lunch, and other times in the car on the way to work or on the way back home. But once a day, for thirty days he quickly checked in and told her he loved her at the end of every conversation.

4. A high Lion spouse who was always good at solving problems went with his wife to a doctor's appointment. It was just a routine visit, but he could tell his wife genuinely appreciated his company. While it's a small thing, now neither she nor his young daughter has gone to the doctor without him for the past two years, and every time it blesses his wife and child that he'll carve out time for something so small as a checkup (even if he sometimes bothers the doctor!).

5. A fast-paced wife, half Irish and half Italian, knew she was too quick at verbally blowing up at her husband. Every day for thirty days her "Good morning, Lord" prayer was, "Lord, help me to ask three questions before I offer an answer or a reaction." When her husband leaves the car running in the driveway, instead of dramatically yelling at him that someone is going to steal the car, she takes a deep breath and then asks her husband questions like, "Honey, did you know the car's still running in the driveway?" and/or, "Are you heading back out right away?" or anything that asks for *information* before her husband gets her instant reaction. She has worked hard at asking these questions with no sarcasm or edge to her voice. One, two, or three questions with a neutral or positive tone of voice—instead of instantly blowing up.

6. One spouse is skeptical of people and situations, and when he's right about something, he tends to gloat and make sure his wife knows he "called it" and predicted her idea or thought would fail. The HeartShift this husband made was to not gloat for thirty days. Every day he prayed that he wouldn't spit out a single "I told you so!" that day. And no "See, why didn't you listen to me" either! Instead, he linked a memory slogan to his HeartShift: "No to gloating—yes to promoting." To him this was a reminder to praise his wife (or kids) every time they tried something rather than waiting to point out the obvious when something failed.

7. A fast-paced person made her prayer and HeartShift a month of weekends. She realized that their biggest fights were over the weekends,

and it came to her—from reading her report—that she was trying to push way too much into each day. This wife had come from a home where her parents did *nothing* for or with the kids when she grew up, and she had made an internal decision never to be that way. So she pushed, planned, overplanned, and overcommitted—even if the family grumbled or rebelled—until she made a HeartShift. "One thing a day is my HeartShift way," was her reminder. For thirty weekends, she did *less,* and she soon became amazed at how slowing down the pace actually made life less anxious and stressful at home. (And to her amazement, her family actually started asking to do more, instead of being resentful for her pushing!)

8. One husband who was a problem avoider realized that television was becoming his escape valve from talking about small or large issues with his wife. He was often bored with the shows, but he'd still sit there for hours. Until the day he went to a men's meeting and heard he needed to make a HeartShift. So he bought a new 120-minute VCR tape and wrote on the label "HeartShift Tape." Now when this man gets home, he puts the tape in the player, pushes record, and then finds his wife and asks about her day. They're actually having conversations now, even some about certain issues he would have naturally avoided. His wife goes to bed early, so if he decides to stay up, then he's got all the shows he missed on tape—even though after fifteen days, he was *amazed* at how little taped *or* live television he was watching.

9. Another husband was a fast-paced risk taker. His HeartShift was to carry a roll of mint-quality quarters in his pocket each day for thirty days. It wasn't for self-defense but because his quick, reactive nature caused him to interrupt his wife during almost every conversation. While he was skeptical at first, he made this HeartShift decision: every time during the next thirty days, if he interrupted his wife and didn't allow her to finish a complete thought before speaking, he'd pull out a brand-new, uncirculated quarter and hand it to her. That's because he knew, internally, that it was costing him dearly when he kept interrupting his wife so much. At first he was convinced this was only a minor problem, but after he went through two rolls of quarters in the first four days, he experienced a dramatic paradigm shift. He had no idea how pronounced and irritating his interruptions were until it cost him several dollars. When he finally saw it, and how costly it was in all ways, it was like a switch flipped. The first few days, two rolls of quarters.

During the rest of the month, he lost three quarters total until the end of the month. He finally saw and felt it enough to change that irritating habit. (And his wife gave him back all the quarters he'd lost—and a gold coin inside a romantic card. It was her way of thanking him for investing in their relationship and for trying to honor her so much.)

10. One wife was naturally skeptical, a "glass is way less then half full" kind of person. She knew in her heart of hearts that this was an area that was dragging down her optimistic, trusting husband, and it became her HeartShift commitment. Her small 2 Degree Change? *Put a smile in her voice.* She had a friend who did radio commercials and was successful at it. As they talked one day, her friend told her the secret of her professional radio success: "I always have a smile in my voice. Even on the radio, people notice." Without telling her husband (who said he didn't want to read this book or go to church at the time), she decided every day for thirty days to put a smile in her voice. (She even got some coaching from her friend on how she sounded.) After day ten, even though nothing else had dramatically changed, her husband asked her what had happened to her. Two days later when he asked again, she talked about going to a Wednesday night class a her home church where they were studying *HeartShift.* On day twenty-eight of her smiling voice, he went with her to that evening class for the first time. A few months later he went with her to church for the first time.

11. A husband was a definite high-procedure Beaver person. As such, he set incredibly high expectations on himself and others, especially his wife. Convicted upon hearing a HeartShift sermon about the need to make small changes in a specific problem area—and knowing his constant criticism was pushing him and his wife apart—his HeartShift was to turn being judgmental into something *positive* for his wife. This husband went to the local party supply store and purchased thirty blue ribbons (like the kind you award to someone at a field day). He would look for one thing a day he judged to be helpful, or positive, or loving that his wife did, and then he'd present her with a blue ribbon, with his thanks (anything from doing the laundry to talking with him about a problem at work). It was funny the first day, still appreciated the second, and it almost brought tears on day three when he presented her a blue ribbon at the table with some of their friends at dinner. Every day for thirty days he pointed out something positive, and that was after twenty-two years of daily only speaking out about the negative. She

kept every ribbon, and a year later they still talk about what it did for their marriage.

12. Have you heard the old saying "a month of Sundays"? That, obviously, means a long time. However, for this wife with a very fast-paced husband, her HeartShift was to line up thirty "I'm yours for two hours" Tuesdays. This woman knew that for years a problem point in their marriage had been his wanting to do something together. But with three small children, she had neither the time, energy, or strength to drop everything and go do something with just him. They did some family things but next to nothing as a couple—until she was challenged to make a HeartShift. Based on being sixty points different in the pace area (she slow; he fast), she made a commitment. While she wasn't naturally spontaneous, she was a great organizer. (She was also a high Beaver procedure person as well.) So she lined up a babysitter for every Tuesday night for two hours for a month of Tuesdays. Just two hours a week, week after week, to do something small. Like go to the mall, run an errand together, go get yogurt, stop at a local coffee shop that had a jazz band on Tuesdays, or go wash his car. Small things that from start to finish took only two hours (babysitters aren't cheap), but she and he were shocked with how much they reconnected.

That's just a dozen small 2 Degree Changes that sprang from a HeartShift decision from a husband or wife to move closer together. And if you want to see a dozen (and more) examples, just go to www.HeartShift.com, click on the "Marriage" label, and print off this month's list. Or, like the 2 Degree Difference quiet times, we'd love for you to submit a small change that made a difference in your marriage. Same rules: they must come with written permission and not be novels but short examples. And we can't post every one we receive. But who knows? Someday perhaps we'll do an entire book of 2 Degree Changes for couples, and your contribution will be right there to help others committed to making a HeartShift.

You've seen how making a HeartShift in your marriage can lead to small changes that make an ongoing, significant impact. That's also true as a parent, as we'll see in the next chapter.

CHAPTER SIXTEEN

The 2 Degree Difference for Parents and Grandparents

We've looked at how making a HeartShift decision, lived out through making 2 Degree Changes, can renew our spiritual life and strengthen a marriage. Now let's apply these same principles to parents and grandparents, and see how, with our parenting partner and our children, small shifts and changes can lead to close-knit relationships.

GETTING ON THE SAME PAGE AS PARENTS

I was out of town, speaking at a conference. This was several years ago, and Kari, our oldest daughter, was only about five years old. I'd already spoken with my wife and daughter earlier in the day, and this call was to talk to Cindy after she'd put Kari to bed.

"How'd it go putting Kari down?" I asked over the phone.

"Fine, but I did learn something interesting," Cindy said.

When I asked her what this new revelation was, she told me, "I learned that Kari hates me. I was helping her brush her teeth before bed, and when I pulled out two feet of dental floss, Kari just exploded."

As I listened, I could get a mental picture of Cindy following one of our family rules, which was to pull out only two feet of dental floss, (more than enough floss for a child or adult). As she continued, I became more and more uncomfortable.

"Mommy, I can't believe you only let me pull out two feet of dental floss. *Daddy doesn't make me do that.*"

Now I was really hoping that static would spring up on the phone connection.

"Mommy," Kari had said, "I don't like you. In fact, *I hate you.* I like Daddy because Daddy doesn't make me keep the rules."

Anyone for teaching their precious five-year-old to be a major sociopath? Obviously, rules do count, but by my actions in ignoring or even flaunting the dental floss rule, Kari was getting a very wrong mixed message.

Thankfully, that phone call led to a *long* discussion between Cindy and me about a major difference we had in parenting. Namely, as a high Beaver (and an excellent teacher), Cindy knows how important structure is for young children. We did have good rules with the kids that we both had talked about and agreed were important, but Cindy was the only one seriously enforcing them. For me, the two feet of dental floss rule might mean three, or five, or who cares how much dental floss. And I'd communicated that clearly to Kari when it was my turn to floss her teeth.

If you'll think back to the last chapter, then imagine how helpful it would have been for us as parents to be able to take that relational X-ray. It would have pinpointed the major area of adjustment we'd just run up against—Cindy wanting clear procedures and rules, and me being at the low end of that scale. Before I have you work through each of those areas as a parent, I'd like to share another reason for being able to identify an area of adjustment and then crafting a 2 Degree Change to pull you and your parenting partner together. It's not only crucial that parents be on the same page but that we also understand our own and our child's strengths.

The Breakthrough Day
the Egg Timer Disappeared

Cindy and I have a friend who is a major real estate salesperson. She's at or near the top in sales every year, and she's a strong Lion/Otter personality. In short, she jumps in, solves the problem of selling a person's house quickly, and then moves on to the next house and the next set of clients.

That same "let's get moving" attitude that has made her so successful as a real estate salesperson was destroying her relationship with her nine-year-old daughter. That's because our friend applied her God-given Lion/Otter strengths to raising her Golden Retriever daughter—with no 2 Degree adjustments—and the results were devastating to their relationship.

Proverbs 22:6 is familiar to many parents: "Train up a child in the way he should go, even when he is old he will not depart from it." That's a general promise that encourages many parents, but here's what it literally says in Hebrew: "Train up a child, *according to their bent.*" When we realize that our child is a unique fingerprint (Ps. 139) and that we're to train them up in a way that factors in their God-given strengths, we work to create an atmosphere that can draw a child back to God's love and our love in the years to come.

Our friend wasn't doing that, and it's not just fathers who have to worry sometimes about exasperating their children (Eph. 6:4). As an example, this mother had her Golden Retriever daughter involved in several different things after school. (High Golden Retrievers typically like to do a few things rather than many things.) This mother knew the schedule was tight to get everything in, so she did what worked for her. Meaning, she set a deadline.

Out came the egg timer, and it would be placed next to her daughter. Then the mother would thunder, "OK, you've got thirty minutes to do your homework, and then we've got to get to soccer (or dance, or the tutor). Let's get going!"

That kind of loud, ticking countdown would motivate most Lions. They'd start racing the clock, saying internally, *I can do it! I can beat that timer!* But put Golden Retrievers under intense time pressure, and watch them slow down. They want to do things right and please their parent or teacher, and now they're being rushed to crank out a formula or paper, and they panic inside and go slower, not faster. It's not just a timer sitting next to them, it's a time bomb. And sure enough, when the bell went off and this young nine-year-old had only half her assignments done, her mother would say she was being defiant! They needed to get going, and her daughter was holding up the real estate closing!

After talking with this mother and hearing her problem with her child, I had her and her child take the Leading From Your Strengths™ report (nine is one year younger than we normally suggest a child take the report; however, the daughter was an excellent reader). As this mother finally saw *objectively* how different she was from her daughter, and as she read page after page about her daughter's strengths of wanting to go slow and needing to ask questions, lightbulb after lightbulb went on.

No wonder they were at war so often! She'd been training up her daughter in the way *she* wanted to go, not even close to a way that honored her daughter's God-given bent.

And that's when this Lion mother walked in and apologized to her daughter and put away the egg timer for good. That nine-year-old is now thirteen years old. She may not be involved in as many things (down to two from five or six), but her grades, her attitude, the quality of her piano and volleyball skills, and her relationship with her mother are right up there at the top of kids and parents her age. All because a wise parent realized that understanding her own strengths *and those of her daughter* could provide a framework for small, specific, positive changes.

Which brings me to you as a parent.

Whether you're a grandparent or noncustodial parent and have your grandchildren or children only occasionally, or if you're a grandparent or parent who's with the kids every day, it's crucial to get on the same page with your fellow caregivers for that child. Not doing so risks having "dental floss" stories of your own that reflect confusion and anger for the child and frustration for the parents who aren't on the same page. You also need to factor in your child's strengths over and against your own. That's key to training them up in the way they should go and building a positive short- and long-term relationship with them as well.

With that in mind, take time to work through the following questions with your fellow parents about your child.

An Important Discussion for Parents and Grandparents

Before we look at 2 Degree Changes to make you a more effective parent, it's crucial to see God's handiwork in your life, in the life of your spouse (or other caregiver), and especially in the life of your child. And one very helpful way of doing just that is working through those four major areas of adjustment, focusing on your role and natural gifting as a parent.

First, on the blank "core" graph at the top of the next page (if your child isn't old enough to take their own report or you choose for them not to), together mark where you think your child would fall on each of the four scales. Then answer this question:

"Are there any 'alarm clock' type issues we're facing with our son or daughter that tie directly into our strengths and theirs being very

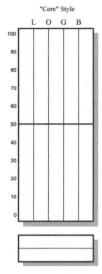

"Core" Style

L   O   G   B

different?" If the answer is yes, take some time to talk through your thoughts about how you could still be the spiritual and relational trainers in your home you're called to be—yet do so in a way that takes into account that child's unique strengths.

As parents, to make sure you're on the same "page," answer the following questions:
1. When it comes to being *aggressive* or *passive* with **problems** . . .

• On a scale of 1 to 10 (with 10 being a great deal and 1 a little or none), how significant a difference and a potential problem do you see this area of adjustment being in how you and your spouse (or other major caregiver, such as a grandparent) parent? (Each person answers and gives a reason for the score they chose.)

• If you scored high on the Lion scale on your core graph, then complete the following statement and share it out loud with your spouse: "When I see a problem situation with our child, I think it's important to . . ."

• If you scored low on the Lion scale, complete this statement, "When I see a problem with our child, I think it's important to . . ."

• Both of you answer this question: "If we're not on the same page as parents when it comes to facing problems, what is one small way we could move closer to each other in this area in the future?" Then both of you come up with one specific area that you think could be a problem in the future (like for Cindy and me, the dental floss area) and talk about how and why things should be different the next time a similar situation comes up.

2. When it comes to being *trusting* or *skeptical* with **people** . . .

• On a 1 to 10 scale, how significant a difference and how much of a potential problem do you see your and your spouse's (or other major caregiver, such as a grandparent) strengths being in this area? (Each person answers and gives a reason for the 1 to 10 score they chose.)

- If you scored high on the Otter scale on your core graph, then complete the following statement and share it out loud with your spouse: "When I see a problem situation with our child, I think it's important to . . ."
- If you scored low on the Otter scale, complete this statement: "When I see a problem with our child, I think it's important to . . ." (If you're in the middle, then still answer the question related to problems or issues that come up.)
- Then both of you answer this question: "If we're not on the same page as parents when it comes to facing problems, what is one small way we could move closer to each other in this area in the future?" Then both of you come up with one specific area that you think could be a problem in the future (like for Cindy and me, the dental floss area) and talk in honor about how and why things should be different the next time a similar situation comes up.

3. When it comes to preferring to go fast or slow in terms of the **Pace** of life . . .

- On a scale of 1 to 10, how significant a difference and a potential problem do you see this area of adjustment being in how you and your spouse (or other major caregiver, such as a grandparent) parent? (Each person answers and gives a reason for the score they chose.)
- If you scored high on the Golden Retriever scale on your core graph, then complete the following statement and share it out loud with your spouse: "As a parent, I think the way we're handling the pace of life issues is . . ." (good, bad, slanted one way or the other, hugely problematic, a minor issue).
- If you scored low on the Golden Retriever scale, complete the same statement: "As a parent, I think the way we're handling pace of life issues is . . ."
- Both of you answer this question: "If we're not on the same page when it comes to the pace of life, what is one small way we could move closer to each other in this area in the future?" Then both of you come up with one specific area that you think could be a problem in the future (like for Cindy and me, the dental floss area) and talk about how and why things should be different the next time a similar situation comes up.

4. When it comes to wanting *rules* or taking *risks* when it comes to procedures . . .

- On a scale of 1 to 10, how significant a difference and a potential problem do you see this area of adjustment being in how you and your spouse (or other major caregiver, such as a grandparent) parent? (Each person answers and gives a reason for the score they chose.)

- If you scored high on the Beaver scale on your core graph, then complete the following statement and share it out loud with your spouse: "Rules are important to me as a parent because . . ."

- If you scored low on the Beaver scale, complete this statement: "I think the reason I'm not naturally as tuned into encouraging the kids to keep rules is . . ."

- Both of you answer this question: "If we're not on the same page as parents when it comes to having an agreed-upon procedure or rule for something, what is one small way we could move closer to each other in this area in the future?" Then both of you come up with one specific area that you think could be a problem in the future (like for Cindy and me, the dental floss area) and talk in honor about how and why things should be different the next time a similar situation comes up.

A Dozen 2 Degree Difference Examples for Parents and Grandparents Who Want to Be on the Same Page

1. One husband and wife were on different pages when it came to problems. For him, problems didn't exist; for her, they needed to be dealt with immediately. This was becoming a major source of irritation for the two of them, so their HeartShift decision was to get closer as parents in this area. As a small 2 Degree Change, the husband bought a small, ruled-lined, notebook. This notebook became their discussion pad. His wife wrote notes during the day that highlighted issues or problems she felt they needed to talk through. If his wife was feeling an issue wasn't getting addressed, she wrote it down in the notebook. Then for thirty days, after the kids were finally asleep, her husband would ask, "Is there something in the book we need to talk about."

That did two things for this couple. First, it kept the wife from blowing up when her husband hit the door because she had so much to say about a problem. (And it kept him from coming home later or trying to avoid talking to her because she was so dramatic.) And it allowed her husband to talk about a situation in a positive way and to feel better prepared to step into an issue that had been talked through. What amazed them both was how every day, day after day for three weeks, she had an issue to talk to him about. And then the writing seemed to stop except for an occasional note. (Picture a cup finally being filled up—in this case with his involvement in talking about issues with his wife.)

2. Another couple had a great deal of problems in the *trusting* and *skeptical* Otter area of adjustment. In a nutshell, the wife didn't like or trust her husband's family. None of his relatives were believers, and his brother allowed their small children to watch R-rated movies at an early age (nightmares and all), and do other age-inappropriate things.

If you've faced a similar situation, it's like walking in a minefield. Go one way and your spouse gets mad at you; go the other and your extended family gets angry with you. So instead of letting this situation become a gaping wound in their relationship (him wanting his son to play with his cousins and her wanting to protect the child from different lifestyle choices), they made a HeartShift decision as a couple. And after making their decision, the 2 Degree action that they committed to for thirty days was that their son could see the cousins once a week, but never without one of them there—no exceptions. And they added one more thing. Every night for thirty nights they would pray together before they went to bed for the brother's family to come to faith. This relaxed the mother enough to let the son see his cousins and opened the husband's eyes to realize that appropriate boundaries need to be set for an innocent child. Praying together kept their focus on making these decisions in a positive, God-honoring way, not reacting to them out of fear or anger.

3. One 2 Degree Change that a Beaver mom made came when she and her husband talked and turned their living room into Kid Heaven. This came about because of the wife's struggle with the kids messing up the house and feeling that her husband didn't help or care or support her desire to keep things clean and in place. As they talked and prayed, they made a HeartShift decision to work on this specific frustration. The small 2 Degree solution? They purchased a long, portable gate that turned the unused living room into Kid Heaven. They sat the kids down

and told them that the rules were different in Kid Heaven. They didn't have to keep that room as clean as the rest of the house (messes were OK within reason), and it gave them a place to romp and not have to worry about breaking or destroying anything. But once they left Kid Heaven, they met a united front (finally) about the importance of keeping their rooms and the rest of the house clean and picked up. This HeartShift decision not only taught their children a valuable lesson about play and work areas, but when the husband took seriously these changes that meant so much to his wife, it made a huge difference in the level of closeness in their relationship.

4. Another high Beaver parent often complained that his high Otter wife was going too much, doing too much, and spending too much. After seeing each other's strengths and his seeing her genuine need for a fast pace and people, he came up with the idea of a Party for Five every week. With his full support, four other moms with younger children brought their kids over to their house once a week for a craft and play time. At other times they'd go on short field trips or to the mall. Instead of being and staying on opposite pages, the wife slowed down the need to go and spend every day, and the husband actively encouraged her to take part in fun Otter times.

5. The HeartShift for one couple was their decision to get on the same page when it came to being the spiritual trainers in their home. Neither one had really done more then just take their children to church, thinking, "Let the experts train them." But in reading God's Word, they couldn't get away from the fact that the parents should "train up" their children. So their 2 Degree Difference was to carve out five minutes every night for a bedtime blessing with their children. In that short time they read a verse or a short story at bedtime (with all of them on their child's bed), and then they closed the night with a prayer and a hug. A short verse, short prayer, and quick hug before bed. Just that small investment in time, and soon they saw those bedtime blessings becoming the times they looked forward to each day.

6. One set of parents are *both* fast-paced Lion parents. But their HeartShift to be more connected with each other and their daughter was to make her their hero. They would pick a child's book, like one of the Chronicles of Narnia or *The Treasure Tree,* and then they'd pick a heroic character in the book. Every time that character's name came up when they read her the story each night, they'd substitute their

daughter's name for that heroic character. Instead of Lucy in Chronicles, they read their daughter's name. Instead of Lance in *The Treasure Tree,* they read their daughter's name. We did this with our daughters, and it's a small way not only to link them to a story but also to put them inside roles that do great things for the Lord or others.

7. Yet another couple who were similar in their God-given strengths (both Golden Retrievers) decided to use pictures to talk to their child. Once a day for thirty days they had their six-year-old son pick out a picture at dinner to use to describe his day. Before dinner they had cut out lots and lots of pictures from old magazines: boats, trains, cowboys, sunsets, waterfalls, submarines, snakes—more than two dozen pictures. Then to connect with their son, model engagement, and help him learn to open up, each person at the table had to pick one of the pictures on the table that described his or her day. I've heard of other families who have done this just by saying, "high/low" before they can leave the dinner table. In other words, tell one high point and one low point about their day. Both are small ways to connect and train our children to open up.

8. A frustrated Lion parent couldn't understand why every question to her junior high child was met with a one-word answer. So a 2 Degree Change this parent started for thirty days was to ask "twenty questions." It was only a ten-minute drive from school back home, but once she picked up her son, her goal was to ask twenty questions before they got home. She rarely got past seven or eight (but it also took at least that many). That's because after, *"What did you do in PACT?"* Nothing. *"What did you have for lunch today?"* Same stuff. *"What happened in practice that was exciting?"* Nothing. *"Did anyone get in trouble today at school and why?"* Finally, instead of a one-word response, a question would hit a nerve from her son's day, and they would be off and talking. That small decision to keep asking questions until she got home built a safe place for her son to open up, and for her those mother-son talks helped her feel that she had a window into his school world.

9. Similar to a husband in the previous chapter who bought the VCR tape and wrote *HeartShift* on the label, this single parent used his VCR as a parenting lifesaving device. Instead of worrying about what he was missing on the television, he felt free to help with homework or housework, knowing he wasn't missing a thing. (And he discovered he could even fast-forward through the commercials!)

10. While this would be a major HeartShift decision for some families, one couple decided that getting a small, loving dog would be a

great way to teach their child about caring and responsibility in small doses. Their son was to fill the doggie's water dish, and they filled the food dish. Then all of them were responsible for playing with the dog. Dogs are tremendous interruptions from the seriousness of the day and wonderful objects of unconditional love. The daily task of taking care of a puppy became a purposeful tool for connecting as a family and teaching responsibility at the same time.

11. One husband who was high in the Beaver area decided that a small way to connect with his son was to keep stats for his baseball team. He also decided to take along a digital camera. Then when this father got home, he would download the photos from the camera into the computer, make one click of the mouse, and instantly turn ten digital pictures into a PowerPoint presentation for his son and other team members to see. (Most new computers have digital photo programs like Iphoto built right in that can do this with a single click of a mouse and no knowledge of technology.) Those pictures and keeping stats ("You're second on your team in doubles, son!") became small ways to keep the father from being bored at all the school and club baseball games and practices, but it also became a powerful, memorable connection point for a father and a son.

12. A Lion and a Golden Retriever parent were both worried about their oldest child entering the junior high years. Their HeartShift commitment was to stay connected with that child in a positive way during those tough junior high days. Their small 2 Degree Change to live out that decision was that they would be the bus. Junior high kids still need mom and dad to drive, so these parents made the decision to be the bus in as many situations as they could. Instead of dreading being the ones to drive, they volunteered—even to pick up a friend on the way. Their son could always count on them to be the bus, and they could see who he was with, what he was doing, and even build close relationships with their son's friends. It was a small decision (that cost lots of gas money), but it was worth every mile and every minute they spent chauffeuring their son.

Once again you can visit www.HeartShift.com to find another dozen (and more) small 2 Degree Changes and ideas that gained ground for parents and grandparents. And while small things can make a positive difference in our spiritual life, marriage, and parenting roles, they can also dramatically affect our health.

CHAPTER SEVENTEEN

The 2 Degree Difference and Better Health

There's an old adage that you teach best what you most need to learn.

If that's really true, then this short chapter on making small changes in your health will be the strongest and most helpful in this book! That's because, without a doubt, I feel the least qualified professionally to tackle subjects like diet and exercise. My training has come in the soft sciences (theology and counseling) rather then in chemistry, physiology, or biology. Therefore, I commend to you the many much more qualified nutritionists and physiology experts who have written acres of "get fit" books.

What I can offer you, however, is a simple insight that sprouts up in every row of that acre of better health books. Namely, in a hundred different ways, you'll hear health experts say, "It's the small things" that make all the difference in your health. As an example, an entire shelf of books cries out, "8 Minutes in the Morning" is all it takes for better health. An article in a major running magazine stated, "29 Small Changes for Big Rewards." That's not to mention "One Minute Abs" or the "One Minute Workout" or countless other books on the shelf that stress the need to start slow, start small, but start now.

I'll leave you to figure out which workout on the Fitness Channel will really get you in Navy SEAL shape, but I'll also leave you with my own convictions and encouragement on why making a HeartShift in your health is so important. In fact, taking small steps toward better health can actually help you live out your God-given purpose in a way that may surprise you.

FEAR OF LOSS, DESIRE FOR GAIN, AND THE
WINNER AND STILL CHAMPION—FREEDOM

There was a time several years ago when I pushed and pushed and wound up waking up in a hospital in San Antonio. While I was given a clean bill of health on my release, that was just a physical clean bill of health. I'd also been read the riot act and told that if I didn't back out of some of the stress and add in things like diet and exercise, I'd be back in the hospital, likely in far worse shape.

Whenever we wake up to the fact that we need to make physical changes, there are three major ways to be motivated to make changes. I heard two of them before leaving the hospital. "Don't you want to be around for your family?" is an appeal to our natural desire for gain. Of course the answer is "Yes, I'd love to be around much longer for Cindy and the girls." But I also heard, "If you don't stop pushing so hard, you're going to implode physiologically," which appealed to a second major motivational factor—fear of loss.

To get a better picture of these two primary motivators, let's look at both in turn. First, when it comes to desire for gain, let's say that someone at your office whispers in your ear a "hot stock tip" that is guaranteed to triple your money overnight. Forget about insider trading laws for just a moment. It's possible that the thought of tripling an investment, a desire for gain, might motivate someone actually to go out and buy shares of that stock.

Then there's a second major motivator. In addition to a desire for gain, there's also the fear of loss that motivates us. For example, let's say (even though it would be extremely unwise) that you had put every cent of your savings in one company's stock. That means all your retirement funds and all your rainy-day savings were in a single company's stock. Then from a credible source, you received a warning that the stock was about to drop 95 percent in value the next day. (Does this sound a little like the call Martha Stewart received that got her in so much trouble?) Do you think someone might be motivated to get on the phone and sell the stock while it still had some value? Fear of loss is motivating, even if you already have a great deal of money in the bank.

In the world, those are the two primary ways people are motivated. These same two motivators fill the self-help book section and shout from their covers, "You can look like me if you'll just buy my book!" That's the desire for gain at work. Other books will appeal to our fear of loss. While I couldn't find a book with the specific title *This Is Your Last Chance Diet* on the shelf, that's what many other books stress if you don't immediately go low carb, or high fiber, or modified low carb/high fiber. Change now or take out a prepaid funeral plan.

Fear and greed motivate book sales every day. And they can motivate us at some levels and for short periods of time. But their motivating power is like dropping a cup of gasoline into an empty engine. It can cause the engine to sputter and come to life for a moment, but it only provides a short *burst* of energy that can move us a short distance. Neither fear nor greed will fill our tanks for the long haul. That's part of the reason the self-help field keeps expanding. We need to keep buying another book, getting another exercise video, ordering another infomercial work-out machine. And that's not all bad. A cup of gas at a time can get us moving toward better health.

But isn't there a better way to build a healthy lifestyle?

I think so. And not surprising, I think it's linked with a HeartShift and 2 Degree Changes made over time.

THE STARTING POINT FOR A HEALTH HEARTSHIFT

There is indeed a better way to stay motivated to change over the long haul, but I don't want to say it's an easier path. It's better because it focuses on who you are *before* you ever start your journey toward better health, and that, believe it or not, is *you are fully accepted and complete.*

When you come to Christ, amazing things happen here on earth and in heaven, where the angels rejoiced that you came to faith. When we talked about being born again, it was in gaining new capacities for love and faith and discipline we didn't have before. Even more, it's like we receive a stamp on our forehead that says in invisible ink, "This person is special and whole and significant, just the way I made them."

In other words, before you ever make a health HeartShift, it's crucial to know that your significance isn't tied up in this or any diet and exercise program. When we're motivated by greed or fear, it's because there's something outside of us that pushed us to get more or makes us afraid that we'll have less.

But what if you were already complete, full, whole, and a special future was already locked up in the heavenly places along with that dwelling place Jesus said he has for you in heaven? That takes away the need for more because we're already full, and it stops the fear of loss because what we have is protected in God's hands. Then what is our motivation for change?

Instead of greed or fear, what motivates a Christian to make health changes, or changes in any other area, is an inexhaustible word that's infinitely more powerful than either fear or greed; it's the word *love*.

Love motivates a person to take risks when she's not a risk taker. It urges a person to follow rules when he's not a rule person. Or face problems when they're not a natural problem solver. Love bears all, outlasts all, is the greatest of all.

And we are incredibly, deeply, forever loved by Jesus—just the way we are. If you really believed that, can you imagine how you'd feel when you look in the mirror? You're his beloved, so where you start when it comes to health (or wealth, or education, or social standing) isn't the issue. It's where he's taking you, and that's to a special future with him and to "fullness of life."

Now I'm sure you won't see a *New York Times* best seller called *The Love Diet*. (Or actually, you might see that title someday because there are so many diet books!) But I don't think it will mean what Christ's love means to us. Namely, that we start out whole, accepted, complete, secure, forgiven; our next step is to get even better, not struggle to measure up.

ONCE WE REALLY KNOW WE'RE LOVED AND ACCEPTED, CHANGE CAN COME FROM A DIFFERENT PLACE

Knowing that we're completely loved and accepted by Jesus and that "He who began a good work in you will perfect it" (Phil. 1:6) sets the stage for positive change as nothing else can. Let me try to highlight one reason.

Have you ever gotten an envelope from Easter Seals or some other organization with address labels bearing your name and address? You didn't order them. They just showed up—a gift for you. Something as small as an address label pushes us to feel indebted in some way. And many people will send a check to support that organization.

Love given produces an imbalance that can make us want to give back. And the more we understand God's sacrifice of his Son for us, and because he loves us, the more we want to love back. There's more.

For all who come to Christ, we get Christ's life within us in ways we can't fully understand. And we get his Holy Spirit to guide and his timeless Word to inspire, teach, and change us. That's a tad more than address labels! And the amazing thing is that God gave us that kind of love when we didn't deserve it.

"For God so loved the world, that He gave His only Son" (John 3:16).

"While we were yet sinners, Christ died for us" (Rom. 5:8).

The fact is, we were imperfect and hostile or indifferent toward God when he died for us, and that makes his love that much more precious and unfathomable. The issue isn't really losing pounds or worrying about wrinkles. He loves us whether we ever drop a dress or pants size because we have incredible value and worth to him.

That's the starting point for better health that those who know Jesus have over all others. And interestingly, when you look at most successful diet books, you'll see that they tell you "attitude" is key. If you hate yourself, the way you look and who you are, then you're not going to be motivated to change. "So start liking yourself" is what you'll see time and again.

But what if you know there are parts of you that are unlikable? And things that you've done that are awful? And thoughts you have had that are indefensible?

We can psyche ourselves out all we want about how wonderful we are, but we know deep inside we're the emperor with no clothes. Which is exactly why we need a Savior who wraps his cloak of love around us—one who knows us, all the good and bad, and still loves us. And who gives us new capacities to love others as we love ourselves.

IF WE'RE REALLY THAT LOVED, WHERE'S THE MOTIVATION FOR CHANGE?

If all that's really true, then where is the motivation for change? If we're really that accepted and valued, unconditionally and just the way we are, then why not just eat the whole dozen Krispy Kreme doughnuts that we were going to share at the office? Why worry or bother about getting up to exercise or eat healthy or set a HeartShift goal of losing a few pounds over several weeks?

That's a similar question to one the apostle Paul answered when he tried to explain how great acceptance (God's grace) doesn't lead to license but to love.

In the book of Romans, Paul confronts those who would say, "If God loves us so much and forgives us when we sin, then why not just sin so he'll love us more!" While their question is a good one because of the reach of God's love, listen to the apostle's answer: "Are we to continue in sin so that grace may increase?" And his answer is classic, "May it never be! How shall we who died to sin still live in it?" (Rom. 6:1–2).

The response to God's unmerited favor, his filling up all our holes and making us whole in his love, doesn't motivate us to go out and sin but to respond in kind, to love him more. To give back to him, which reflects his glory!

Put another way, the apostle Paul tells us, "Do you not know that your body is a temple of the Holy Spirit who is in you, whom you have from God, and that you are not your own? For you have been bought with a price: therefore glorify God in your body" (1 Cor. 6:19–20).

In short, we were loved and set free for a purpose—to glorify God in our body.

Not because doing so will get us to heaven or will make us one bit more acceptable to God. But because a healthy body gives us the freedom to serve others and to worship and glorify God.

Think about the last time you were sick. *Really sick,* like with the flu that pounded you for days. Cold sweats each night. Aches and pains and no energy during the day—and for days. And then just when you thought you were going to expire, you suddenly noticed that you felt slightly better.

An incredible sense of freedom comes when you leave a sickbed. The world opens up again, and while it's easy to forget how sick you were (a gift from God), life holds more options and opportunities to glorify God when you're finally out of bed. God wants us to have good health because it opens up more doors for us to be his vessels on earth and live out his purpose for our life.

Let's bring this section to a close with this summary.

There is absolutely some value in responding to either the fear of loss or the desire for gain when it comes to motivation to change our health. Both motivators provide a brief rush of energy. But the power to make long-term changes in our health and life comes from knowing we are deeply, unconditionally loved. We're already complete, but we're deeply indebted because of his great love to be more loving. And better health provides us the freedom to live out our purpose and his purpose for our life more fully—to be a giver and lover like he is, and thus glorify God each day. Getting in shape then isn't just for us. It's a reflection of our love for God as well. And while you may not have looked at it this way before, your choice to pursue better health is a reflection of God's love for you and your love for him.

HeartShift Health Ideas and Journal

While this isn't a diet and exercise book, I do want to provide at least some tangible health pointers to those who are looking to make a HeartShift in their health for the next thirty days. First, keep in mind what we've said about making HeartShifts all along. Be specific and realistic in your commitment, and take small steps to reach your goals.

For example, when I set out to run the marathon, that goal really sprang from one of the most embarrassing moments in my life. I was at a pre-party during the weekend of my twenty-five-year high school reunion. There were close to forty former classmates in a living room, all of whom had gone to Young Life back in high school. Our old leaders were there as well as fellow classmates. There was Jan Webb, a tremendous woman who was the girls' senior leader during my years in high school. And there was one of my closest of friends, Doug Barram, our Young Life leader and the one who led me to Christ.

Remember, this was a twenty-fifth reunion. It had been a quarter century since I'd seen the people in this room. At one point Doug called everyone together to say a few words. He began his talk by saying, "It's great to see so many of the old gang. There's Debbie and Suzie, there's Chuck Savale and Hayes Button. And it's great to see Jeff Trent, who looks like he could still play football, and of course John, who looks like he swallowed the football."

Jeff is my twin brother, and yes, he did look in better shape than I did that day. Even though I had gone on the "two days before the reunion crash diet" that obviously didn't work. Laughter filled the room, and I started looking for a back door. Like never before in my life, I felt embarrassed and fat in front of friends I hadn't seen in decades. Doug later apologized, and I accepted his apology, but I couldn't shake the sadness and shame I felt until I started taking steps to change.

First, I went back to basics.

"Jesus loves me, this I know," even if I'd swallowed a football or two. But Doug's comments pointed to the prominent truth. I was way out of shape. So instead of the crash diet program, I began with a commitment to change—a HeartShift.

My 2 Degree Change was just to leave my job a few minutes a day, four days a week. I dusted off the old tennis shoes and jogged and walked around the block to begin. (We live on a cul-de-sac, so it was a short block.) That was about all I could muster that first day. But I had a group of friends whom I'd shared my HeartShift commitment with, a 33 Group of two wonderful friends. They prayed with and for me as I started.

I worked up to where I'd jog for one minute and then walk for two minutes. Then over time, I'd jog two minutes and walk one minute. Over the days and weeks and months, I built up to jogging eight minutes and still walking one minute. At that point I ran my first 5K race (or 5K shuffle in my case). A few months later I nearly passed out in the heat on a boiling afternoon in Wisconsin (of all places), when I ran my first 10K (coming in just behind the lady with the jogging stroller she'd pushed the whole way). And then several more months of running eight minutes and walking one until I ran the Valley of the Sun half marathon. One year later I ran and finished the Rock 'n' Roll marathon. A blazing 5 hours 21 minutes 54 seconds. The winner from Kenya that year nipped me at the finish line by a measly three hours. But it didn't matter that I'd finished in 10,581st place. I finished the race. And amazingly, so many people run the Rock 'n' Roll, there were more than 10,000 people behind me!

Running the marathon started with a HeartShift commitment, a 33 Group to pray and encourage me, and a few steps around the block.

How about you?

Is the HeartShift you want to make prompted by a physical wake-up call like I received in San Antonio? Or a slam at your twenty-fifth reunion? For whatever reason, getting healthy isn't about acceptance; it's an act of loving God and getting in shape for service in his army.

Think small if you're serious about making a health HeartShift. For example, here's a list of small 2 Degree Changes you could make.

2 DEGREE STEPS TOWARD GAINING BETTER HEALTH

1. Drink eight glasses of water each day.

2. Do something aerobic at least once or as many as three times a week.

3. Without regard to how much weight you're lifting, do some strength training once or twice a week.

4. When you jog, build in walk breaks every five to eight minutes. (I highly recommend Jeff Galloway's *Complete Book on Running*. He's a former Olympian who encourages even competitive runners—and slow joggers like me—to build in walk breaks. It was his book that told me to start with "run a minute, walk two minutes" and then work up to eight minutes jogging, one minute walking. For five years I've been injury free following his method. I've had the chance to meet Jeff, and he's a strong believer as well!)

5. Read an exercise book once a year.

6. Get several friends to exercise with you (perhaps your 33 Group could get together once a week to exercise or aerobic walk before your meeting).

7. Enlist your spouse as a support person for your goal.

8. Say to yourself when you get up in the morning, "I feel great! I think I'll go exercise!"

9. Realize that eating is really about portions. Eat the equivalent of a nine-inch plate of food at least three times a day, with half of the plate being fruits or vegetables; a quarter of the plate containing protein, like chicken or fish and cheese; and a quarter of the plate having whole grain breads or some other type of carbs.

10. Pray that God's love will inspire you to get in better shape to serve him and others. With nothing to prove, since you're already fully accepted, you have more to give others, and getting healthy physically becomes another way to serve him and others more!

A trip to the bookstore and any one of those acres of diet and exercise books can give you another one hundred or more small steps you can take toward better health. And to help track these small changes in your health, here is a HeartShift health journal you can feel free to copy and use. It gives you a place to write down your specific decision to change and one or two items from the list above (or from your own list) that will put your decision into action this week and for the next thirty days.

HEARTSHIFT JOURNAL

My HeartShift health commitment for the next 30 days is to _____

_____

_____

For week 1 my 2 Degree Changes to my health will include _____

_____

_____

For week 2 my 2 Degree Changes to my health will include _____

_____

_____

For week 3 my 2 Degree Changes to my health will include _____

_____

_____

For week 4 my 2 Degree Changes to my health will include _____

_____

_____

May the Lord bless your small steps toward better health. And as with each of the other major areas of this book, please feel free to share your 2 Degree health suggestions at www.HeartShift.com. If it proved to be helpful to you, then there's certainly someone else it will inspire as well. May the Lord bless you as you take your first steps, and may we all be diligent to be in our best shape possible to serve our Commanding Officer!

CHAPTER EIGHTEEN

Final Thoughts on Making a HeartShift and Long-Term Change

I remember beginning J. R. R. Tolkin's classic tale *The Lord of the Rings* by reading the author's preface. Including *The Hobbit,* I knew there were four books to read, each hundreds of pages long. But as I read his preface, I laughed out loud when he shared that his only regret was that he wished he had made these tales *longer*! Of course, when I finished the last page of *The Return of the King,* I agreed with him. There was so much about that imaginary world of Middle-Earth that had become real in his telling the tale that made me want to know more and more.

In some small ways I pray this idea of making a HeartShift and living it out through small 2 Degree Changes has opened a new world for you—one based in reality instead of fantasy, and one that despite the length of this book has left you feeling that you've just scratched the surface of this concept. That's certainly the way I feel.

There is still so much that could be said about the power of being "faithful in a little"—that is still waiting to be said. My prayer is that others come along and do outstanding research on the power of small things that can be added to later editions of this book and posted at www.HeartShift.com.

I also pray that there will someday be a whole book of 2 Degree quiet times sent in by readers just like you who are more in love with God and his Word by taking small spiritual steps. And additional workbooks and small group studies that shed further light on making a HeartShift in a marriage, or as a parent, and when it comes to strengthening our health. (For example, I'm praying about meeting a Christian fitness expert who falls in love with the HeartShift idea and works with me on that book!) In every area the challenge to make small shifts and changes of the heart that gain the "compound interest" Lewis spoke about can be fleshed out more and more.

In closing, I'd like to share one final thought about making a HeartShift and long-term change. I've pushed for a thirty-day commitment to make small changes in a specific area. But what happens beyond that short period of time? Is this idea really adaptable to long-term change?

Consider two things about whether this idea of small changes can be sustained over the long-haul of a life, or ministry, or marriage, or career. First, I have in my office a plaque that says I completed the San Diego Rock 'n' Roll Marathon—all 26 miles 258 feet. What it doesn't say is that distance was traveled one step at a time. Long successful journeys are made up of small steps, whether it's a marriage, a ministry, or a marathon.

Second, because you have Christ's life within you as a believer, there will *always* be an area to change—a need or conviction to make yet another HeartShift. That's because a body that is alive is always in a state of self-repair. That's one mark of a living organism. At least to some degree, it's able to repair itself. And when the Holy Spirit lives within us, then the daily process of being renewed and sanctified and turned into the heavenly creature he is making us will usher in a lifelong process of small changes, not a short-term fad.

It has been nearly two years since I first spoke with Broadman & Holman and shared with them this idea for challenging men and women to make a HeartShift. I can't begin to thank Len Goss, my patient, long-suffering editor, and Ken Stevens, Broadman's exceptional publisher, and the entire team at Broadman for their unwavering belief in the message of this book and its potential to change lives. They have been my 33 Group, supporting me every step of the way, and I am incredibly grateful to them.

Now finally, I ask God's blessing on your life and the HeartShift commitment you've made. In the words of Aaron, "The LORD bless you, and keep you; The LORD make His face to shine on you, And be gracious to you; The LORD lift up His countenance on you, And give you peace" (Num. 6:24–26) one small step toward him at a time.

–John Trent, Ph.D.

APPENDIX A

Seven Keys to an Effective HeartShift Small Group

Conducting a quality HeartShift small group requires developing a style that works best for you. The following ideas may be helpful as you plan the format of your meetings. These suggestions need to be tailored to your particular meeting and leadership style. In fact, you may be able to improve on them considerably by allowing God to lead you in a slightly different direction.

The following suggestions are based on a meeting of no longer than two hours. This includes the seven basic components of a HeartShift small group. We don't encourage a meeting length consistently longer than two hours because it breeds burn out and a lack of enthusiasm. Consider varying your format from time to time to avoid staleness. The suggested time breakdowns are not meant to be rigid limits, only guidelines.

KEY 1. CORE GROUP MEETING

Approximately thirty minutes before your HeartShift small group meeting starts is an excellent time to meet with your host and any others who will be helping you lead the group. Explain what you are planning for the meeting and what you expect from each person. Spend some time praying for the people coming to the meeting.

KEY 2. WELCOME GUESTS AND FELLOWSHIP TIME

Be ready about ten minutes before the meeting starts to welcome the guests at the front door. Show them where to hang their coats (where appropriate), lead them to the coffeepot and refreshments, and introduce them to others. Everybody likes a friendly face at the door and appreciates a few moments of conversation before entering right into a meeting. This is especially necessary for new people! Consider some soft music in the background at this time. This period usually lasts about ten to fifteen minutes.

KEY 3. GROUP BUILDING

Get the meeting started on time after an appropriate amount of fellowship. People came to the group to engage in discussion and receive support in areas where they want to make a HeartShift, or are considering making one. Make sure that an atmosphere of acceptance and kindness is fostered so people will feel safe as they share.

- Icebreakers are an excellent way to get the group relaxed, talking, and participating. They provide an opportunity for everyone to "buy in." An example of an icebreaker might be to go around the room and have everyone share a favorite snack food. Icebreakers can range from simple, like the preceding example, to something relating to the discussion for that night.
- Testimonies are another excellent option. Sharing what the Lord is doing gives glory to him and allows members of the group to speak freely in a safe environment. This is not a time for problems or prayer requests. The leader may have to gently direct the flow of the conversation to prevent one person from dominating the group or to keep the conversation on track. This group-building time might take fifteen to twenty minutes.

KEY 4. DISCUSSION TIME—PUTTING HEARTSHIFT INTO ACTION

Bible or topic study and discussion are a vital part of a successful HeartShift meeting. This is the time where we learn to apply the Word and the HeartShift principles in our lives. It is important that as many people participate as possible, so it is often necessary to break into smaller groups. Everyone can participate at his or her own pace and comfort level. Gently direct the conversation away from fruitless and directionless discussion. Develop questions ahead of time for each small group around the HeartShift topic you will be discussing. This is a good time to discuss the commitment sheet and have the topic center on what commitment each person made and how that commitment is working. This will take around thirty to forty-five minutes.

KEY 5. PRAYER TIME

You may want to provide time at the end of the meeting for people to pray and interact with the Lord. Most of the time, break into groups of three for prayer. At times you may separate men and women for better disclosure or remain together in a group as you are led. The most important thing is to be sensitive to each person's needs and make sure everyone feels cared for and listened to. This prayer time will take whatever remaining time you have left to finish the two hours. Make sure you end the meeting on time so people are left wanting more and will come back the next time. If people think a meeting is going to drag on every week, they will begin to dread it (and may stop coming). Child-care issues also become more relevant if a meeting runs late.

KEY 6. FELLOWSHIP

Sharing a cup of coffee and cookies is a great way to get to know one another after the meeting is over. This especially helps visitors feel comfortable and welcome. Although some individuals might need some encouragement to participate, share the responsibility of bringing snacks. A sign-up sheet for snacks on the coffee table with specific dates and times is a good way to encourage people to help with the refreshments. A sign-up sheet for child care might also be appropriate. You might also want to have a paper for e-mail, addresses, and phone numbers of each member in the group.

KEY 7. FOLLOW UP AFTER YOUR HEARTSHIFT SMALL GROUP

Small groups function best when one person is designated as the coordinator for the group. This person should contact each member of the group every week to confirm the meeting place and time. This is usually a person who has a heart to care for others and can effectively use this contact time to inquire about how people are doing with their HeartShift goals for that week (in a caring, nonprying way). Having a coordinator for the group lets everyone relax, knowing that any details relating to child care, refreshments, meetings that are postponed to another day, or a change in the location of the meeting will be relayed each week. It also just helps people feel that someone in the group cares about them.

Three Sermon Outlines for a HeartShift Series

WAKING UP MILES AWAY FROM WHERE YOU WANT TO BE

I. "How Did I Get Here?" The Character Asks.

A. It's a formula that's been used in classic children's tales, adventure novels, and feature films for generations. Someone wakes up, opens his or her eyes, and discovers that everything has changed.

B. In literature, it's Rip Van Winkle waking up to discover himself covered with the dust of decades after lying down under a tree for a short noontime nap. It's a New England blacksmith in Mark Twain's *A Connecticut Yankee in King Arthur's Court* who opens his eyes to find an armor-clad knight's lance point leveled inches from his heart. For Gulliver it meant awakening to find he'd been tied up by hundreds of tiny evil creatures bent on his immediate demise.

C. In movies, you see the same situation pictured time and time again. It's Bill Murray waking up to find another day stuck on rewind in *Groundhog Day,* or a mother and daughter waking up to discover they've traded bodies in *Freaky Friday,* or Joe waking up to find out that he doesn't have a body at all in the black-and-white classic *Mr. Jordan* (which was remade as *Heaven Can Wait* in the 1980s and remade again in 2003 as *Down to Earth*!).[1]

D. Why do so many novelists and producers rely on this tried-and-true plot device? Because, as implausible and even impossible as it may seem, it still rings true with us at many levels. For in a way, people every day—*perhaps even you*—wake up to find that in a critically important area of life, everything has changed. In the blink of an eye, you're miles from where you ever thought you'd be.

E. Examples

    1. Illustrate the point by telling William's story (pp. 4–5). For some readers, discovering that they can indeed make important health changes will be the most important shift they make in their life story. But for many others it won't be the fear of clogged arteries or shortness of breath that opens their eyes to the fact that important things have changed. It will be waking up to find a treasured relationship in ruins. Every day far too many people wake up miles from where they ever thought they'd be in their marriage or family relationships.

    2. Share the example of Sarah's story (pp. 5–7). Sarah isn't alone. There are far too many Sarahs and increasingly more and more Toms all across the country who wake up one day to discover they're in a marriage that's in ruins. To top it off, what's so confusing is that there was never a clear-cut wrecking-ball reason for the collapse. In the marriage, there was no adultery. No drug or alcohol addiction issues. No job loss that caused incredible financial pressures. No piling on by intrusive in-laws that finally became so heavy it shattered the relationship. Despite all this, the relationship was in ruins and seemingly over small things.

    3. Tell Ray's story (pp. 7–8). *How did I get here?* he asked himself as he turned and looked at his wife, her hands open and eyes shut in worship. His own eyes stayed open as he battled with that terrible, nagging emptiness.

F. Transition: Granted, William, Sarah, and Ray represent people in crisis. But have you ever felt that one of them? In your health, or home, or even in your heart for God, have you ever felt that the place you're at isn't *close* to where you ever thought you'd be? If so, then you're not alone, and you've come to the right place. On the other hand, if you've never once been where these three have, then you've *absolutely* come to the right place. To draw from the apostle Paul's words, "Let him who thinks he stands take heed that he does not fall" (1 Cor. 10:12).

    Dr. Trent shares in his *HeartShift* book, "In my own life, and after spending twenty-five years counseling with hundreds of Williams and Sarahs and Rays across our county, I have found it is incredibly easy for all but a few of us to drift away in one or more important areas of our lives. In fact, it's not just individuals who wake up one day far from where they want to be. In the Scriptures, *an entire home church* got a wake-up call that despite all their good works, things were terribly wrong."

II. A Church That Fell Prey to Lucifer's Fall

A. Read from *The Message*, Revelation 2:1–2

    1. "Write this to Ephesus, to the Angel of the church. The One with Seven Stars in his right-fist grip, striding through the golden seven-lights' circle, speaks." And that Person who looks down and speaks to this church we know in any translation or paraphrase is the resurrected Lord Jesus himself.

    2. Tell the story of what Jesus said to the church at Ephesus (pp. 9–11). Somehow, in the process of doing so many good things over such a long period of time, this church had ended up at Satan's, not heaven's, doorstep!

        Doesn't that seem almost incredible based on all the good they had done? The question the Lord puts to them, "Do you have any idea how far you've fallen?" (v. 5 *The Message*) points to the fact that they didn't know! There was a collective wake-up call that day as the message was delivered, and people must have looked around and thought, *But we've worked so hard! Done so much! Done so many things right! How did we get here?*

    3. Even for a church or a small group, it's not enough to put even good actions on autopilot and just assume we'll end up where we want to go. For in the midst of doing all those good things, they had drifted from what's best. They had ended up closer to pride and emptiness than God's heart and the warmth of a first love.

    4. "Turn back!" the Lord says. "Recover your dear early love. No time to waste, for I'm well on my way to removing your light from the golden circle" (v. 5 *The Message*).

III. Conclusion

A. Can you hear that sense of urgency from the Lord who calls those in the church to make a shift before it's too late? There's no time to waste! Now is the time to wake up and see that our collective light as a small group or congregation has grown ineffective and dim, like a candle moved farther and farther from a table it once brightly lit.

    Like it or not, realize it or not, far too many of us are like William, or Sarah, or Ray in our personal and spiritual lives, and, if we're honest, like the church of Ephesus when it comes to our corporate worship and church relationships. We've drifted toward a place we never wanted to be, even in the midst of making sincere efforts. It is time we turned back to our families or toward better health or a vital, real personal faith or to a loving connection with our brothers and sisters in Christ.

B. Like an echo from the writer of Hebrews, "Today if you hear His voice,
do not harden your hearts" (3:7–8). Today is the day to wake up and
begin the journey back toward God's best and what's best for our family,
our friendships, and even our fellowship with other believers.

It's time we made a HeartShift.

HOW A 2 DEGREE CHANGE CAN RUIN
OR RENEW YOUR LIFE

I. Introduction

A. When asked to share about their life story, people overwhelmingly
describe special occasions and singular events.

1. If we're still in school, the things that mark pages in our life story
tend to be a graduation, the prom, opening an acceptance letter
from that hoped-for school, or winning (or losing) a basketball
championship.

2. If we're a believer, it's often the night we came to Christ or the day
we were baptized or confirmed.

3. As we get older, it may be the birth of a child, a wedding, a funeral,
a divorce, a promotion, or even the day we were fired from a job.

B. The same thing is true with our view of history. Dramatic events are most
often picked as having the greatest ability to turn the pages of history.
And in truth, that's often the case.

1. For example, the picture of a mushroom cloud rising over
Hiroshima, the sounds of rifle shots ringing out and striking down
President Kennedy, or the terrible replayed image of a plane being
flown into the twin towers of the World Trade Center can indeed
shift the plates that lie under entire nations. Viewed another way,
these dramatic, often unparalleled historical events can act like huge
levers that shift world actions and attitudes.

2. In the world of modern-day presidential politics, we've all witnessed
how the smallest of margins can dramatically swing an election. In
the 2000 election between George W. Bush and Al Gore, if less than
two votes per polling place in Florida had swung the other way, it
would have moved the state from the blue column to the red, and
Al Gore would be in the White House today. Nationally, a 2 percent
change in four of the most closely contested swing states could have
changed the outcome of the election as well.

3. If small things matter in the conflict of arms or in the fate of a
national election, they are incredibly powerful when it comes to our
personal lives. For while there are certainly global wild cards that

force us to change; for many of us, it will be the smallest of actions that bring the greatest change. In fact, they can ruin or renew our life.

II. How a 2 Degree Change Can Ruin Your Life

A. Tell Dr. Trent's story of sitting next to a NASA engineer on a plane and discovering that being the tiniest bit off course over time can result in great destruction (pp. 16–18).

1. Dr. Trent says, "I finally left my new NASA friend in peace, but I've never forgotten his conclusion or what it can tell us about the most important relationships and areas of our lives."

2. Add in enough time and distance, and be just two degrees off, and you'll miss your target by miles.

3. Dr. Trent adds, "In my counseling practice, that same explanation fit like a frame around many troubled marriages I'd seen. Be just a few degrees off as a couple and don't bother to make any genuine course corrections over the months and years, and then watch how you wake up one day and discover you're emotionally miles apart."

4. Example: I recall a successful red-haired banker and his wife whom I'd met with in my office. Like Sarah's story in the first message, their marriage had gotten off to a great start. But seventeen years had passed, and now they stood at emotional opposite ends of the equator. To make matters worse, a female coworker at the banker's office now factored into the husband's equation. Tragically, from this banker's perspective, it all seemed to add up. After all, what's easier to do? Make a 180-degree change (or even a 90-degree change) back toward his wife? Or just turn 2 degrees toward a stranger?

B. Transition: That NASA conversation on a plane years ago first began to form a tangible picture in my mind and provide an answer to so much of the emotional, spiritual, and even physical wreckage I'd seen for decades. What's more, it opened my eyes to passage after passage in Scripture that talks about the importance of small things in a life of faith, peace, and rest. As I began to share these ideas, first with those in counseling and then with many at my conferences over the years, you could see the heads nod and the eyes open.

People instantly *"got it."*

They understood almost intuitively the idea that a small 2 Degree Change could change their life for the worse, given the gradual workings of time. But then they began to understand that the *reverse* was true as well. Amazingly, even small shifts in a positive direction could move a person from ruin to renewal.

III. How a 2 Degree Change Can Renew Your Life or Relationships

A. In your mind, picture any one of the couples I've mentioned who woke
up one day with their marriage in ruins. (Or feel free to substitute
your own marriage, if you've been there, or any couple of your own
choosing.) If you've spent any time viewing a conflicted couple, it's like
they're standing on opposite banks of a deep, fast-flowing river. The mere
thought or encouragement from others to move toward each other seems
to bring with it a strong, involuntary emotion akin to having to plunge
into that icy cold river and exert tremendous effort to get across. No
wonder so many couples settle for tossing loud, angry words across the
chasm, trying to get the other person to take the plunge. And no wonder
so many people then feel justified with walking away because, "Well,
I tried to get him (or her) to move, but it just never happened."

But what if there were a way to bridge that gap between a couple in
conflict?

What if there already were a bridge, a footbridge really, between
these two people—so narrow it had gone unnoticed and unused? What if
there really were a way to move closer so that any need for shouting
could stop because they were now inches instead of a football field apart?

And the answer to all those "what ifs" is that such a footbridge does
exist, though it is too often ignored, unseen, or less traveled.

There is a narrow way that our eyes tend to miss in all the noise
and emotion of our lives. A bridge that can provide a way back to closeness and caring for couples or to a renewed faith or good health for an
individual.

That "bridge" is what I call a HeartShift, and the way we cross it is
through 2 Degree Changes. For example, C. S. Lewis uses the word *charity* to describe just such a secret path.

B. What does charity have to do with change?

For Lewis, "charity" wasn't a token gift given to help those less fortunate. It was a heartfelt decision to choose action over emotion or natural preference as well as a daily "virtue" that should mark a Christian as
set apart from nonbelievers. Here's how Lewis illustrates "charity" in
action: "The difference between a Christian and a worldly man is not
that the worldly man has only affections or 'likings' and the Christian has
only 'Charity.' The worldly man treats certain people kindly because he
'likes' them, the Christian, trying to treat every one kindly, finds himself
liking more and more people as he goes on—including people he could
not even have imagined himself liking at the beginning."

C. Now go back to that picture of a conflicted couple.

> The idea of not being able even to imagine liking their spouse again is exactly the mind-set most couples hold on to with white-knuckle grips when they first walk into my counseling office. They can't even imagine rekindling warm feelings of attachment, much less regaining a genuine love for that person they're so angry with.

> But again, what if there really were a bridge that still existed between these two, even with all the arguments they've had? What if, over time, they could pick a path that could lead them up to a level of closeness they couldn't dream of reaching in that first counseling session? What if there were a way of relating to each other that could even result in their gaining back a first-love attachment for each other?

D. Sound impossible?[2] Yet, in fact, such a bridge back to each other does exist, as C. S. Lewis points out: "The rule for all of us is perfectly simple. Do not waste time bothering whether you 'love' your neighbor, act as if you do. And soon as we do this we find one of the great secrets. When you are behaving as if you love someone, you will presently come to love him. If you injure someone you dislike, you will find yourself disliking him more. If you do him a good turn, you will find yourself disliking him less."

E. Doesn't that sound simple?

> Almost childish, foolish, or shallow? And yet Lewis's conclusion is absolutely true, is understood only by the mature, is undeniably biblical, and is fathoms deep.

> There is indeed an amazing secret at work when we take even the smallest steps toward what's right and good.

> Lewis continues, "Good and evil both increase at compound interest. That is why the little decisions you and I make every day are of such infinite importance. The smallest good act today is the capture of a strategic point from which, a few months later, you may be able to go on to victories you never dreamed of. An apparently trivial indulgence in lust or anger today is the loss of a ridge or railway line or bridgehead from which the enemy may launch an attack otherwise impossible."

> Lewis expounds the thought that it is the little decisions we make every day that will move us gradually toward more good or further toward evil.

IV. Still Not Convinced?

A. Still uncertain that great relationships and successful life changes should start with a HeartShift that puts us on the right path and then becomes habit and undeniable reality by small acts, small 2 Degree Changes? Then instead of looking at the calculations of a NASA engineer or at the arguments of C. S. Lewis, let's look at a time when the Lord Jesus himself clarified to the disciples how the path to the heights of greatness begins with the smallest of steps.

B.   Watch how Jesus challenges his disciples to first make what I'd call a HeartShift, to realize they were off course and make a decision to move in a different direction. And then look at how he lays out for them a path that will allow them to arrive exactly where he wants them to be. For Jesus, such a path or bridge to real greatness isn't crossed by taking big steps or doing big things but by the smallest of actions, 2 Degree steps. That comes out as the lesson begins.

   Read Mark 9:33–37: "Sitting down, He called the twelve and said to them, 'If anyone wants to be first, he shall be the last of all and servant of all'" (v. 35).

C.   Whether you call it a HeartShift or mind shift or paradigm shift or any other kind of shift, Jesus begins by challenging them to make a huge shift in their mental and emotional perspective. That day along the road, they may have been on the right road to their destination, but they were way off course in regards to the subject of their discussion—greatness. Jesus goes even further to give them a picture of just what he (and his heavenly Father) meant by *greatness*. "Taking a child, He set him before them, and taking him in His arms, He said to them, 'Whoever receives one child like this in My name receives Me; and whoever receives Me does not receive Me, but Him who sent Me'" (v. 37).

D.   Servants do the small things, the little things that help others succeed. Servants focus on the small, often uninspired tasks that make something better or cleaner or closer. To powerfully illustrate his point, he gives them a living object lesson.

   It's so like *us* to think it's the big things that matter the most.

   It's so much like *Jesus* to sit down with us, tell us we need to make a HeartShift, and to point out that it's the little things that are really important. For Jesus, it was faith the size of a mustard seed that could move a mountain. It's the tiny bit of leaven in the loaf that could raise the whole lump of dough. It's reminding Martha that it wasn't all about doing extra credit things for Jesus; it's that one thing her sister Mary did right.

E.   C. S. Lewis wasn't exaggerating. He was echoing the words of Scripture when he wrote about how the smallest of acts and smallest of decisions could set us on the right course and keep us on the right path. It's the small acts of goodness that can move us *increasing* toward doing more and more good until we reach our heavenly home. "Good and evil both increase at compound interest. That is why the little decisions you and I make every day are of such infinite importance."

   1.   It's the small things that take advantage of the incredibly powerful "secret" of compound interest.

2. It's things like reaching out and putting our arms around *one* child.
3. Or opening one car door for our spouse (instead of giving her that look that says, "What's the matter, is your arm broken?").
4. Or skipping one dessert.
5. Or reading one verse a day in our Bible or uttering one sentence prayer at night.

TAKING THAT FIRST STEP INTO A KINGDOM OF CHANGE

I. Introduction
A. Today let's take a closer look at two terms that have surfaced throughout the first two messages: HeartShift and the idea of making a 2 Degree Change.
B. Because it's always best to show and tell, I'd like to let two dramatic biblical examples help show off and define both terms and demonstrate practically what they can mean to your life and mine. Both stories are found in the Old Testament. In the first, we'll see a man who indeed woke up one day to find his world radically and tragically changed.

II. When Small Things Lead to Great Things
A. In God's Word, there was a soldier who had earned a place of great power, prestige, and influence. Here's how the Scriptures picture him. Read 2 Kings 5:1–12 and tell the story of Naaman as told by Dr. Trent on pages 33–40.
1. The tipping point for real change—I've pointed out before, when we think of change, we think of wild cards and big things and dramatic events. But it's Naaman's servants who are so attuned to doing small things themselves that they point out the obvious thing Naaman had missed. "Then his servants came near and spoke to him and said, 'My father, had the prophet told you to do some great thing, would you not have done it? How much more then, when he says to you, "Wash and be clean"?'" (v. 13).
2. It's easy to see where Naaman had gone wrong. After all, it's only natural for us to think that if there's a big rock to move, we need a big shovel. It's so foreign for successful people, or almost any person, to think that the little things count. The same thing is true for us living in a world where bigger is better and where our press blows almost everything out of proportion.
3. This servant's words were so plain. No drama. No shouting. No waving. No screaming. Holy men of Naaman's day often added emphasis to their incantations. There is none of that here.

4. Elisha doesn't say a word, and his servant says very little. *Just go bathe in the River Jordan.*

5. There is something inside us that automatically says, "It can't be that easy." There is something deep within us that warns us, "It's got to be trick, a joke, some sort of scam."

6. But neither Elisha nor the God he served was about to humiliate a man of honor who was dying. And because of the courage of Naaman's servants to speak up, *because of his tremendous support system,* he finally gives it all up.

7. On the banks of the River Jordan, Naaman lays down every sword and weapon that had earned him his place in his kingdom. He strips off every symbol of success and authority, and listens to the words of a servant who carried God's word. "So he went down and dipped himself seven times in the Jordan, according to the word of the man of God; and his flesh was restored like the flesh of a little child, and he was clean" (v. 14).

B. To comment on the scale of such a miracle is unnecessary. God alone could effect such an incredible cure. So instead, let me go back to how we started this message, and how I mentioned both ideas of a HeartShift and a 2 Degree Change.

1. Had Naaman not made a HeartShift, one that required him to drop his anger and pride and admit he was on the wrong road, he never would have changed and certainly would have died of leprosy. The first step he took in the right direction was to do something small. A 2 Degree step of bathing (baptizing) himself in that river. Seven times, going under the water and coming up, the number of completion, and a picture of going from death to life.

2. Dipping himself in the river was such a small step that initially that fact alone held Naaman back from entering the river. He almost missed his chance for change by demanding, expecting, waiting for some great thing to effect change and demonstrate the great God of Israel's power.

C. Obviously, the purpose of Naaman's story in Scripture is to show God's power, not illustrate a point in a message. But as I mentioned in the first message of this series, time and again in Scripture, you'll see how a significant need was met by the need for an individual to make a HeartShift, to lay down his or her pride and pretext and to take that first small step. Which is certainly something we'll see in our second Old Testament example.

III. Many People in Peril and the Small Step That Could Save Them

A. From one dramatic story of a leper who is given new skin and a new life, let's look at yet another life-and-death story. Only this time, there were many people in peril, and the cure put before them was perhaps even smaller and more difficult to accept.

1. Read Numbers 21:4–9 and tell the story about the nation of Israel as told by Dr. Trent on pages 40–44.

2. *Once again, a huge problem is met in Scriptures with the encouragement to do something incredibly small.*

3. It doesn't get much easier then just lifting our eyes. But can you imagine what went through these people's minds?

B. While the Scriptures are silent on this fact, I wouldn't be surprised if there were people who died instead of doing something so silly as looking up at a pretend snake. Perhaps some simply wouldn't believe that it could be so easy. Perhaps some balked at the thought that all their pain could go away by doing something as small as shifting their gaze up to the long wooden pole and crossbeam and what was fastened to it.

C. Remember, the reason these people had been bitten in the first place was because of their vocal unbelief. They were up front in questioning God's direction for their lives and his provision for them on their journey. Now in order to live, they had to make a HeartShift. They had to, at least internally, admit that *they* were the ones on the wrong road by complaining and accept that the right road, the only road that led to life, was by believing God's Word and his provision for them.

D. Once they'd made that HeartShift, then it still took a small 2 Degree step to stop their pain. They still had to look up to find hope and healing.

IV. When Jesus Had a Pharisee "Look Up"

A. If you're not familiar with this Old Testament story, then you might not know that Jesus used this example to help picture for a doubting Pharisee his need to make a HeartShift.

B. Read John 3:1–16 and tell the story of the event that happened early in Jesus' ministry. Dr. Trent's insights can be found on pages 43–44.

C. John 3:16 is without a doubt one of the most quoted passages in all the Bible. Yet few know that just two verses before, Jesus himself gives a picture that illustrates its meaning, drawn from that life-and-death time in the desert. For those in the desert, bitten and dying with the venom of "fiery serpents," that small, insignificant act of looking up at a bronze serpent provided their only cure. For those in Nicodemus's day, and for all people since, only by looking up *in* faith—even the new or small faith of a fellow thief on the cross—was the only place to find the antidote to sin and the way to be born again into eternal life.

V. How, Exactly, Do These Two Stories of Faith and Small Acts Help Me Change?

A. In each story above, in order for someone in a serious situation to make a much needed change, they first had to face up to the greatest sin.

B. According to Christian teachers throughout the ages, the greatest sin was the thing responsible for Satan's fall—pride. Through pride Satan lifted himself above God, and for that choice he was tossed down from heaven. Think of any sin or evil. Anger. Lust. Greed. Abuse. Neglect. In each of these, and all other vices and evils, you can extract trace elements of pride's DNA.

1. Pride always puts itself above change, above caring, above wanting another's best. Pride says, "I win (or deserve to win), and you lose." "I know the answer; you don't." "It's not my problem; it's yours." "It's what I want, not what you need." "God may say otherwise in his Bible, but I know best. And besides, he'll forgive me."

2. C. S. Lewis addresses the ultimate problem of pride bluntly: "As long as you are proud you cannot know God. A proud man is always looking down on things and people; and of course, as long as you are looking down, you cannot see something that is above you."

3. Proud people don't feel the need to change, any more then they realize they're off course. For proud people there's no need to see a counselor, or get a new direction, or even turn to a Savior. They're above all that. And so, little by little, they'll continue to drift toward darkness instead of light and death instead of life.

4. It takes the opposite of pride—humility—to make a HeartShift.

C. There's a second everyday lesson that springs from those two biblical stories.

1. Anger and a lack of forgiveness will also cut us off from any real change.

2. If pride is our ultimate enemy when it comes to change, then it's younger twin cousins are anger and a lack of forgiveness.

3. For Naaman, it was his anger at Elisha and his servant that almost kept him from accepting or seeing that small step toward change. For those who were dying in the wilderness, it was anger at Moses and even God that led to their being bitten by snakes in the first place.

4. The more anger you carry as a person, the less likely you'll be able to see that small path toward change, or accept it as real. Why? First, because anger always pushes us into darkness.

D. Read 1 John 2:9–10.

1. If making a HeartShift requires facing our pride, it also demands that we be honest about the degree of anger we carry in our lives. And that anger could be directed toward a parent who abandoned us, or a prodigal child who hurt us so deeply, or an insensitive spouse who doesn't cooperate or seem to care, or an unfeeling boss who passed us over for promotion, or an unethical partner or corrupt financial

planner who ruined us financially, or—and this is crucial—anger and a lack of forgiveness with ourselves.

2. Anger turned inward or toward others pushes us into darkness and blinds us to something as small as a 2 Degree Change. And linked with anger, is the issue of forgiveness.

3. Explain how anger and forgiveness affect out ability to make a HeartShift and a 2 Degree Change. Dr. Trent provided this information on pages 46–47.

VI. Personal Application

A. Now you can see why those two biblical stories hold so much everyday application to our lives and why they also represent the starting point for being able to make a HeartShift.

1. For any person in a situation where they need to make a change, a HeartShift requires us first to lay down our pride and admit we're on the wrong road. And hand in hand comes the understanding that unless we lay down our anger and untie the knot with forgiveness (for others and ourselves), we won't see or feel that we're making any positive movement at all.

2. Am I suggesting that the reason some of us struggle with our weight is because we're still tremendously angry with our parents and have yet to forgive them? Absolutely. (Not excuse their sinful behavior, which isn't forgiveness at all, but forgive them. Drop the anger and turn them over to God so that we aren't the ones tied up in emotional knots and, as such, easily prone to try to eat away those negative feelings.)

3. Am I suggesting that the reason some are getting nowhere in their marriage is because they haven't forgiven their spouse for investing in that "can't miss venture" and losing so much of their retirement funds? Absolutely.

4. Am I suggesting that some of us have seen our love for God grow cold because we're actually angry at him for sending us out in the desert? Absolutely.

B. Many of us must stop right now before going a step further toward change. If there are pockets (or deep wells) of anger, or if we're still tied up in knots from a lack of forgiveness, then now is the time to put down this book and go to the Lord in prayer. Indeed, if we're serious about change and have been deeply hurt, then it might take days or weeks or months of clearing the deck each day of anger as the best way to begin to make a HeartShift.

VII. Challenge to Congregation

A. Suggested approach: Hand out a HeartShift memorial marker certificate. (Yes, you have permission to go online at www.HeartShift.com, download the certificate, and then print off as many as you need of that one page for your congregation or group.)

B. Ask them prayerfully to fill out one area in their life they need to work on. (Remember to tell them that if they can't think of a single area to work on in their life or most important relationships, then they need to pick lying!) With that one focal point picked out, then urge them to think about one, two, or three small things they could do to move them closer to the Lord, or their family, or even better health, over the next thirty days. Then have a time of prayerful commitment, praying in faith in advance that the changes we can't see today will be changes that do happen when God takes our little and does his work over the next month.

C. A HeartShift is the conviction that we're on the wrong road and in need of making a turn back to better health, stronger relationships, or a deeper faith.

D. A 2 Degree Change is taking the smallest of positive steps, actions, or corrections to begin, sustain, or move us toward a needed change.

Notes

Chapter 1, Waking Up Miles Away from Where You Want to Be

1. These movies are used as examples, not recommendations.

Chapter 2, How a 2 Degree Change Can Ruin or Renew Your Life

1. I had the honor of spending a week with Dr. Dixon and his family and was greatly impressed with his insights and commitment to Christ. His outstanding book on future trends is *Futurewise: Six Faces of Global Change* (London: Profile Books, 2003).

2. For a full picture of this failed attempt to take Hitler's life, see William L. Shirer, *The Rise and Fall of the Third Reich: A History of Nazi Germany* (New York, N.Y.: Touchstone Books, 1981), chapter 29, as well as the excellent History Channel special depicting the same event.

3. The English detonator was silent whereas the German one made a hissing noise that could have been heard in the room.

4. C. S. Lewis, *Mere Christianity* (New York, N.Y.: HarperCollins, 1952, renewed 1980, 2001 Edition), 131.

5. Don't be too quick to answer no. If you've ever been in a hugely conflicted marriage or relationship, or worked closely with those who have, you'll find that on an emotional level, such a shift certainly sounds and *feels* impossible!

6. Lewis, *Mere Christianity,* 132.

7. Ibid.

8. Ibid., 119–20.

9. Dr. John Trent, *The Blessing: Giving the Gift of Unconditional Love and Acceptance,* revised and updated (Nashville, Tenn.: Thomas Nelson Publishers, 2004). See the chapter on "Appropriate Meaningful Touch."

Chapter 3, Taking That First Step into a Kingdom of Change

1. Lewis, *Mere Christianity,* 114.

Chapter 4, Nine Reasons You'll Never Change—and the One Reason You Must, Part I

1. Connie Cone Sexton, *The Arizona Republic,* 9 March 2004, A1.

2. James Gleick, *Faster: The Acceleration of Just about Everything* (New York: Pantheon Books, 1999), 279.

3. And don't forget to keep reading, for indeed God calls on us to "measure" our days.

4. Science journalist, James Burke, source unknown.

5. Even if you feel like a defective product, don't give up. There is a way to change.

6. Gary and Barbara Rosner, *Divorce-Proof Your Marriage* (Carol Stream, Ill.: Tyndal House, 2003).

7. Juliet Schor, *The Overworked Americas* (New York, N.Y.: Basic Books, 1992), 3.

8. Ibid., 36.

CHAPTER 5, NINE REASONS YOU'LL NEVER CHANGE—AND THE ONE REASON YOU MUST, PART II

1. Neil Postman, *The Disappearance of Childhood* (New York, N.Y.: Knopf Publishing Group, 1994).

2. Ibid.

3. Matthew Barakat, Associated Press, "MCI makes $74 bil adjustment," reported in *The Arizona Republic,* 13 March 2004, D1.

4. Again, don't write me letters until you've read the whole chapter! There are indeed ethical companies and trustworthy people who help people manage their money. My wife, Cindy, and I have a trusted financial advisor, Lori Davis at the Ron Blue Company, who has been totally ethical and committed to helping and protecting our retirement funds. I'm sure there are Lori Davises in every state and city.

CHAPTER 6,

1. Lewis, *Mere Christianity,* 159.

CHAPTER 8, GETTING A CLEAR STARTING POINT FOR CHANGE TODAY

1. After nearly twenty years in print, I just had the privilege of updating this book for a new generation of parents. See John Trent, *The Blessing* (Nashville, Tenn.: Thomas Nelson Publishers, 2004).

APPENDIX B

1. These movies are used as examples, not recommendations.

2. Don't be too quick to answer no. If you've ever been in a hugely conflicted marriage or relationship, or worked closely with those who have, you'll find that on an emotional level, such a shift certainly sounds and *feels* impossible!